WHITE HAT

WHITE HAT
THE MILITARY CAREER OF CAPTAIN
WILLIAM PHILO CLARK

MARK J. NELSON

UNIVERSITY OF OKLAHOMA PRESS : NORMAN

Publication of this book is made possible through
the generosity of Edith Kinney Gaylord.

Library of Congress Cataloging-in-Publication Data

Name: Nelson, Mark J., 1959– author.
Title: White Hat : the military career of Captain William Philo Clark / by Mark J. Nelson.
Other titles: Military career of Captain William Philo Clark
Description: Norman, OK : University of Oklahoma Press [2018] | Includes bibliographical references and index.
Identifiers: LCCN 2018011927 | ISBN 978-0-8061-6122-8 (hardcover)
ISBN 978-0-8061-9369-8 (paper)
Subjects: LCSH: Clark, W. P. (William Philo), 1845–1884. | Indians of North America—Wars—1866–1895—Biography. | United States. Army. Cavalry Regiment, 2nd—Biography. | United States. Army—Officers—Biography. | Soldiers—United States—Biography. | Explorers—West (U.S.)—Biography. | Ethnologists—United States—Biography.
Classification: LCC E83.866.C55 N45 2018 | DDC 973.8092 [B] —dc23
LC record available at https://lccn.loc.gov/2018011927

The views and opinions expressed herein are solely those of the individual author(s) and do not reflect the policy, opinions, or positions of the University of Oklahoma its regents, officers, or employees.

The paper in this book meets the guidelines for permanence and durability of the Committee on Production Guidelines for Book Longevity of the Council on Library Resources, Inc. ∞

The manufacturer's authorized representative in the EU for product safety is Mare Nostrum Group B.V., Mauritskade 21D, 1091 GC Amsterdam, The Netherlands, email: gpsr@marenostrum.co.uk

Copyright © 2018 by the University of Oklahoma Press, Norman, Publishing Division of the University. Paperback published 2025. Manufactured in the U.S.A.

All rights reserved. No part of this publication may be reproduced, stored in a retrieval system, or transmitted, in any form or by any means, electronic, mechanical, photocopying, recording, or otherwise—except as permitted under Section 107 or 108 of the United States Copyright Act—without the prior written permission of the University of Oklahoma Press. To request permission to reproduce selections from this book, write to Permissions, University of Oklahoma Press, 2800 Venture Drive, Norman, OK 73069, or email rights.oupress@ou.edu.

To the memory of my sons,

Boyd Washakie Nelson
and
Justin Isaac "Zack" Nelson

CONTENTS

List of Illustrations ix
Preface xi
Acknowledgments xv

1. Native Son of New York and West Point Cadet 3
2. Regimental Adjutant 15
3. Big Horn and Yellowstone Expedition 27
4. Powder River Expedition 40
5. Surrender of Crazy Horse 48
6. Dog Feasts and Failed Diplomacy 59
7. Death of Crazy Horse 74
8. Washington Delegation and Relocation 105
9. Fort Keogh and the Miles-Hoyt Expedition 118
10. Little Wolf's Surrender 131
11. Fighting Sitting Bull's Band 147

12. Fort Keogh and the Big Horn Mountains 155
13. Fieldwork for *The Indian Sign Language* 167
14. Yellowstone National Park Explorations 182
15. Final Months in Washington, D.C. 197

Notes 207
Bibliography 237
Index 247

ILLUSTRATIONS

FIGURES

Cadet William Philo Clark, United States Military Academy. 97

Grand Duke Alexis buffalo-hunting party at Camp Alexis 98

Brigadier General George Crook and headquarters staff 98

Helen "Nellie" Larrabee 99

First Lieutenant Clark and Little Hawk 100

First Lieutenant Clark 101

Brigadier General George Crook 101

Lakota and Northern Arapaho delegation in Washington, D.C., 1877 . . . 101

Miles-Hoyt party in Yellowstone National Park 102

Lieutenant General Philip H. Sheridan and party at Old Faithful 102

President Chester A. Arthur and party in Yellowstone National Park . . . 103

Captain William Philo Clark, circa 1884. 104

MAP

Western locations important to Clark's Military Career 14

PREFACE

During his rather brief military career Captain William Philo Clark undertook a variety and array of assignments perhaps unmatched by any army officer of his time. Clark the soldier performed a number of important duties during his years as an army officer. Shortly after arriving in the West he began a lengthy stint as a staff officer with the Second Cavalry, serving as the regiment's adjutant. After years of service as an administrative officer he finally received his chance at field duty and joined Brigadier General George Crook's infamous "Starvation March," a rather cruel initiation into the rigors of Indian Wars campaigning. Clark gained the trust of Crook and was later assigned the task of recruiting and supervising Indian scouts at Camp Robinson, Nebraska. This duty placed Clark, known as White Hat to the Indians, in the tenuous position of playing a critical role in the life and subsequent death of the Lakota leader Crazy Horse. During his time with the army Clark participated in his share of fighting, playing a prominent role in the battle of Slim Buttes in September 1876, commanding Indian scouts at the Dull Knife Fight in November of the same year, leading a charge at Index Peak against the Bannocks in August 1878, and heading a detachment fighting Sitting Bull's band the following year. Late in his career Clark served at Lieutenant General Philip H. Sheridan's headquarters, first at Division of the Missouri Headquarters in Chicago and later at Army Headquarters in Washington, D.C., eventually becoming a member of his staff.

Clark the diplomat secured the surrender of Crazy Horse and many other Lakota and Northern Cheyenne people in 1877. Following Crazy Horse's death, Clark led a delegation of Lakota and Northern Arapaho leaders to Washington, D.C., to negotiate a permanent location for their reservations. He returned to the northern plains and continued the cause of peace. In 1879 he brokered the surrender of the Northern Cheyenne leader Little Wolf after his band's return north from Indian Territory.

Clark the explorer ventured into the area of Sybille Canyon in southeastern Wyoming in 1875 to prepare a map of the region. Years later he would explore the Big Horn Mountains in northern Wyoming, providing the information needed for fellow officer Captain James F. Gregory, chief engineer of the Division of the Missouri, to draft a map of the mountain range. Clark participated in three explorations of Yellowstone Park: the first in 1878 with Colonel Nelson A. Miles and Colgate Hoyt, the second in 1882 with General Sheridan, and the third in 1883, when he accompanied President Chester A. Arthur's party to the national park.

Clark the ethnologist spent a number of years studying the sign language used by the Plains Indians to communicate with each other and became a recognized expert in utilizing their hand gestures. He also studied their cultures in much broader terms. In 1881 Sheridan assigned Clark the task of conducting a detailed study of the Indians of the northern plains. These various efforts resulted in the posthumous publication of his book, *The Indian Sign Language*, in 1885.

I began my research on Captain William Philo Clark's life a number of years ago. From reading *The Indian Sign Language* it was evident that Clark had maintained a diary during his lifetime. I knew that if I could locate Clark's diary it would serve as the cornerstone to his biography. While researching all of the readily available information, I embarked on a quest to find this elusive source. Time passed, no one that I had contacted knew anything about the whereabouts of the item, and all progress on the project eventually ceased.

Years later, while I was attending a history conference at Fort Robinson, Nebraska, in 2013, a colleague politely and professionally called me out for stalling on completing the Clark biography. Diary or no diary, Clark's story needed to be told and shared. I redoubled my efforts to dig deeper into the paper trail that did exist. Slowly but surely the details of Clark's life as a soldier revealed themselves.

The product of my research is limited almost exclusively to an official view of Clark's life. The documents used to reconstruct his past came largely from military records and official correspondence. The one great exception is the information contained in *The Indian Sign Language*, which in addition to being a manual for Plains Indian sign language also serves as something of a memoir of the captain's years on the plains.

ACKNOWLEDGMENTS

This book would never have become a reality without the assistance and support of numerous people. Eli Paul provided the motivation needed to get me working on Clark's story once again. Douglas C. McChristian was kind enough to offer his advice, guidance, and support. Vonnie Zullo of the Horse Soldier Research Service provided outstanding assistance in obtaining documents from the National Archives and elsewhere. My late friend Thomas R. Buecker of the Nebraska State Historical Society shared information that he had collected on Clark, which benefited the project. Thomas Powers, Tom Lindmier, Kingsley Bray, and Ephriam Dickson proved eager to contribute their information, knowledge, and insight. Dr. James S. Brust was instrumental in sharing material concerning the Miles-Hoyt Yellowstone Expedition.

When I began this project some years ago, Laura Prievo, historian for the Village of Carthage, New York, assisted me with material on Deer River, New York, and the Clark family. During the same period Lisa Becker, Lewis County, New York, historian, and Jason Ischia of the Lewis County Historical Society provided valuable information concerning the Clark family. More recently Jerry Perrin from that same institution provided his assistance.

Tom Mooney of the Nebraska State Historical Society provided copies of material from its collections. Joshua Caster of the University of Nebraska–Lincoln Libraries supplied documents from its archives. The staff of the Morris Museum in Morristown, New Jersey, provided records concerning Clark and his ethnographic collection. The interlibrary loan staff at the Salt Lake City Public Library assisted me in acquiring both primary and secondary sources from all over the United States. The staffs at the Department of the Army's United States Military Academy and U.S. Military History Institute contributed to material used in my research. Finally, I thank the staffs at the National Archives and the Smithsonian Institution's National Anthropological Archives for their efforts in securing information utilized in this book.

WHITE HAT

❖ 1 ❖

NATIVE SON OF NEW YORK AND WEST POINT CADET

William Philo Clark's ancestral roots can be traced back to England. The Clark family first came to America in the seventeenth century and settled in the Boston area, becoming New Englanders. At some point around 1800 Clark's grandfather William left Massachusetts and settled in Deer River, New York. The Black River region of northwestern New York was unsettled country at that time. William's brother, Daniel, also ventured to the area. The two pioneering brothers were among the area's first settlers.[1]

Clark's father, William Durant Clark, was born at the homestead in Deer River in 1808 and would spend his entire life living in the home he was born in. He became a farmer, highly esteemed and respected by those who knew him and described as "a quiet, industrious man, simple in life and habits."[2] He married Prudency Taylor of nearby Champion, New York, at some point in the 1830s. The couple had five children, beginning with Harriet A. in 1838, followed by John W., Frances M., Sarah P., and finally William P., who was born on July 27, 1845.[3]

The village of Deer River is nestled among a number of other small communities and hamlets. During the third quarter of the nineteenth century it was a diminutive but thriving community with a population of 175 in 1865.[4] Deer River offered its citizens a limited number of social amenities. During Clark's lifetime the village supported two churches, a school, a store, and a hotel. The Deer River Hotel served as the social center for the community, a popular place for hosting dances.⁵

The surrounding area provided excellent soil, plentiful water, and abundant timber to support its farms and industries. The river attracted grist mills to grind grain into flour. Sawmills, various woodworking businesses, and the production of steel plows and other farm implements also fueled the local economy. Denmark Township, encompassing Deer River, boasted of such nonagricultural businesses as a stove factory; a tin, sheet iron, and copper producer; and an ashery producing potash.⁶

Farming and dairy farming in particular, however, played a very important role in the area.⁷ The Clark farm in the mid-1860s consisted of seventy-four improved acres and twenty-four acres of unimproved land. Forty-four acres served as pasture land, while just over three acres were plowed. The farm produced fifty tons of hay, which served as an important cash crop in addition to feeding stock. Crops raised on the farm included barley, Indian corn, potatoes, and peas. Maple trees provided maple sugar. The Clark's owned seventeen milk cows that produced large quantities of butter and cheese. Other livestock on the Clark farm included nine sheared sheep, eight lambs, two horses, and two pigs. Cash value for the farm was placed at $5,780, with an additional $1,100 value placed on their livestock. The family lived in a frame home valued at $500. Compared to other farms in the area, the Clarks did not stand out on either side of the economic spectrum.⁸

This rural agrarian life shaped Clark during the first nineteen years of his life. The son of a farmer, he knew what it was like to work hard and became very familiar with animal husbandry. It is uncertain just how deeply religious the family was, but Clark's brother John spent his entire life as a member of the Presbyterian Church. Clark may have followed that denomination as well.⁹ The family placed a high value on education. Clark received his schooling at the Lowville Academy in the nearby town of Lowville.¹⁰ At the age of eighteen he became a teacher in 1863.¹¹ Clark's sisters gravitated toward careers in the field of education as well, with all three of them serving in that profession. Sadly, two of them died very young. Harriet passed away in 1862, followed by Sarah in 1867.¹² The *Lewis County Democrat* eulogized the young Lowville Academy teacher on July 8, 1867, referring to her as a zealous and respected teacher.

John Clark also had an influence on his brother. The Civil War erupted when Philo was still a teenager. His older brother, however, heeded the call of his country and enlisted as a private in the Fifth New York Heavy Artillery

Regiment in September 1862. Before long he was promoted to second lieutenant in Company L. Within a few months he received another promotion, to first lieutenant of the same company. On May 29, 1864, he attained the rank of captain and was transferred to Company I of the regiment. Following his years of service, John was mustered out in September 1865 and eventually became a prominent merchant.[13]

Philo also looked toward the military, but not through enlistment. He preferred to be commissioned as an officer after graduating from the United States Military Academy. On March 2, 1864, Congressman Ambrose W. Clark, a northern New York newspaper publisher, nominated him to fill the cadet vacancy for the Twentieth Congressional District of New York. The congressman, however, did not include Clark's age on the nomination. At the bottom of the form he penned: "I have not his exact age, though he comes within the requirements. Though a namesake he is not a relative."[14] In a letter dated the following day, Clark's father wrote to the secretary of war, Edwin M. Stanton, applying to the United States Military Academy on behalf of his son, and also provided his son's current age. On March 5 Clark received the news from Stanton that President Abraham Lincoln had given him a conditional appointment as a cadet. Clark promptly notified Stanton of his acceptance.[15]

Clark also wasted little time in getting to West Point, situated on the western bank of the Hudson River about fifty miles north of New York City. He must have viewed his new surroundings with a sense of awe, as he walked among the classic and English Tudor gray stone structures of the academy. While his official admittance to the academy dated from July 1, 1864, Clark was treated at the facility twice during the month of March and once in April, according to the records of the post hospital at the academy. He may have been taking his entrance examinations there in March. The ailments that he suffered from during that month were minor: a bruise and a headache. The problem in April, however, was more serious, as Clark had contracted gonorrhea.[16] Deer River is located about 250 miles from West Point, so Clark may have preferred to receive treatment for his condition at the post hospital rather than from a local doctor. In any case, on June 3, 1864, about two months before turning nineteen, Clark reported to the academy and confided to himself that "I now must fight the battle alone."[17]

Cadets had to undergo formal examinations twice each year, in January and June. After the June exams the cadets would begin their summer encampment in lieu of vacation. The only exception was cadets finishing their Third Class year, who went on to enjoy a two-month summer furlough. All other cadets had to report to West Point before June 25 for the summer encampment even though the academic program did not begin until September. Cadets were formed into companies and participated in the summer encampment for a period of three months. The commandant of cadets was in charge of the cadets during the encampment, where they learned practical lessons in field soldiering. Among other duties, the commandant, who was an army officer, was responsible for tactical training, oversaw discipline, and issued demerits.[18] When Clark reported to the academy in early June, Major Henry B. Clitz served as commandant of cadets. A month later he was replaced by Colonel John C. Tidball, a Union artillery officer who served at West Point for less than three months and then returned to field duty in the Civil War. During the rest of Clark's tenure at the academy the commandant was Major Henry M. Black, Seventh Infantry. Black had served in the Seventh and Ninth Infantries and was a veteran of the Mexican War. He served in the Northwest from 1857 to 1861, dealing with Indian problems there. During the Civil War he was stationed on the Pacific Coast until 1864, when he arrived at West Point.[19]

Hazing was part of a plebe's life at West Point, and Clark was abundantly hazed.[20] Hazing activities took place primarily during the summer encampment before the Civil War but later became a year-round ordeal and also increased in intensity. Superintendents frowned on hazing, while faculty members and alumni supported it.[21]

The cadets embarked upon their scholarly pursuits in September. The academic board maintained oversight of the academic program and examined cadets. The board consisted of permanent professors and the superintendant, who was the equivalent of a college president. Superintendents generally originated from the Corps of Engineers, and the academy stressed the field of engineering.[22] During Clark's four-year course of study the academy had three different superintendents: Zealous Bates Tower, George Washington Cullum, and Thomas Gamble Pitcher.[23] Clark's engineering training would serve him well at least once later in life, on the Powder River of southeastern Montana in 1876.

The curriculum was much the same as it had been for young cadets who had preceded Clark decades earlier. In many cases the classes were being taught by the same instructors. Notable among the academy's longtime professors when Clark attended the institution were men like Dennis Hart Mahan, professor of engineering since the early 1830s; math professor Albert E. Church, who began teaching at the academy in 1828; and noted artist Robert W. Weir, who had served as the drawing instructor since joining the faculty in 1833.[24]

In addition to offering classroom instruction and tactical training, the academy was also doing what it could to produce Christian soldiers. Attention to religious development dictated mandatory attendance at Sunday chapel services and optional prayer meetings twice each week.[25] Clark's upbringing in northern New York near a region of religious fervor, his education at Lowville Academy, and his attendance at West Point combined to influence his thinking for the rest of his life.

At the United States Military Academy class ranking was all important: the merit roll determined a cadet's service placement.[26] Clark's Fourth Class year proved challenging for the young plebe. Clark ranked thirty-second of sixty cadets in the class. He performed respectably in mathematics, but his English and French scores brought him down. The 116 demerits that he received also detracted from his ranking.[27] That number tied him for fourth most in the class and was the highest number of demerits that he would receive during a single year over the course of his four years at the academy. Examples of his transgressions and their associated punishments included "Laughing in ranks marching out to parade—confined to quarters when not on duty one Saturday" and "Not ceasing to swing arms when ordered to do so—two extra tours of Saturday or Sunday guard duty." Clark may have been a practical joker: he also received demerits for "Making unnecessary noise with pitcher at mess."[28]

Summer encampment activities commenced after the June examinations. On June 19, 1865, Clark found himself assigned as a corporal in Company C of the Battalion of Cadets. Having survived his plebe year at the academy, Clark's academic performance improved during his Third Class year. He completed the year ranking twenty-ninth out of fifty-seven cadets. Mathematics proved to be his best subject, in which he finished twenty-ninth. He placed thirty-third in drawing and managed to finish forty-fourth in his French class. His conduct improved as well, tallying seventy demerits, which placed him a little below the middle of the class for number of demerits.[29] Infractions during the year included "Giving information at black board in French academy" and "Idling, laughing, and talking in Drawing academy."[30] As usual the delinquencies were punished with either confinement to quarters or extra tours of guard duty. With his examinations completed in June 1866, Clark and the rest of the Third Year cadets enjoyed their much-anticipated furlough. It is not known definitively where Clark spent his vacation, but he is presumed to have returned to Deer River for at least a portion of it.

During his Second Class year Clark's position among the Corps of Cadets continued to rise, as he served as the senior first sergeant. Shortly after the cadets returned to the classroom, Clark fell victim to cholera morbus, also known as acute gastroenteritis or stomach flu, being admitted to the post hospital on September 16, 1866, and released two days later.[31] Clark would suffer the ailment again later in life, with tragic and fatal consequences.

After his release from the hospital Clark resumed his Second Class year. He continued to improve his ranking among his fifty-seven classmates, ending the year in the twenty-second position, the highest placement that he would obtain during his career as a cadet. His course of study during the year consisted of classes in artillery tactics, chemistry, drawing, infantry tactics, and philosophy. He excelled in infantry tactics, with the sixth best score in the class, but performed poorly in artillery tactics, with a class standing of thirty-second. Clark's behavior during the course of the year, however, did not continue to improve: he racked up ninety-three demerits, twelfth most in the class.[32] Clark was cited on more than one occasion for the offense of being in or on his bed at inspection. Other violations included being "Absent from drill" and "Entering mess hall after battalion at supper."[33]

Clark's First Class year at the academy proved to be an eventful one. To his credit, he had the distinction of serving as the first captain in the Corps of Cadets,[34] the highest rank possible for a cadet to achieve. On the negative side, he found himself facing a court-martial. Special Order No. 456, Headquarters of the Army, dated September 30, 1867, appointed the general court-martial scheduled to meet on October 4 at West Point for Clark's trial. On that day the court convened with retired Brevet Lieutenant Colonel J. C. Clark serving as president. As the proceedings began the defendant listened to the order appointing the court and then was asked if he objected to any member assigned to hear his case. He objected to Brevet Lieutenant Colonel S. N. Benjamin, Second Artillery, being on the court because that officer had expressed an opinion on the case some three weeks earlier, stating that Clark should be dismissed. Benjamin replied that he had no opinion in the case and had never expressed one except perhaps in jest, not referring to Clark's case in particular. After Benjamin's explanation Clark withdrew his objection.[35]

The judge advocate of the court, Brevet Major William Sinclair, then read aloud the charge and specifications against Clark. The charge was "Conduct to the prejudice of good order and military discipline." The first specification stated that Clark went beyond cadet limits and visited Cozzen's Hotel, near the village of Highland Falls, New York, between tattoo on September 16 and reveille on the following morning. The second specification claimed that Clark was at Cozzen's Hotel in citizen clothing, a dress not prescribed for cadets. The charge and specifications were signed by Captain John Egan, Eleventh Infantry. Clark pled "not guilty" to the charge and both specifications. He then introduced to the court fellow cadet James B. Mackall, who would serve as his counsel for the proceedings.

The next order of business was to hear the testimony of Captain Egan, witness for the prosecution. According to him, he had seen Clark at Cozzen's Hotel near Highland Falls, about a mile from West Point, between the hours of 11:00 P.M. on September 16 and 1:00 A.M. on September 17. He spotted Clark, dressed in citizen's clothing, on the south piazza, on the north piazza near the main entrance, and on the path leading to the bar at the hotel. Egan stated that he had called out to Clark by name and ordered him to halt. Clark did not reply or stop, however, and kept walking at an ordinary gait along the path leading to the bar before and after his name was called out. Egan watched Clark until he disappeared under the piazza.

Under cross-examination, Egan was asked why he thought that it was Clark. He replied that from the moment he saw the man walking toward him and passing a few feet from him in the bright moonlight he knew that it was a cadet and looked at him closely. From the individual's figure, walk, size, and profile Egan suspected that it was Clark. He looked around the piazza for Clark and saw him again near the main door when the light fell upon him, convincing Egan that it was Clark. When asked if he could be mistaken, Egan replied that Clark had been in his company since May 3, 1865, and that he knew Clark better than any cadet in the corps and had no doubt that the person he saw was Clark. Contradicting himself, Egan went on to say that the person he saw was wearing citizen clothing and had his face concealed, so he might possibly be mistaken and thus would not swear to the person's identity. When asked to describe how the man was dressed, Egan replied that he wore a dark coat and light pair of pants and a slouched hat, carried a cane, and had a moustache. Contradicting himself yet again, Egan ended his testimony by stating that the side view of

Clark's face that he saw removed all reasonable doubt as to his true identity. The prosecution then closed. Clark requested that he be given until 10 the following morning to prepare his defense. The court granted the request and adjourned.

The proceedings were complicated once again the following morning before the court-martial resumed. Brevet Lieutenant Colonel Benjamin's participation in the court was once again objected to, this time by the judge advocate of the court, Brevet Major Sinclair. According to Sinclair, after the court's adjournment on the previous day Benjamin had remarked that he would never vote to dismiss a cadet for the offense for which Clark was being tried. Benjamin countered that his opinion had nothing to do with his ability to sit on the court, adding that the statement was made only in the presence of one or two members of the court and was made on general principles. Sinclair replied that he himself had heard Benjamin make the comment near the entrance to the building as the members of the court were leaving. Benjamin retorted that Sinclair must have partially misunderstood him. The remark was made in general conversation and could not affect his eligibility by expressing an opinion regarding the nature of punishment to be inflicted. Each member had a right to propose a sentence, which was not an expression of Clark's guilt or innocence. After deliberating on the matter, the court concluded that Benjamin would not be excluded from the proceedings. Clark then asked for a delay until the morning of October 7 owing to the absence of an important witness for the defense from the post, Brevet Colonel Henry M. Black, commandant of cadets. The request was granted and the court adjourned for the day.

The court reconvened once again at 10:00 A.M. on October 7 with Brevet Colonel Black testifying. He stated that he had known Clark since the fall of 1864. In his opinion Clark's character had been very good from a military point of view, as shown by the offices that he had held under Black: corporal, senior first sergeant, and first captain. Black mentioned that Clark would not have attained the position of first captain if he himself had not had great confidence in Clark. Contradicting Egan's testimony, Black stated that Clark had been in Egan's company since about June 18, 1866, over a year later than Egan had stated. Black went on to characterize Clark's military conduct while on duty with him as excellent. The defense then closed, and Clark requested that he be given until 11 the following day to prepare his final defense. The court granted his request and adjourned until the next morning.

The court opened the next day with Clark's counsel, cadet James B. Mackall, reading the written defense. According to the statement, Clark was placed under arrest on September 17 and kept in close arrest until his trial began. Clark confessed: "In my defense I have taken the broad, just, and liberal ground 'Innocent until proven guilty.'" He thereby admitted his guilt in a backhanded manner while challenging the system to prove it. He also pointed out that the only evidence against him was Egan's testimony and that for an entire year out of the two and a half years that Egan had testified to Clark's having been in his company he had actually belonged to the other wing of the battalion and had nothing to do with Egan or his company. If that information was erroneous, what good was the rest of Egan's testimony? Clark then set about discrediting Egan's accuracy. Among a number of other things he pointed out that Egan did not state that the moustache was fake and noted that cadets could not have whiskers of any kind. Clark closed his defense by arguing that the specifications for which he was charged should have been addressed through the United States Military Academy Regulations. The case was being prosecuted under the Ninety-Ninth Article of War, which Clark claimed was both unjust and illegal.[36]

Having heard Clark's defense the court cleared for deliberation. The court returned its verdict, finding Clark guilty of the two specifications and the charge. The sentence imposed proved severe: Clark was to be suspended from the academy until July 1, 1868, and to join the First Class cadets upon his return. Additionally, all his pay and allowances were to be forfeited until that date.[37]

In his summation of the case to the adjutant general dated October 23, 1867, Judge Advocate General Joseph Holt confided that the written defense questioning the identity of the accused had been argued ingeniously "but, in view of the fact that, had the accused been in his quarters, as required by the regulations of the Academy, it could readily have been shown and no witness being called by him in that behalf, it has little weight."[38]

Dismissals and suspensions from the academy were a rather common occurrence. The affected cadet generally appealed his case to the secretary of war, who would then reinstate him. Unfortunately, in Clark's case the secretary of war, E. D. Townsend, upheld the court's ruling. Determined to fight the court's decision, Clark spent his days in Washington, D.C., trying to get someone to assist his cause. In November 1867 he penned a plea for help to General Ulysses S. Grant. In his letter Clark stated that his punishment was overly severe for such an offense. Stressing the seriousness of the situation, he noted that the punishment would hinder him for the rest of his life. "I ask to be punished as though I had not held the highest position in the Corps of Cadets, which is the reason as I am informed that I am treated in so severe and harsh a manner."[39]

Clark then composed a letter to President Andrew Johnson dated November 8, 1867, also written from Washington. The letter reiterated that his punishment was too harsh for the nature of his transgression: "I would respectfully request that this sentence be remitted."[40] Clark's plea for revocation was forwarded from the president to the judge advocate general for comment. Holt's reply to the president on November 9 was swift and to the point. He called attention to the report of October 23 made after a careful review of Clark's case. Holt pointed out that Clark's appeal did not set forth any new evidence but simply complained that the sentence was too severe. He concluded: "The sentence was not a light one, but is conceived to have been merited," adding that "no sufficient reason is exhibited to remitting it at present."[41] President Johnson thereby made his decision on November 16, declining to take any action in the matter.

During the next two weeks the situation changed for Clark for unknown reasons (there is a gap in the written record). On December 4, 1867, President Johnson commuted the sentence, stipulating that Clark "will rejoin his class at the U.S.M.A. and remain until they graduate, when, if his conduct in the mean time is satisfactory to the Superintendent of the Military Academy, this sentence is hereby revoked from the date of this order, otherwise the sentence of the Court will be carried into execution."[42]

Clark clearly knew that his case was receiving attention. On December 5 he wrote to Townsend, informing the secretary of war that he could be reached at the Metropolitan Hotel in Washington.[43] On the same day Inspector General Edmund Schriver issued a War Department memorandum to the adjutant general concerning the president's order in Clark's case: "In the same order it will be directed that Cadet Clarke [sic] shall be confined to the Cadets' Barracks until further orders."[44]

With the commutation of his sentence Clark left Washington, D.C., and traveled to West Point to resume his final year at the academy. His absence from the academy in the fall of 1867 certainly did not benefit his performance in the classroom for the year. Clark placed thirty-second of the fifty-five graduating cadets in the class of 1868 in three of his courses: engineering, ordnance and gunnery, and ethics and law. He did slightly better in mineralogy and geology, finishing twenty-ninth. Clark did not perform well at all in his final foreign language class: his Spanish score ranked thirty-eighth. The one course he excelled in was cavalry tactics, where he placed third among the First Year cadets. Interestingly, Clark accrued only sixty-four demerits during the year in which he suffered the agonies of a court-martial, his lowest single-year total as a cadet. He ended his career as a cadet with an overall ranking of twenty-sixth, placing him near the middle of the graduating class.[45]

On June 25, 1868, Clark and the other First Year cadets graduated from the academy. With their West Point days behind them, the graduates bought their uniforms, were assigned their duties, and went on furlough. Clark's one and only preference for assignment was the Second Cavalry. His wish was realized when he received his commission as a second lieutenant in that regiment.[46]

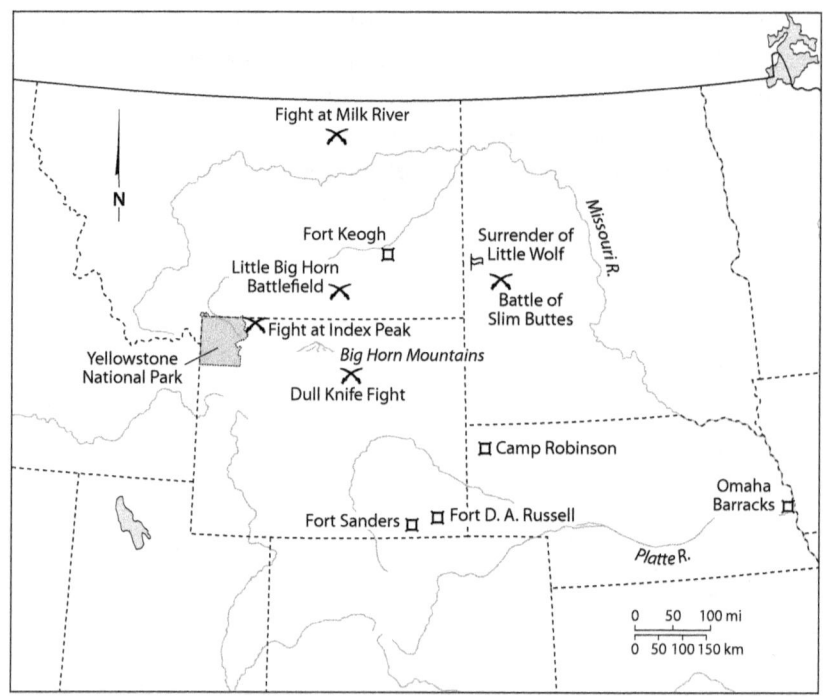

Western locations important to Clark's military career.
Cartography by Bill Nelson.

☙ 2 ❧

REGIMENTAL ADJUTANT

In the years following the Civil War, America's continued expansion into the largely unsettled West necessitated a military presence in the region. The primary obstacle to the country's aims in the area was the ever-present threat of Indian opposition to incursions on their lands. Many challenges faced the military at the time, including the railroad construction crews who needed protection, telegraph lines that had to remain functional, and emigrants and settlers who required security. To serve the needs of the country and enforce the will of the government, the military established a number of frontier posts throughout the West. This was the environment that Clark entered when he left the academy and began his career as a military officer.

Clark received his commission in early July 1868 and was then assigned to his company as a second lieutenant on July 21. He formally accepted the commission and took his oath of office in early August. The new lieutenant signed the commission before a justice of the peace in Denmark, New York, near his hometown of Deer River.[1] After leaving West Point, Clark spent the remainder of the summer and a portion of the fall enjoying a leave of absence, presumably among his family and friends in New York.

Following the completion of his leave of absence Clark ventured west to his first duty station, Fort D. A. Russell in Wyoming Territory, reporting there on October 1, 1868, to serve with Company A, Second Cavalry.[2] Described as "5 feet 10 inches in stature, and exceedingly well made,"[3] Clark was physically well suited for the rigors of frontier duty. Throughout his years of service in the army Clark was known by different names. Fellow officers simply called him "Philo." Enlisted men referred to him as "Nobby," a traditional British nickname for a person with the surname of Clark and an army slang term meaning "stylish." Indians called him "White Hat" because he wore a white felt hat when in the field.

Fort D. A. Russell, located along the north bank of Crow Creek in the southeastern portion of Wyoming Territory, sat amid low hills and prairie. Crossing the plains not far from the post, the newly laid Union Pacific Railroad route had been established in the area almost a year before Clark arrived there. The city of Cheyenne was situated just three miles east of the post. The fort served the purpose of protecting the railroad and other routes of travel in the area as well as the citizens of Cheyenne and the surrounding vicinity. The post and its associated depot became an important staging point for supplies and soldiers serving the region.[4]

The officers' quarters at D. A. Russell faced the fort's diamond-shaped parade ground and were primarily constructed as duplex units, with a company captain living in one half and his two lieutenants occupying the adjoining space. Clark's immediate superior commanding Company A was Captain Thomas B. Dewees, a Pennsylvanian who started his military career as a private before the Civil War and worked his way up the ranks.[5] The company's first lieutenant, Henry S. Pearce, was under arrest but not confined when Clark arrived at the garrison. The lieutenant had been found guilty of being drunk while serving as officer of the day. By early December 1868 Pearce would be cashiered (dismissed from the army).[6]

During his time at the post Clark assisted Captain Dewees in commanding Company A as it performed the mundane tasks associated with garrison duty: roll calls, guard mounting, fatigues, drills, and dress parades. As the sole lieutenant in the company, Clark's workload must have been heavy. In March 1869 he also took on the added responsibility of post adjutant.[7] As such, Clark took on the clerical and administrative duties assigned to him in supporting the post's commander, Major James Van Voast of the Eighteenth Infantry. Like Clark, Van Voast came from New York and graduated from West Point, albeit sixteen years earlier than his new post adjutant.[8]

On two occasions during his assignment at the fort Clark served as judge advocate in general court-martial cases.[9] The role of judge advocate was important. It became Clark's responsibility not only to serve as the public prosecutor in such cases but to ensure that the defendant received a fair trial. As judge advocate, Clark recorded the court's proceedings and had to be ready to offer his opinion when any point of law was raised. If any deviation from the law should become evident, it was up to Clark to point it out.[10] While the judge advocate supervised the proceedings, it was the responsibility of the officers serving general court-martial duty to determine guilt or innocence.

After serving at Fort D. A. Russell for six months, Clark and Company A were assigned detached service duty in April 1869 at Fort Sanders, Wyoming Territory, about fifty miles west of D. A. Russell. Clark remained at Fort Sanders for two months. In early June he was assigned to serve as acting regimental adjutant for the Second Cavalry, which necessitated his move to regimental headquarters at Omaha Barracks, Nebraska. His new duty station was situated near the west bank of the Missouri River overlooking the city of Omaha, three and a half miles away.[11] By the middle of the month Clark not only served as the regiment's adjutant but performed the additional duties of post adjutant.[12]

On July 10, 1869, via a letter of instruction from the Adjutant General's Office, Clark received promotion to first lieutenant. At the end of the month his temporary status as regimental adjutant became a permanent appointment.[13] Clark did not sign the oath of office for his new commission until late January 1870.[14] In June 1869 Clark had left behind service in a field company and had become a staff officer under the Second Cavalry's commander, Colonel Innis N. Palmer, a fellow New Yorker and a respected veteran of both the Mexican-American War and the Civil War who now commanded the regiment and Omaha Barracks.[15] Clark would serve as the regiment's adjutant for seven years.

The assignment revealed Palmer's high regard for Clark. As a former regimental adjutant himself, the colonel knew the demands and rigors of the position. The role required an officer who had a thorough knowledge of field exercise, army regulations, and the inner workings of his regiment. The demands now placed upon Clark were many and varied. As adjutant he would assist Palmer in the administration of the regiment. His duties included communicating Palmer's orders to the command, maintaining the regiment's records, and supervising the men of the headquarters, including the regimental band. Clark also inspected the soldiers assigned to escorts or guards before they went on duty.[16] One former regimental adjutant, Captain Charles King, who in later years would become a well-known novelist, summarized the position: "We all know what the adjutant should be,—a soldier in everything, in carriage, form, voice, and manner, the soul of parade and guard-mounting, the reliable authority on tactics and regulations, the patient student of general orders, the rigid scrutinizer of returns and rolls, the scholarly man of the subalterns, the faithful adherent and executive in spirit and in letter of the commanding officer."[17]

Clark's life at Omaha Barracks settled into administrative routine as he fulfilled his duties in the dual roles of post and regimental adjutant. There were a few exceptions, mostly instances when he served in various capacities in general court-martial cases, usually as judge advocate and always in Omaha.[18]

Clark did receive a brief respite from his military duties in January and a portion of February 1871, when he was granted a thirty-day leave. The young adjutant traveled to New York. Enjoying his stay, he received permission to extend the leave ten more days. He returned to resume his duties on February 13.[19]

In May 1871 Clark and a guard consisting of eight infantrymen were ordered to proceed by train to San Francisco. Shortly after their arrival, Clark and the men in his detachment returned to Omaha as an escort to special officers of the Treasury Department.[20] The exact nature of this assignment remains unknown, but by early June Clark was once again performing his regular duties.

The most noteworthy experience for Clark during his tenure at Omaha Barracks occurred in January 1872 when Grand Duke Alexis of Russia ventured to the plains of America to participate in a buffalo hunt during his tour of the United States. On the morning of January 12 Alexis and his entourage of Russian officials arrived in Omaha aboard his imperial train and were greeted by former Nebraska territorial governor Alvin Saunders, Lieutenant General Philip H. Sheridan, local dignitaries, and an assortment of army officers from the Division of the Missouri and Department of the Platte, including the flamboyant and self-assured lieutenant colonel of the Seventh Cavalry, George A. Custer. Also on hand to greet Alexis were Colonel Palmer, Clark, and the rest of Palmer's staff. The group retired to the Saunders home, where they enjoyed fine food and drink. After the festivities those dignitaries who were to participate in the hunt left Omaha for North Platte Station, arriving there the next morning.[21]

Awaiting the hunting party was the chief scout from Fort McPherson, William F. Cody, popularly known as "Buffalo Bill," who had been selected by Sheridan to lead the party. Cody had successfully performed the same duty in the same area the previous September and October for Sheridan and another group of distinguished hunters. Members of the grand ducal hunting party left North Platte Station, riding on cavalry horses or in army wagons for the eight-hour journey to the hunting camp located on Red Willow Creek, aptly return to Nebraska so that he could attend to some unknown regimental business in New York. Clark and Private Riley left Omaha Barracks on June 27, 1872, for the east. While in Washington, Clark resided at the Ebbitt House, a stylish hotel popular with military officers. On July 8 the Adjutant General's Office notified him that his request for the twenty-day delay in returning to his station had been approved. Presumably Clark ventured to New York to take care of business there. By July 22 he had returned to Omaha.[30]

In early September Regimental Headquarters for the Second Cavalry received orders to proceed to its new duty station at Fort Sanders, Wyoming Territory. On September 25 Clark was relieved from his duty as post adjutant at Omaha Barracks. The members of the headquarters, staff, and band left Omaha on October 10 and arrived at Sanders two days later.[31]

Fort Sanders, established in 1866, was located on the high plains along the Union Pacific Railroad about three miles south of the town of Laramie. The post protected emigrant trail routes and the Denver–Salt Lake stage route. During the building of the transcontinental railroad the garrison provided protection to Union Pacific Railroad construction crews. The buildings of the post were in large part constructed of log. A nearby reservoir created from Spring Creek provided water to the garrison, carried throughout the post by a series of ditches. The water system also fed an artificial pond at the fort that allowed the men to enjoy boating in warm weather and skating during the winter months.[32]

As was the case at Omaha Barracks, Clark served in the dual role of regimental and post adjutant. One of Clark's additional duties as post adjutant at Fort Sanders was supervising the post garden. The vegetables produced by the garden supplied the needs of staff officers and the post hospital. Each company at the post also had its own garden.[33]

Clark's daring and composure were exemplified when a fire broke out on April 23, 1873, in the kitchen of the southeastern set of officers' quarters at Sanders, completely destroying them. Many men unsuccessfully fought the blaze, but "of the officers Lieut. Clark Adj't. 2nd Cavalry excelled in zeal and judgement."[34] At a board of survey convened the day after the fire Clark took the affidavits of the Second Cavalry enlisted men who fought the blaze. Such boards would convene after a loss of public property in order to determine both the responsibility for the loss and the amount of property lost. A substantial number of enlisted men had their clothing either damaged or destroyed in their attempts to fight the fire, so the secretary of war petitioned Congress to authorize the issue of replacement clothing at government expense.[35]

The Second Cavalry Regimental Headquarters at Fort Sanders found itself in something of a scandal in the fall of 1873. Accusations of wrongdoing at the post sawmill ultimately led to court-martial cases for Colonel Palmer and the regimental quartermaster, First Lieutenant William C. Rawolle. Clark, in his role as regimental adjutant, took an active part in both cases. He recorded the sworn statements of a number of individuals involved, submitted a statement of his own, and also served as a witness.[36]

The basic contention was that from July 1873 through February 1874 government property and soldiers had been used at the sawmill, located some twenty miles from the post, in order for a private contractor to profit from the production and sale of railroad ties manufactured there. The court-martial trial for Rawolle took place in May 1874, charging the lieutenant with conduct to the prejudice of good order and military justice. Eight specifications were attached to the charge. The court found Rawolle guilty of the charge and four of the specifications. It concluded that he had allowed the sawmill to be used for the manufacture of railroad ties to the benefit of private interests, had permitted enlisted men to be employed for the benefit of private interests, and had loaned out property of the United States for private purposes. The court then sentenced Rawolle to be suspended from rank and command for six months and to be confined for the same six-month period to the limits of the post where he was stationed. It should be noted, however, that eight members of the court signed a paper asking for clemency for the lieutenant, stating that circumstances at frontier posts sometimes required actions that strayed from strict interpretations of the law.

Unfortunately for Rawolle, the secretary of war, William W. Belknap, did not agree. Following Rawolle's court-martial Belknap determined that Palmer should face trial as well. His court-martial commenced on September 3, 1874. Palmer faced the same charge as his regimental quartermaster, with nine accompanying specifications. Eight days later the court announced its findings. Palmer was found guilty of the charge itself but innocent of eight of the nine specifications. The sole exception, according to the court, was that Palmer had failed to investigate the situation at the sawmill when first reported to him in September 1873. As a result, Palmer was sentenced to be suspended from rank and command for one month.[37]

In March 1874 Clark took on the added duties associated with serving as post signal officer, charged with maintaining the various means of communication at the post, especially the telegraph line. To add to his burden, on the last day of the month he was also placed in command of a detachment of Second Cavalry recruits at Fort Sanders. Clark performed his various duties throughout the spring and then left the post on June 17 for a twenty-day leave of absence that was further extended by ten more days.[38] It remains unknown where he traveled on this particular leave. Despite the extension, he came back prematurely.

Clark returned to Fort Sanders on July 6 and resumed his duties as post and regimental adjutant. In the middle of October he took command of Company G, Fourth Infantry, for a short period of five days, as the company's only officer remained in his quarters due to illness. Clark was called away to Camp Douglas near Salt Lake City, Utah Territory, to serve general court-martial duty. Clark served as judge advocate in the court-martial of Captain George W. Dost and then returned to his post in Wyoming on October 28.[39]

Just days after his arrival at Fort Sanders, Clark once again departed on an extended leave of absence that would keep him away from the post for two months.[40] His whereabouts during the leave remain a mystery, but it is speculated that he traveled to Deer River.

On January 10, 1875, Clark entered the familiar and probably cold and windswept surroundings of Fort Sanders. He remained there for the winter with only one opportunity to leave: a brief assignment some ninety miles to the west to equally foreboding Fort Fred Steele, Wyoming Territory, to serve as a member of a court-martial case.[41] In late April Clark and Lieutenant Joshua L. Fowler relieved the monotony of garrison duty ever so briefly when they led the regimental band to the train tracks near Sanders and lined it up along the rails so that the band could play as Brigadier General George Crook and his aide Second Lieutenant John G. Bourke slowly passed by the fort en route to Omaha.[42] Both Crook and Bourke would later play major roles in Clark's life and military career.

During the final two weeks of June Clark commanded Fort Sanders due to the absence of both Colonel Palmer and Lieutenant Colonel Albert G. Brackett. He was relieved of command on July 1, 1875, when Brackett returned to the post. On that day tragedy struck the small Wyoming fort: Captain Elias B. Carling of the Quartermaster's Department committed suicide at the post early that morning. He reportedly cut his own throat after having suffered from depression for some time due to financial concerns. Two days after Carling's death, Clark fulfilled one of his responsibilities as post adjutant by officiating at the officer's funeral service at Sanders. Pallbearers included an assortment of army officers and the mayor of Laramie.[43]

Clark busied himself with his everyday routine at Fort Sanders until offered another chance to leave the confines of the post. That opportunity came on September 19, 1875, when Clark, Captain William H. Powell, Fourth Infantry, Regimental Quartermaster Joshua L. Fowler, Second Cavalry, and an escort of eight men were ordered out on a scout in the vicinity of Sybille Pass and the area's most prominent mountain, Laramie Peak, to examine all roads and passes leading from the Black Hills (the modern Laramie Mountains, not to be confused with the Black Hills of South Dakota) to the Laramie Valley. The range of mountains created a natural barrier between Fort Sanders and Fort Laramie to the northeast. The small detachment was instructed to record an itinerary of the march, complete with odometer readings, and also to submit a detailed report and map of the country covered on the scout.[44] A great deal of information about the geography, geology, flora, and fauna of the American West resulted from such military explorations of the region, and it would not be the last time Clark participated in such a venture.

A few days before the issuing of this order, English soldier, author, and sportsman Major Sir Rose Lambart Price, the third baronet of Trengwaiton, arrived at Sanders while on a tour of South and North America. Lieutenant Colonel Brackett, commanding the post in Palmer's absence, offered to arrange a hunt for Price, resulting in the order for the scout. The group left Fort Sanders on the wet and snowy morning of September 20. For transportation the party utilized a four-mule wagon and light ambulance with led horses, accompanied by a mounted eight-man escort. The group was well armed with Springfield rifles, express rifles, and a number of shotguns, along with a thousand rounds of ammunition. At the end of the first day's march the men had covered twenty-seven miles of territory.[45]

During the first days of the trip the group traveled east near the Union Pacific line. Large sheets of tin, torn from the roofs of rail cars by high winds, lay strewn about their path. The party then turned to the north and at the end of the third day established a camp on the North Fork of the Laramie River about nine miles from Laramie Peak. After setting up the camp Price, Clark, and Fowler rode up a nearby canyon where they spotted four elk. Their attempts to get close to their prey were foiled when the mule Clark was riding let out a hideous bray, frightening the elk and setting them to flight. Even so, Price and Clark each managed to kill an elk. "Had it not been for C.'s musical mule I believe we should have killed the entire band," Price lamented.[46]

On the next day the men toiled to get the elk from the previous day's hunt into camp, followed by an attempt at bear hunting. Having seen plenty of fresh signs indicating the presence of a bear in the area, the men were keyed up to confront it. The tenseness in the air was broken when Clark's dog, a setter, came bounding out of a thicket and ran right between Clark's legs. The scene provided a moment of comic relief for the hunters. Price pointed out that "C.'s back was turned at the time, and I never saw a fellow hop round quicker, as he certainly thought the bear was right upon him."[47]

In the following days the detachment continued its hunting and exploring activities in the Laramie Peak area. On one occasion Clark went off exploring while hunting mountain sheep, leaving Price with a sergeant from the escort. The two men became lost and spent hours wandering the rugged terrain. By sheer luck they stumbled upon their camp about nightfall, reuniting with Clark and the others. When the members of the party returned to Fort Sanders on September 29, they had racked up an impressive tally of animals killed during the hunt: two elk, seventeen antelope, thirty-five blue grouse, fifty-four sage hens, twenty-eight ducks, twenty-five rabbits, two rattlesnakes, and a badger. Upon their return to the fort the men were informed that three men had been killed and scalped in the vicinity of their hunt while they had been out.

Following his adventure into the mountains Price remained at Fort Sanders for a few days. During his stay President Ulysses S. Grant passed through Laramie aboard a train. Price, along with Clark and the other officers of the garrison, were allowed to board the president's car and pay him a visit. According to Price, Grant hardly spoke a word to anyone. Mrs. Grant exhibited more cordiality.

On October 8 Clark left Sanders en route to Fort Hartsuff, Nebraska, to serve as a member of a general court-martial. Clark invited Price to join him. The two men traveled by rail, stopping first at North Platte and then at Grand Island, where they were joined by five other officers, including Lieutenant John G. Bourke, detailed to the same duty. From Grand Island the group utilized a trap carriage and light spring wagon for the two-day drive to the post on the Loup River. Seizing another opportunity for sport, Price and the others shot prairie chickens along their route.[48]

About halfway between Grand Island and Hartsuff the group stopped at Beebe's Ranch, a humble structure at least partially dug into a hillside. The small party of seven men spent the night there in a twelve-foot by fourteen-foot room furnished with a sparse three beds. The group passed the evening chatting and smoking until late into the night. On the following morning the officers drove the rest of the way to their destination, again shooting prairie chickens as they went along the trail, arriving there at dinnertime.[49]

After completing his duties associated with the court-martial in Nebraska, Clark returned to Fort Sanders on October 19, 1875. The next few weeks passed quietly for the young lieutenant until the night of November 27. On that evening two Second Cavalry recruits stole two government horses by breaking into the post stables and then deserting. Clark was identified as the officer responsible for the loss and spent the next three days pursuing the deserters.[50]

Clark spent the winter of 1875–76 at Fort Sanders performing his customary duties as regimental and post adjutant. In April he received a subpoena to testify as a witness in the general court-martial of Captain James T. Peale, Second Cavalry. Clark accordingly left Sanders on April 27 for Fort D. A. Russell and remained there until May 17. Shortly after his return Clark took on the additional responsibility of acting assistant quartermaster, supporting the quartermaster in his endeavors to satisfy the building, storage, transportation, and clothing needs of the garrison as well as to disburse funds to meet a variety of expenses. At about this same time he also assumed the role of acting commissary of subsistence, providing soldiers with foodstuffs and a plethora of other goods such as candles and matches. Clark held the temporary positions until June 13, 1876.[51]

Clark's military career and life were about to change drastically. Some months earlier, in early March 1876, First Lieutenant John G. Bourke at Fort Fetterman, Wyoming Territory, found time to answer a number of letters from friends, including Clark.[52] Bourke and Clark had a familiarity with each other dating back to their West Point days, when Bourke was a member of the class of 1869. The two men's paths had crossed a few times on the frontier. It is uncertain whether or not they were close during their time at West Point, but by early 1876 Bourke considered Clark a friend. In the coming months their friendship would be solidified as they shared a campaign experience that no participant would ever forget.

⋇ 3 ⋇

BIG HORN AND YELLOWSTONE EXPEDITION

Clark's long-standing role as regimental adjutant came to an end when Colonel Palmer accepted his resignation on June 13, 1876, to date from July 1. Clark was then assigned to temporary duty with Company F, Second Cavalry, until a vacancy occurred in the grade of first lieutenant, at which time he would be given a permanent assignment.[1] By coincidence, between the middle of June and the first of July events in southern Montana and northern Wyoming would alter the course of Clark's military career.

That summer the army found itself actively engaged in its Sioux War of 1876, a large-scale operation against the Lakotas and Northern Cheyennes of the region. The strike force consisted of three imposing elements. The Montana Column commanded by Colonel John Gibbon advanced eastward along the Yellowstone River; the Dakota Column under the leadership of Brigadier General Alfred H. Terry proceeded to the west from Fort Abraham Lincoln; and the Wyoming Column led by Brigadier General George Crook marched northward from Fort Fetterman. The intended purpose of the campaign was to force roaming bands of the tribes onto their assigned reservation lands and to coerce them into conceding their claims to the Black Hills. Among the leaders of the opposition were famed Lakota headmen Sitting Bull and Crazy Horse. Crook faced the Northern Cheyenne and Lakota warriors in battle on June 17 at Rosebud Creek in southeastern Montana and then returned to his old base camp on Goose Creek in northern Wyoming. A week later Lieutenant Colonel

George A. Custer and the Seventh Cavalry, part of the Dakota Column, met these same warriors at the Little Big Horn and were thoroughly whipped. Custer's debacle prompted military officials to send additional troopers to the theater of operations.

Clark's first assignment since leaving the regimental staff placed him in charge of a group of thirty Second Cavalry recruits bound for Montana to join various companies of the regiment serving in the field. Clark left Fort Sanders on July 5 and arrived with his recruits at Fort Ellis, Montana Territory, seventeen days later.[2] Situated in the Gallatin Valley of southwestern Montana near Bozeman, Fort Ellis served as the staging area for Gibbon's Montana Column, which included the Second Cavalry's Montana Battalion. While Clark and the recruits were at Ellis, Colonel Palmer issued an order from regimental headquarters transferring Clark to Company H. In a letter to the adjutant general asking for approval of the transfer, Palmer noted that it would "leave him [Clark] with the portion of the Regiment in Montana, where I think he desires to remain, as he has seen but little company duty in the field."[3] The transfer received formal approval.

Clark and his small party of recruits left Fort Ellis on August 4. Two days later they embarked from the small settlement of Benson's Landing twenty-seven miles from Ellis aboard mackinaw boats for their long journey down the Yellowstone River to join General Terry's command in the field, which was now composed of the combined units from the Montana and Dakota Columns. Clark's contingent of recruits now consisted of twenty-six Second Cavalrymen and eight recruits for the Seventh Infantry.[4] The mackinaw boats used by Clark were rather large vessels generally used to transport freight. The Yellowstone River served as an important transportation route during the Great Sioux War and later, as the army utilized steamboats to carry men and supplies to various points along the river in order to conduct its operations in the region.

On the afternoon of August 6, after loading supplies and recruits aboard three boats, Clark and the others left Benson's Landing. Second Lieutenant Francis Woodbridge of the Seventh Infantry had left days before. The two groups rendezvoused later that evening. Another Seventh Infantry officer, First Lieutenant William I. Reed, commanded the flotilla. A former Crow trader now turned opportunistic sutler, Matthew "Cy" Mounts, joined the fleet in his own boat, loaded with goods for the soldiers in the field. After a relatively uneventful journey of five days down the river, on the morning of August 11 the group reached the mouth of Rosebud Creek.[5]

A camp known to the soldiers as "Fort Beans" had been established there. The mariners reported to its commander, Captain Louis H. Sanger, Seventeenth Infantry. Not long thereafter Colonel Nelson A. Miles arrived aboard the steamer *Far West*, the same vessel that had been used to transport a number of wounded soldiers from the Seventh Cavalry after the fight on the Little Big Horn. Miles, the Fifth Infantry's fiery and outspoken commander, had recently been dispatched from Kansas along with six companies from his regiment to the northern plains. He was now charged with the responsibility of distributing soldiers at strategic points along the Yellowstone River in an attempt to prevent the enemy from fleeing to the north. Miles gave instructions that the mackinaw boats were to be loaded with forage and then sent downstream to the mouth of Powder River. Additionally, Miles ordered Clark to take his recruits and some of the Crow allies selected from the approximately 450 expected to be present to scout the north bank of the Yellowstone to the Powder River.[6]

When the Crows arrived on August 12, Clark held a feast for them, consisting of one day's rations. He then requested volunteers for the scout down the north bank. The Crows were reluctant but promised Clark an answer the following morning. The attitude of the Crow allies angered Clark's superior, Captain Sanger. The following morning the Crows asked for five days' rations for the entire group in exchange for scouts. Sanger refused the offer. When the Crows requested ammunition instead of food, Sanger agreed to issue it only to those who participated in the scout. With Sanger insisting on imposing his terms in securing scouts and thereby squelching the plan, Clark attempted to purchase thirty Crow ponies for his recruits. But the Crows had no interest in the food and blankets offered them. The ill-tempered Sanger therefore ordered the Crows back to their agency.[7]

Having failed to acquire Crow auxiliaries, Clark and his recruits once again boarded Reed's mackinaws. While Clark had been dealing with the Crows, the vessels had been emptied of their contents and then reloaded again with grain. The fleet left the camp at the Rosebud on the afternoon of August 13, 1876. In addition to the cargo of grain the small fleet also added a passenger, *New York Herald* correspondent James J. O'Kelly.[8]

The fleet remained on the river until 7:00 P.M., when the boats stopped and spent the night of August 13 on a sandbar. The mackinaws proceeded downriver the next morning to Captain Andrew S. Bennett's camp on Tongue River. Later that evening Colonel Miles arrived there aboard the *Far West*. He ordered the group to continue down the Yellowstone at daylight. Leaving Tongue River as ordered, Clark and the others finally arrived at the mouth of Powder River late on the morning of August 15 and from there floated down another mile, where the group had been instructed to make camp. Shortly after their arrival, Miles appeared once again on the *Far West* and had a Gatling gun unloaded, which was placed in the rear of the camp. Additionally, large quantities of supplies were unloaded from the steamship to bolster the stores of provisions held at the Powder River depot on the south side of the river.[9]

A diary or itinerary of the trip down the Yellowstone is preserved among the collections of the Montana Historical Society. For many years the manuscript has been known simply as the "William P. Clark Diary." It now appears that the document has almost certainly been misidentified. Three officers journeyed downriver in the mackinaws: Clark, Reed, and Woodbridge. The author of the diary identified Woodbridge as having left Benson's Landing before the main group, thus ruling him out as the author. An indication that Clark did not write the diary is found in the second sentence of the itinerary: "The command consists of myself, Lieut. W. P. Clark, 2d Cav., 26 recruits for 2d Cav. & 8 for 7th Infy."[10] The *New York Herald* correspondent accompanying the group, James J. O'Kelly, referred to the boats in his August 24 article as "Lieutenant Reed's Mackinaw boats." On August 11 Colonel Miles ordered the author of the diary to load the boats with forage and take them to the mouth of Powder River, while on the same day he instructed Clark to scout the north bank, which is additional evidence that Clark was not the author. Finally, an examination of a page from the original handwritten diary reveals that the writing does not match known examples of Clark's handwriting but does resemble the penmanship of Reed. Thus it is fairly certain that Reed authored the diary.

Before leaving Powder River Miles instructed Clark to remain at the depot with his recruits. Awaiting the expected arrival of Terry and Crook with their troops, which had united on Rosebud Creek five days previously, and feeling rather exposed and vulnerable, Clark took action. Finally having an opportunity to utilize his engineering training from his days at West Point, he led his men in making the depot more secure by constructing a defensive lunette at the site.[11] Clark's engineering efforts failed to impress Bourke, who commented that the lunette "was rather a parody upon the lunette of the text-books and would have made old Dinny Mahan gnash his teeth with rage had he lived long enough to see it."[12] Dennis Mahan had been Clark's engineering professor at the academy.

On August 17 Clark and the others could see dust in the distance and feared that it might signal the approach of enemy warriors. He felt, however, that

Black Hills. With only a few days' rations left and an estimated seven or eight days' hard march ahead of them to reach their destination, they all knew the grim task that lay before them.[19]

Survival now became the primary goal for the command. On September 5 Crook ordered that abandoned horses be shot for food and later that evening reduced the men to half rations, stretching their food supply to four days. Out of respect for the horses, the men initially ate mule meat but began to consume horses a few days later. According to Clark, for its first equine meal the command was issued eight boxes of hard bread, also known as hardtack, and six horses. The men also attempted to supplement their rations by living off the land, but with limited success.[20]

Years later, when a reporter asked Clark how he liked horse meat, he replied: "Oh, it goes pretty good, if the animal isn't too old."[21] In *The Indian Sign Language* Clark commented on conditions during the march, with the men hoarding what little they possessed. "I have seen white men reduced to the last 'hard tack,' with only tobacco enough for two smokes, and with no immediate prospect of anything better than horse-meat 'straight.' A portion of the hard tack bread was hidden away, and the smokes were taken in secret."[22]

On September 6, 1876, the command marched during a constant drizzling rain, crossing both branches of the Cannonball River. On the following day, with both men and animals dropping from exhaustion, the soldiers advanced as far as the North Fork of the Grand River, enduring rain again. At this point Crook made the decision to send a detachment mounted on the strongest available horses to escort the pack mules to the nearest Black Hills settlements in order to obtain supplies. He chose Captain Anson Mills of the Third Cavalry to lead the 150-man escort, which left Crook's camp that night.[23]

Crook pushed his command forward the next morning through wind and rain to a point on the South Fork of the Grand. The command had been without firewood for days, but this camp offered fuel for campfires. That evening Clark and the other officers gathered to celebrate Crook's forty-eighth birthday, although the mood remained rather gloomy.[24]

By the afternoon of September 8 Captain Mills's command had advanced to the vicinity of Slim Buttes, where scout Frank Grouard, riding ahead of the column, spotted a small herd of Indian ponies. Knowing this to be a sure indication of the presence of a nearby village, Mills hid his soldiers in a ravine. After deliberating with his fellow officers, Mills persuaded them that the best course of action to take would be a dawn attack on the village.

In the early morning light of September 9 the soldiers struck the camp. The surprise attack sent the village's inhabitants fleeing, some scattering into surrounding bluffs and others finding temporary safety in a nearby deep ravine covered in dense underbrush. The fighting lasted for roughly half an hour. Then the action became defensive as Mills attempted to defend his gains from the warriors on the bluffs and in the ravine who were sporadically firing at his men. One soldier had been killed in the fighting, and five or six were wounded. Mills sent messengers to Crook to inform the general that he had taken the Lakota and Northern Cheyenne camp and that he needed help in holding it. Mills knew that the lodges contained large quantities of dried meat, berries, and other provisions. But with Indian snipers firing into the village he felt that he would have to wait until Crook's arrival before the village could be thoroughly searched.

As far as the warriors were concerned, the fight was far from over. Once they had assisted their families to safety, some of the men returned to fire upon the soldiers. They felt no need to flee because they knew that other camps were in the area and that eventually additional warriors would join them in ousting the white invaders.

Crook's column started out at 5:00 A.M. on September 9, marching yet again in the rain. After covering five miles of soggy terrain, Mills's messengers arrived and informed Crook of the attack on the village, located some seventeen miles away. Crook ordered cavalrymen with horses fit for pursuit to join him in advancing on the village. The rest of the command would straggle behind. The relief party consisted of 250 men and 17 officers. Crook's men arrived at the village around noon, with the rest of the command reaching the site throughout the afternoon.[25]

Shortly after Crook's arrival the soldiers began going through the thirty-seven lodges composing the village, looking for provisions. An impressive assortment of goods was discovered: five thousand pounds of dried meat, freshly killed game, flour, corn, fruit, beans, salt, pepper, and tobacco. Other items of use to the soldiers included saddles, canvas, ammunition, and blankets. The men also found a number of objects of Seventh Cavalry origin, convincing the soldiers that the inhabitants of the camp had been participants in the fight at the Little Big Horn. As the Lakotas who remained in the narrow ravine continued to menace the command, Crook turned his attention to clearing the snipers from their stronghold, who had already killed one soldier. Due to the density of their cover, Crook had no idea how many warriors concealed themselves there. The soldiers sent a volley into the ravine, which was answered with a hail of bullets that forced the soldiers back. During the early exchange scout Charles White, who was something of a sidekick to Bill Cody and known to the soldiers as "Buffalo Chips," was fatally shot in the chest. Two soldiers received wounds in the affray.[26]

At this point Crook turned to Clark and ordered him to take a group of volunteers and attempt to clear the ravine. Twenty soldiers answered Clark's request for men to join him. The group moved forward to the ravine. Clark's call for surrender was answered with volleys of fire that sent the detachment into a rapid retreat. A large group of onlookers had gathered around the ravine by this time, hampering the efforts of Clark and his volunteers. Clark and his men advanced to the ravine a second time, going dangerously close to the edge of the ravine, where they delivered a withering fire into the dense cover.[27]

First Lieutenant Charles King, Fifth Cavalry, witnessed Clark's actions at the ravine. King maintained that the two men had been close friends during their days together at West Point. He described Clark in extremely glowing terms as "one of the handsomest, bravest, manliest cavalrymen it was ever my lot to know." While the volunteers took positions along the right and left sides of the stronghold, Clark positioned himself at the mouth of the ravine. To King, Clark appeared to be oblivious to the danger he faced. Despite calls from his comrades to get down, he maintained a smile on his face and pushed forward to rally his men to action. King concluded that "I had seen some Indian fighting before this affair, and have been in one or two campaigns since, but I recall no piece of individual daring and bravery and consummate coolness under fire to eclipse Philo Clark's exploit at Slim Buttes in 1876."[28]

This latest barrage of fire brought forth screams and cries from women and children concealed in the stronghold, alerting Clark, Crook, and the others that noncombatants were in the ravine. The general promptly ordered a cease-fire, but the angered men were worked up into such a frenzy that it took great effort on the part of Clark and other officers to control them. When the firing finally ended, Crook sent scouts Baptiste "Big Bat" Pourier and Frank Grouard forward. Their efforts resulted in the surrender of one warrior and about twenty women and children.[29]

The remaining warriors in the ravine refused to come forward and fired on the soldiers, once again sending the men scampering for cover. Crook called up a large number of infantrymen and cavalrymen to the opening of the ravine and ordered them to fire into the position. The men fired an estimated three thousand rounds of ammunition at the warriors. When the shooting stopped, another offer of surrender was issued to the concealed foes. After an hour passed Pourier and Grouard, along with one of the captive women, approached the ravine again. The captive Lakota woman managed to convince one warrior to surrender. Shortly thereafter Pourier went into the ravine and emerged with another warrior and American Horse, a Lakota leader also known as Iron Plume, Iron Shield, and Black Shield. American Horse suffered a severe abdominal wound and carried his own bowels in his hands as he came forward. These men were followed by two more warriors, one of them wounded. With the ravine cleared, soldiers found the bullet-riddled bodies of a warrior, three women, and a child. Of the twenty-eight Lakotas who had sought refuge in the ravine, twenty-three had somehow survived the ordeal.[30]

After the fighting at the ravine had ended Lieutenant King gazed upon General Crook and his aides and pondered on their appearance. He noted the ragged and worn look of Crook, Bourke, and First Lieutenant Walter S. Schuyler. But of Crook's third aide he commented: "Clark is unquestionably the show figure of the staff, for his suit of Indian-tanned buckskin seems to defy the elements, and he looks as handsome and jaunty as the day we met him on the Yellowstone."[31]

The quiet that followed did not last long. At about 4 in the afternoon some of the village's warriors returned to the area with reinforcements from Crazy Horse's camp. The six hundred to eight hundred warriors had expected to find Mills's detachment but were welcomed instead by the entirety of Crook's command. The Indians fired down on the soldiers from nearby bluffs and hilltops as the troops set the camp ablaze. Gunfire continued until around 7. By nightfall the soldiers had forced the warriors to withdraw. The evening fight had resulted in five or six soldiers being wounded, with estimates ranging from seven to eighteen Lakotas and Northern Cheyennes killed and wounded.[32] The army had finally achieved a significant victory in the Sioux War. Clark had survived his initiation into fighting the Plains Indians.

That night the soldiers enjoyed the warmth of campfires and robes and also filled their stomachs. The dried meat was set aside, to be placed on pack mules for the remaining march, but a number of Indian ponies were killed and consumed by the men.[33] "After the capture of the village," Clark recalled, "we had a little more to eat, and we got 8,000 pounds of meat and a little flour, and young ponies were issued to the troops to eat, instead of the worn out horses of our command." When asked how many horses were issued to the men, he replied: "I think sixty-two."[34]

The next morning the command continued on its journey to the Black Hills, some seventy miles away. Despite sporadic fire from lurking warriors in the vicinity of the village, the men pushed onward. After a short march the column stopped in the early afternoon to make camp. On September 11 the soldiers crossed over Slim Buttes in the midst of another rainstorm, with heavy mud adding to the men's already crippling fatigue, and advanced until they established camp on Owl Creek.[35]

While Crook's command was camped along the creek, newspaperman John F. Finerty of the *Chicago Times* witnessed Clark issuing portions of Indian pony to the troops and later recalled: "I saw a heap of the hind-quarters of Indian ponies in front of the Fifth Cavalry headquarters—a few wicky-ups—during the halt on Owl Creek, and the late Capt. W. Philo Clark of the Second Cavalry, acting as commissary, distributing the 'beef' to the soldiers of the different commands."[36]

September 12 proved to be the most grueling day of the entire expedition. The command departed Owl Creek at 5:30 A.M. and marched through a horrendous rainstorm with its accompanying mud. The men and remaining animals were driven to the point of exhaustion but managed to reach Willow Creek, about six miles from the Belle Fourche River. Many in the command who had fallen by the wayside during the day came straggling into the camp throughout the night.[37]

Crook allowed the command to rest until about noon the following day, then the soldiers moved toward the Belle Fourche. En route the men spotted a small herd of beef, in advance of the relief party bringing provisions to the starving and weary command. The sight of the cattle brought forth cheers from the famished soldiers. In a short time the men went to work cooking and filled their stomachs with a double ration of beef and a full ration of other various edibles. To brighten the scene even further, the sun came out for the first time in ten days.[38] The harrowing ordeal endured by Crook and his men would henceforth be remembered by them and by history as the Starvation March, the Mud March, or the Horse Meat March.

The command remained in camp at the Belle Fourche all of September 14 and enjoyed a bright and beautiful day resting, cooking, and eating. The next morning the soldiers moved to Whitewood Creek near Bear Butte and went into camp.[39] On the morning of September 16 Crook, Clark, Bourke, Schuyler, and a number of other officers along with newspaper reporters John F. Finerty and Joseph Wasson, protected by an escort headed by Second Lieutenant

Frederick W. Sibley, left the command to make their way to Fort Laramie, where Lieutenant General Philip H. Sheridan had previously ordered Crook to meet with him.[40]

The soldiers traveled along Whitewood Creek to Crook City, where they were greeted with cheers from the gathered miners and townspeople and enjoyed the hospitality of the citizens, who bestowed food and drink upon Crook and the others. From Crook City they continued on their journey, heading toward Deadwood. About four miles from the mining community the mayor and city council met Crook and escorted his group into the town. When the soldiers entered Deadwood they were greeted by a large crowd, with cheers and blasting steam whistles adding to the excited atmosphere of the moment. That night the officers resided at the Grand Central Hotel, where they enjoyed hot baths and changes of underclothing. Crook gave two speeches, one in front of the hotel and the other at the McDaniels Theatre. In the evening the officers attended a performance of Miller's Grand Combination Troupe and later went out about town.[41]

It is uncertain just how much of Deadwood's nightlife Clark took part in. He did not have the opportunity to join the other officers in exploring the town during the late evening hours. His duties prevailed upon him to secure the services of farriers in order to get the group's horses shod. Newspaperman Finerty noted: "As nearly every horse-shoer in Deadwood happened to be on a spree the night of Crook's reception, Lieutenant Clark, our acting quartermaster, had to go around with a posse of soldiers and sober up sufficient of the boys to get our horses shod. This operation consumed several hours and it was nearly daylight before we got to bed."[42]

Crook and company pressed forward on their trek to Fort Laramie, arriving first at Camp Robinson on September 20. Crook and twenty-two soldiers then went ahead to Fort Laramie and arrived there on the following day.[43] Clark and other staff members remained behind at Camp Robinson. On the evening of September 21 the officers of the camp gave the expedition's officers a reception at the sutler's store. The men conversed freely among themselves regardless of rank and enjoyed the fullest camaraderie. Among the officers joining Clark in the festivities was First Lieutenant John A. McKinney, who would tragically lose his life in an upcoming confrontation with the Northern Cheyennes. Speaking of the two officers, Finerty once again recalled that "no two men were more beloved in that brilliant assemblage."[44]

On September 24 Clark and the others joined Crook at Fort Laramie, where he had been reviewing the previous campaign with General Sheridan.[45] In addition, the two men discussed plans for an upcoming winter expedition against the Lakotas and Northern Cheyennes. For all practical purposes the summer campaign now came to an end, although Crook did not officially terminate the expedition until October 24 at Camp Robinson.[46]

❈ 4 ❈

POWDER RIVER EXPEDITION

Shortly after reuniting with Crook at Fort Laramie, Clark received instructions from the brigadier general to travel to Cheyenne. One of Crook's scouts, Frank Grouard, had fallen drastically ill and had left the fort by stage the day before, en route to Cheyenne for medical treatment. Grouard made a rather sudden and unexpected recovery, however, so Clark's time in Cheyenne was short.[1]

After disbanding the Big Horn and Yellowstone Expedition at Camp Robinson on October 24, 1876, Crook and his staff returned to Fort Laramie on October 26. Clark may have accompanied the general back to the fort or, in light of his upcoming duty, may have remained behind at Red Cloud and Spotted Tail Agencies in northwestern Nebraska during the final days of October. Regardless, at Fort Laramie on November 4 Crook announced the organization of the Powder River Expedition. Clark found himself assigned to command the Lakota, Northern Cheyenne, and Northern Arapaho scouts from the agencies during the forthcoming campaign. It was probably about this time that Clark received the name "White Hat" from the Indians. Second Lieutenant Hayden De Lany, Ninth Infantry, was charged with the task of assisting Clark.[2] Just five months older than Clark, De Lany served in the enlisted ranks during the Civil War with the Thirtieth Ohio Infantry before attending the academy at West Point for two years, receiving his commission as a second lieutenant in 1867.[3]

In addition to the Indian scouts, the newly formed expedition commanded by Crook consisted of eleven companies of cavalry, eleven companies of infantry, and four artillery companies utilized as additional infantry units.[4] The expedition, intended to apply continued pressure on the nonreservation bands until they submitted to the will of the government, left Fort Laramie later that day. As the command departed, brothers Frank and Luther North, well known for previous exploits while leading their Pawnee scouts and now once again commanding the Pawnees, remained in their tent shielding themselves from the snow and wind outside with no idea that the command was on the move. According to Luther, Clark appeared at the tent and made a wisecrack to Frank: "Hello Major, are you going on the expedition?"[5]

Crook arrived at Fort Fetterman, situated on a plateau overlooking the North Platte River roughly eighty-five miles from Fort Laramie, on November 7. Much of the command came in the following day. The men drew additional supplies and made final preparations for the expedition. About a week after arriving at Fetterman Clark and Frank North engaged in a mildly heated confrontation. The trouble started when Clark and First Sergeant Three Bears, a Lakota scout, were discovered taking Frank's bay horse from the herd of ponies that had been captured by Pawnee scouts from the camps of Red Cloud and Red Leaf on October 23 when the Lakota leaders defied orders issued by their agency. Frank protested, but Clark stood up for Three Bears, who needed a new mount because his was played out. The men decided that Crook should settle the matter. They located the general at the sutler's store. After hearing the point of contention, he ruled in North's favor. Unbeknownst to Clark, Crook had previously allowed the Norths and their men to select specific animals from the captured herds and had also secured an additional seventy head to be used by the Lakota scouts as needed. Crook determined that Frank could keep the bay and Three Bears would pick an animal from the seventy surplus ponies, which were cut from the North herd and moved to the Lakota scout camp and turned over to Clark.[6] Whatever differences Clark and North may have had, the two men did converse in the future: Frank provided information on the Pawnees that was later used in Clark's book on Indian sign language.

On November 14 the Powder River Expedition left Fort Fetterman en route to its supply base located at Cantonment Reno, a small post recently constructed on the west bank of the Powder River, about eighty-five miles to the north. The expedition presented yet another imposing force against the remnants of the free-roaming Lakotas and Northern Cheyennes. The command consisted of 363 Indian scouts, approximately 1,500 military personnel, and some 300 civilian employees. The contingent of scouts included members of the Pawnee, Lakota, Northern Cheyenne, Northern Arapaho, Shoshone, and Bannock tribes.[7]

The command endured cold temperatures and snow on its march to the cantonment, arriving there on the morning of November 18. Later that evening a small number of Lakota and Northern Arapaho scouts were sent out to the vicinity of the Big Horn Mountains in an effort to locate the enemy. On the following day Crook gathered his Indian allies together for a council and presented them with his customary message when addressing Indians: the Indian way of life was dying and in order to survive they would have to adapt to the white way of living. The general also pointed out that he wanted all of the scouts from the various tribes to get along with each other and be friends.[8] Clark shared Crook's philosophy concerning the survival of the Indians, which guided his dealings with them for the rest of his life.

On November 20 the command remained in its camp at Reno. On the following day Lakota scouts returned with a captured Northern Cheyenne. From their prisoner they learned that a village of his tribe could be found in the Big Horn Mountains and that Crazy Horse and his people were camped on the Rosebud. Armed with this intelligence, Crook decided to move his command in pursuit of the Crazy Horse village. On the morning of November 22 the soldiers marched twenty-three miles to Crazy Woman's Fork and encamped there for the night. Early the next morning Sitting Bear, an Indian ally, arrived with new information for Crook. He passed along two vital pieces of news to the general. First, he said that Crazy Horse was being warned of the military presence in the area. Hearing this, Crook knew his chances of a successful attack were greatly diminished. Second, Sitting Bear disclosed to Crook the location of the main Northern Cheyenne camp a short distance southwest of the command. Given the circumstances, Crook decided to change course and strike the Northern Cheyennes.[9]

Later that same day Crook ordered most of the cavalry companies under Colonel Ranald S. Mackenzie, Fourth Cavalry, and the Indian scouts commanded by Clark, to seek out the Northern Cheyenne village and destroy the camp. The detachment, consisting of 350 Indian scouts and approximately 750 cavalrymen, left the rest of the command on Crazy Woman's Fork and advanced ten miles south before encamping for the night. The next morning the soldiers and their allies continued an additional ten miles when scouts reported the location of the Northern Cheyenne camp nearby. Mackenzie made the decision that the soldiers would remain where they were until nightfall and then conduct a night march to the village.[10]

When it was nearly dark the detachment moved out through rugged and broken terrain and navigated its way toward the enemy camp throughout the night, which was exceptionally dark and bitterly cold.[11] Sharp Nose, one of the headmen of the Northern Arapahos, led the contingent, with Clark "in the lead at the heels of Sharp Nose."[12] Just before dawn on the morning of November 25 the detachment reached a point about a mile from the Northern Cheyenne camp. From that distance the soldiers could hear the pounding rhythm of drums emanating from the village. Inside the camp, headed by Dull Knife and others, including Little Wolf, the Northern Cheyennes celebrated a recent victory over the Shoshones. The camp, located along the banks of the Red Fork, consisted of 173 lodges protected by approximately 250 warriors.[13]

Years later Clark remembered:

> During the Sioux and Cheyenne war of 1876–7, in November 1876, I found myself in command of some three hundred friendly enlisted Indian scouts of Pawnee, Shoshone, Arapahoe, Cheyenne, Crow [Bannock], and Sioux tribes; six tribes having six different vocal languages. I had, of course, before known of the sign language used by our Indians, but here I was strongly impressed with its value and beauty. On the march, by their camp-fires at night, and in the early gray of morning, just before charging down on a hostile Indian village, I took my first lessons in this language and in Indian tactics.[14]

Clark's interest in Indian sign language would never sway. It would become both his passion and a legacy in the future.

At daybreak the drumming ceased as the Northern Cheyennes withdrew to their lodges for rest. Moments later the order to attack was given, and the cavalrymen with their Indian auxiliaries charged upon the village. Clark and Lieutenant De Lany commanded about 150 Lakotas, Northern Cheyennes, and Northern Arapahos, the North brothers headed the Pawnees, and Tom Cosgrove and First Lieutenant Walter S. Schuyler, Fifth Cavalry, led the Shoshones and Bannocks.[15] Clark recalled the scene: "One cold, wintery morning in the late fall of 1876, while yet the gray shadows of darkness hovered mistily over crag and gorge, some enlisted Indian scouts and regular troops charged down upon a hostile Indian village sleeping in fancied security in a cañon of the Big Horn Mountains."[16]

With Clark leading his scouts in another demonstration of his daring, the soldiers and their allies descended upon the village. Many of its occupants were able to flee from the opposite side of the camp, while others remained to face the onslaught. Those warriors who escaped found suitable defensive positions in the rocky ridges and hillsides above the valley floor and from there poured defensive fire on their attackers. In addition to taking the camp, the capture of the sizable Northern Cheyenne pony herd presented another prize. Efforts to seize the herd were met with resistance, and in one area of the battlefield the fighting degraded into hand-to-hand conflict. When secured, the captured herd numbered about seven hundred ponies. Following the initial charge and attack, the encounter then turned into a drawn-out long-distance skirmish that continued into the night, allowing the Northern Cheyenne noncombatants to vacate the area.[17]

In the aftermath of the assault a portion of the soldiers, including Clark, and their allies began a thorough search of the village, while Northern Cheyenne sharpshooters continued their harassing fire. The lodges were set ablaze. A large quantity of meat, robes, and hides were secured by the scouts or later burned by the soldiers. A sizable number of firearms and ammunition were discovered in the lodges. The search also yielded an array of trophies that the Northern Cheyennes had gathered from their recent raid against the Shoshones, including the severed right hands from a dozen infants, in addition to a large number of personal effects taken from the bodies of Seventh Cavalry soldiers slain at the Little Big Horn.[18] Clark acquired a fine Northern Cheyenne pipe from the village for his collection. Months later, while stationed at Camp Robinson, Clark displayed the pipe in his quarters. Northern Cheyenne headman Standing Elk came into the quarters one day to visit Clark and noticed the pipe. He informed Clark that the pipe had belonged to him but said that Clark could keep it as long as he had tobacco on hand: Standing Elk wanted to smoke the pipe whenever he came to visit. The lieutenant replied that he would look forward to Standing Elk's visits and that he could have all the tobacco he wanted.[19]

The price paid by both sides in the fight proved steep. The army had lost one officer, First Lieutenant John A. McKinney, and five enlisted men killed, with another twenty-six wounded. One of the army's Shoshone scouts had been wounded. The Northern Cheyennes lost an estimated forty killed and eighty wounded at the battlefield, with an unknown number dying from wounds and exposure in the days following the conflict. Dull Knife suffered the loss of three sons during the fight, while Little Wolf received a number of wounds. The survivors fled the scene in an appallingly destitute condition, left to face a harsh Wyoming winter while in search of a place of refuge.[20]

On the morning after the fight the destruction of Northern Cheyenne property was completed, resulting in the total annihilation of the village and its contents. At this point Mackenzie ordered the command to return to its base camp on Crazy Woman's Fork. A heavy snow fell as the detachment made its way from the village. The soldiers and their allies spent the next few days tracing much of the same route used on their journey to the fight, marching roughly ten miles each day until arriving at their supply camp on November 29.[21]

The command remained on Crazy Woman's Fork until December 2, 1876, when it moved to Cantonment Reno. On the next day the soldiers marched to the head of the Dry Fork of the Powder River. The men set up camp and remained there for a few days. From this location the sick and wounded of the command were sent to Fort Fetterman, reducing the size of the force by about 250 soldiers. The rest of the men continued to be plagued by snow and cold winds. By this time the deteriorating condition of the command's animals had started to become a concern.[22]

In addition to losing the sick and wounded, the command also suffered the loss of the Shoshone scouts, who left the camp on Dry Fork in order to return to their people. Clark observed: "Some of the tribes seem to revel in smutty personal names, and particularly is this the case with the Shoshones, though at every agency, I think, there are many names which civilized taste will not permit to be used in printed or vocal form."[23]

Despite all this, Crook decided to continue his pursuit of the Lakotas and Crazy Horse and revealed his plan to take the command east following the Belle Fourche River to an area on the northwestern edge of the Black Hills. He would then proceed according to the reports of his Indian scouts. The column commenced its eastward march on the morning of December 6 and reached the vicinity of the Black Hills in an area west of Inyan Kara Peak on December 9.[24]

For the next two weeks the command camped on the Belle Fourche as Crook awaited word from his scouts in the vicinity and also the return of a group of Indians sent to Red Cloud Agency. Life for the soldiers at the camp became a monotonous military routine broken by efforts to pass the time and socialize. Days were generally characterized by cold winds and snow, although the men did enjoy a two-day break from the extreme weather. Clark and the other officers busied themselves with their usual duties but also found time to play cards, chat, read, and pursue other interests.[25] Clark probably took advantage of the situation to continue to expand his knowledge and refine his skills in Indian sign language.

By December 20 it had become painfully clear that the winter campaign would have to come to an end due to a lack of supplies for both men and animals. On the following day Crook held a council with the leaders of the Lakota, Northern Cheyenne, and Northern Arapaho scouts and urged them to take it upon themselves to try to get the enemy to surrender before the upcoming spring. Additionally, the general informed the headmen that Clark would also be at Camp Robinson and that the lieutenant would be in charge of the scouts there.[26] Interestingly, in describing his interaction with the Indian scouts at the time of the council, First Lieutenant John G. Bourke mentioned the use of sign language and described Clark as being "proficient" in its use.[27] The intensity of Clark's interest must have been great, as exemplified by how quickly he learned the hand gestures used by the scouts after expressing an interest in them only a month and a half earlier.

In writing about the campaign years afterward, Clark touched upon the use of these allies, revealing much about his attitude toward them and his general disdain for interpreters. While camped on the Belle Fourche, Crook relied on intelligence gathered by his scouts. According to Clark:

> The scouts returned and reported that the hostiles had gone north; had, in fact, crossed the Missouri River. Subsequent events proved that the hostiles had *not* crossed the Missouri, but had crossed to the north of the Yellowstone, and these hitherto reliable scouts were credited with lying and mischievously bringing in a false report with the deliberate intention of deceiving. As a matter of fact the scouts were honest and had faithfully performed their work, and the mistake grew out of the ignorance of the interpreters.

Clark went on to explain that the Indians referred to the Yellowstone River as the Elk River until it reached the mouth of the Powder or Rosebud and then called it the Big Muddy, the same name applied to the Missouri. "The scouts said the hostiles had crossed the Big Muddy going north; the interpreter, not knowing the distinction made by the Indians, naturally supposed they had gone north of the Missouri River."[28]

Writing from the camp on the Belle Fourche on December 21 Clark informed Camp Robinson's commander, Major Julius W. Mason, Third Cavalry, that the Lakota, Northern Cheyenne, and Northern Arapaho scouts serving with the command had been ordered to his post. Clark added that the scouts were to retain possession of their ponies and their firearms. "The General desires that they should be treated kindly and considerately, in fact in such a way as to show them that their recent valuable services are appreciated."[29] Crook was clearly laying the groundwork for the continued grooming of his Indian allies into loyal servants of his will and entrusted Clark with the task of directing and overseeing their ongoing service in accomplishing the army's goals. Clark, for his part, embraced the opportunity, as he shared Bourke's view that Indian policy should be characterized as "justice backed by power."[30] With this new assignment Clark would be able to make his own contribution to the ongoing implementation of an Indian policy that he felt would ensure the survival of the Indians.

The command departed its camp on December 22 en route to Fort Fetterman, with the men suffering in the cold and snow. The inclement conditions plagued the soldiers day after day as they made their way toward the post. By Christmas Eve they had advanced approximately thirty-six miles, with the officers having nothing more to mark the occasion than the hot whiskey punch offered them by Crook. The column continued its march for another miserable five days and eighty-four miles until it reached Fetterman on December 29. The following day Clark joined Colonel Mackenzie's cavalry companies as they marched first to Fort Laramie and then onward to Camp Robinson, arriving there on January 9, 1877.[31] Clark later remarked: "The campaign ended. I was ordered to Red Cloud Agency, and remained there and at Spotted Tail Agency for a year, my duties bringing me in close and constant contact and intercourse with the Sioux, Cheyennes, and Arapahoes—in their camps, at their festivals, and funerals, and in the field with scouting-parties."[32]

⋄ 5 ⋄

SURRENDER OF CRAZY HORSE

Camp Robinson, located on the White River in northwestern Nebraska near the base of a series of pine-covered chalk bluffs, was established in March 1874. Named in honor of First Lieutenant Levi Robinson, killed earlier that year by Indians in the vicinity of nearby Laramie Peak, the post provided protection for the government employees and property associated with Red Cloud Agency, which was situated about a mile and a half from the garrison. The soldiers of the camp were also charged with the task of preventing any outbreak by the Indians of the agency.[1] In the spring of 1877 Camp Robinson and Camp Sheridan at Spotted Tail Agency, located forty-five miles east, witnessed an unprecedented number of surrendering northern Indians. It fell largely upon Lieutenant Clark's shoulders to manage them.

Clark's official duties were to enlist and command the Indian scouts at the agencies. An examination of his actions during this time, however, reveals that the lieutenant became involved in one way or another with most of the military's dealings with the Indians there. His friend First Lieutenant John G. Bourke referred to Clark's activities as "other very important business."[2] Not long after Clark's arrival at Camp Robinson steps were taken to implement Crook's plan to secure the surrender of the remaining roaming bands of Lakotas and Northern Cheyennes. In late January or early February Hunts the Enemy and Few Tails, along with a small number of Lakota warriors, were sent as emissaries his people's homeland against the military in a war that ended in 1868, in an effort to obtain the headman's assistance in securing Crazy Horse's surrender.[11] The lieutenant also realized Red Cloud's usefulness in controlling the Indians at Red Cloud Agency. Clark used the term "working" the Indians in describing his method of managing and controlling them. Simply stated, he attempted to secure the trust of powerful men in the various tribes and convince them that the military's aims were in their best interest. He would then rely on these leaders to influence those under their stewardship to think along the same lines. While successful in a number of instances, this approach had the unintended consequence of becoming a source of added friction among various tribal factions, especially among the Oglalas. For example, Crook ousted Red Cloud as leader of all the reservation Lakotas back in October due to his defiant attitude and replaced him with Spotted Tail. Red Cloud sought opportunities to get back into his former position of power, which in turn caused unrest at the Nebraska agencies. Clark, however, knew about Red Cloud's ambitions and sought to take full advantage of the situation. He understood tribal politics but seemed to underestimate both the depth and the intensity of the struggle for tribal power, a conflict that would destroy the harmonious atmosphere that he intended to create at the agencies.

One of the interpreters at the agency, William "Billy" Garnett, witnessed the meeting between Clark and Red Cloud. In recounting the meeting many years after the fact, Garnett recalled that Clark pledged to help restore the headman to his former position of prominence if he would hasten the surrender of Crazy Horse. He also outlined the benefits of serving as a scout and promised Red Cloud a high rank if he decided to join. In talking to Red Cloud, Clark reached out to the Lakota leader on a personal level and discussed the matter of fatherhood. He knew that Red Cloud's position with the military and federal officials had been compromised when it was discovered that Red Cloud's son, Jack Red Cloud, had clearly fought against Crook and his men at the Rosebud. Clark reassured Red Cloud that he did not blame him for the actions of his son and that he fully understood his position as a father.

During this same conversation Clark revealed something of his own story to the Oglala leader. Garnett remembered Clark stating that his father

> wanted my name pretty well known so he got me in this position; but after I was out in this country he began to see the danger I was in, and he wanted me to resign; but I liked the service so well that I would not quit it. Red Cloud, the money that my father puts in the bank for me brings

me $250 a month. I get $125 a month for this work. I am spending my official salary among you Indians as fast as I get it. This is one reason I have not married; I do not wish to leave any orphans; for a man in my place is liable to be killed any time.[12]

Red Cloud had in fact joined the ranks of Clark's scouts by the latter part of March. In a letter to Bourke, Clark mentioned that he had completed the enlistment of scouts at Camp Robinson and would now be going to Spotted Tail Agency for the same purpose. He was pleased with the men of influence that he had signed at Red Cloud Agency: "most excellent material," as Bourke described them.[13] He had also managed to enlist about twenty-five of the best Lakotas used in the previous winter's campaign. In regard to Red Cloud's recent enlistment, Clark confided: "I am quite convinced it was a good thing to take Red Cloud." He went on to explain: "He has felt keenly and bitterly his downfall and he will work hard and earnestly to regain something of his former prestige and power." Clark concluded his endorsement of the Oglala headman by stating: "I was convinced he could be used to advantage."[14]

Crook apparently was not as enthusiastic as Clark concerning the use of Red Cloud. In an effort to reassert himself as a power among his people, Red Cloud approached the brigadier general and offered to go out and speak to Crazy Horse to hasten his surrender. Crook seemed lukewarm to the idea but assented to the plan after making it clear that the Oglala headman could go if he wanted to but could not do so as his representative. Just days after Spotted Tail's return from his journey north in early April, Red Cloud embarked upon his pursuit of Crazy Horse.[15]

On March 29 Clark set out for Spotted Tail Agency, accompanied by the Oglala leader Little Wound. The lieutenant spent the next couple of days recruiting scouts from that agency and returned to Camp Robinson on April 2 after having signed an additional forty Lakota scouts. As with the other scouts he recruited, Clark had explained to these men that their service would provide them with a better chance for self-government and opportunities for exciting service in the field, thus allowing these former warriors once again to live like fighting men. Clark also outlined the immediate duties of these scouts: to maintain peace and harmony in their villages, to assist the agent on issue days, to take the arms and ponies away from northern Indians when surrendering at the agency, to protect Indian ponies from white horse thieves, and to preserve the peace between their young men and the whites. In his report to Bourke concerning his time at Spotted Tail Agency, Clark noted that the Indians there voiced their hope that their agency would not be moved.[16] Debate over the future location of the Lakota agencies would grow in the months ahead as one of the most pressing issues facing the government and the Indians.

In organizing his Indian scouts, Clark placed influential men in positions of high rank. Both Red Cloud and Spotted Tail were among those who commanded companies as first sergeants. Other prominent men served in leadership roles as sergeants and corporals.[17]

After recruiting approximately 120 Lakota, Northern Arapaho, and Northern Cheyenne scouts, Clark then set about arming his force. On April 2 he requested 150 Sharps carbines with 20,000 rounds of ammunition and 200 Colt revolvers with 10,000 rounds for use by the Indian soldiers at the two agencies. Crook approved the request and it fell upon Major A. W. Evans, commanding officer at Fort Laramie, to provide the firearms and ammunition. Major Evans was able to fill Clark's requisition with the exception of the pistols. Evans could only contribute fourteen of the Colt revolvers; the rest would have to come through the Department of the Platte.[18] In addition to acquiring firearms and being allowed to own ponies, the scouts also were issued military clothing and received the pay of a soldier.

Clark continued to fraternize and socialize with the Indians at the agencies. On April 11 he was asked to attend a dog feast at one of the camps. The invitation stipulated that the lieutenant could bring along a friend. Clark extended the offer to Bourke, who declined because he was too busy.[19] Nothing more is known about Clark's initiation into eating dog. Judging from at least one future experience (discussed later), he was not a fan of the prized delicacy. He did, however, extol the benefits of dog meat in his book on sign language: "The meat combines the flavors of bear and pork, and is wonderfully nutritious; one can undergo a great deal of hard work, especially hard riding, after a hearty meal of dog, without inconvenience, and I verily believe could go longer without special desire or need for food than after a meal of almost any other substance."[20]

Crook, Bourke, Clark, and others gathered at Camp Sheridan in the middle of April in order to receive the surrender of the Miniconjous under Touch the Clouds and the Sans Arcs under Red Bear and High Bear. These northern Indians, numbering approximately one thousand, were the same people who had promised Spotted Tail that they would surrender when he encountered them on the Little Missouri some weeks earlier. When the general met with them in council he emphasized the futility of any further resistance and the necessity for all the roaming bands to submit to reservation life. He also assured the gathered assemblage that he would do what he could to represent their interests to the powers in Washington. During his speech at the council Crook also mentioned that after all bands had surrendered he would allow the reservation Indians to go north, under the protection of soldiers, and conduct a buffalo hunt.[21] This assertion, however, would prove to be a significant point of contention in the months ahead.

At about this time Clark acquired a ring from a recently surrendered northern Indian. As it turned out, the ring came with a very interesting history. In the aftermath of Custer's defeat on the Little Big Horn, the victors ransacked the bodies of the fallen soldiers for anything that they found useful or of interest. One of the items taken that day was a ring worn by Second Lieutenant William Van Wyck Reily, Seventh Cavalry. The distinctive gold ring sported a bloodstone etched with the head of a griffin with a key in its mouth, said to be the heraldic seal of the Key family. Apparently Reily, on his father's side, was related to that family and its most famous member, Francis Scott Key, who wrote the lyrics of the American national anthem.[22]

After receiving the ring, Clark suspected that it had been taken at the Little Big Horn and promptly composed a letter to the editor of the *Army and Navy Journal*, which appeared in its April 14, 1877, edition. He described the ring and offered to return it to a friend or family member of the then unknown slain owner. The letter was dated April 3 in the journal, which may be a typographical error. Clark may have received the item in late March or early April, but contemporary evidence suggests that he did not acquire the ring until some days later.

The circumstances and details surrounding Clark's acquisition of the ring are conflicting. Bourke's diary entry for April 12, two days before the Camp Sheridan council, mentioned that Clark showed him the ring that day and Bourke specified that it belonged to Reily. In writing about the ring years later, Bourke's version of events changed. His recollection then was that in a meeting with the assembled northern Indians at Camp Sheridan Crook stressed the necessity of returning all objects taken at the Little Big Horn so that they might be returned to family members. He "referred very pointedly to Lt. Riley's [sic] ring, a description of which had just been received from Col. Sharp in Washington." Bourke went on to assert that after hearing the description one of the headmen located the ring and passed it along to Clark.[23] His later account established Reily as the owner of the ring before Clark gained possession, completely contradicting Clark's letter to the editor.

A related story published on April 14 in the *National Republican* (carrying the dateline April 13) identified Reily as the owner of the ring. According to the article, Clark received the ring that day from one of the northern Indians surrendering at Spotted Tail Agency.[24] A number of other newspapers printed the same story. Whatever discrepancies exist concerning how Clark obtained the ring, it is clear that the mystery surrounding ownership did not last long after Clark acquired it.

Reily's forlorn mother, Ellen Roche Reily Johnson, had written to both the commissioner of Indian affairs and the secretary of war on April 3 and 9, respectively, just days before Crook's arrival at the Nebraska agencies. Her plea for the ring's return included a facsimile drawing of the heraldic seal so that a detailed description of the ring could be provided to Indian agents and army officers throughout the west.[25] Through her efforts the ring's description reached the Nebraska agencies, making it possible for Clark to identify its owner. The timing of the grieving mother's letters to government officials and Clark's acquisition of the ring could not have been more fortuitous.

According to Clark's April 22 endorsement associated with official correspondence concerning the matter, he sent the ring to Omaha with Major Horace B. Burnham, who had attended the recent council at Camp Sheridan. Major Burnham was then to forward the ring by express to Reily's mother in Washington. Clark contacted Mrs. Johnson directly and closed the endorsement by stating: "I have notified her of my action."[26]

After his return to Camp Robinson from Spotted Tail Agency, Clark witnessed the arrival of members of Crazy Horse's camp. On the evening of April 17 he met with six warriors from that village and continued to speak with other new arrivals in the following days in an attempt to learn all he could concerning Crazy Horse and his camp. From all those interviewed it became clear that Crazy Horse's followers wanted peace and that the Oglala leader was disposed to follow the will of his people.[27]

The number of northern Indians coming in continued to increase. On April 21 Clark and interpreter William Rowland led Dull Knife's band of surrendering Northern Cheyennes into Red Cloud Agency. The mile-long caravan approached from the north, with some of the Northern Cheyennes firing their rifles while others sang. The 109 families constituted 524 people. With their surrender the total number of northern Indians at both agencies rose to 2,200.[28] As in all similar cases, the Northern Cheyennes relinquished all their arms and ponies as soon as they came in. In this instance, six hundred ponies, thirty-four pistols, and sixty-eight carbines and rifles were confiscated.[29] Clark reported: "These Indians are in a very destitute condition and truly represent a most wretched state of poverty—even for Indians. Some are still suffering from limbs frozen in their flight across the Big Horn and Wolf Mountains after the fight on Bates Creek [Red Fork] last winter."[30]

On the following evening runners from the Crazy Horse camp arrived at Red Cloud Agency and confirmed reports that the village was moving toward the agency. Five days later the anticipation surrounding the arrival of Crazy Horse increased when couriers from the Oglala headman brought news to the agency that he would arrive in eight or nine days and that the village was moving slowly because of the poor condition of their ponies.[31]

The opening days of May brought daily reports concerning the approach of the famed Crazy Horse, whose name would forever be associated with Custer's defeat at the Little Big Horn. While Clark would have the honor of accepting the Oglala leader's surrender, the distinction of being the first military officer to shake hands with Crazy Horse went to Second Lieutenant J. Wesley Rosenquest, Fourth Cavalry, who had been sent out with wagons full of provisions for the surrendering band.[32]

On the morning of May 6 Clark and a detachment of his Indian scouts finally rode out and met Crazy Horse and his people about five miles west of the agency on Soldier Creek. Clark later described the event: "When the Sioux chief Crazy Horse came in and surrendered in 1877, he formed all of his warriors in line, in advance of the women and children; then, in front of this line, also mounted, he had some ten of his headmen; and then in front of these he rode alone. I had been sent with Indian scouts to meet him."[33]

Crazy Horse clearly had dictated just how the surrender would proceed, as Clark explained: "He sent me word requesting a similar formation on our part, and asked that I should ride on in advance alone. Then we were to dismount and first shake hands, while seated on the ground, *that the peace might be solid.*" He continued: "After all of this had been done his headmen came up, the peace-pipe was produced, and we solemnly smoked. One of his headmen put a scalp-shirt and war-bonnet on me, and presented me the pipe with which peace had been made."[34] The headman Clark referred to was Crazy Horse's trusted friend He Dog. Crazy Horse made a similar gesture to Red Cloud.

During the proceedings, Clark raised his hand skyward and offered a prayer, interpreted for the assemblage by William Garnett. The essential message of the lieutenant's words was that the bloodshed should end, the past should be forgotten, "and that from this day forward we will live in a peaceful way."[35]

Clark also delivered a brief speech, as reported by the *Chicago Times*, in which he outlined the upcoming procedures for the surrender. The message revealed something of Clark's understanding of the Indian psyche. The lieutenant addressed the gathering:

> We have come to make a lasting peace, never to be broken. We had a rain last night that has washed out all bad feelings that have ever been between us. The sun is now shining brightly. All shows the Great Spirit is pleased with our actions. To insure this lasting peace it is necessary to give up arms and ponies. This afternoon, when we reach camp, I will take the names of all Indians who turn in ponies and arms, and will send them to the great father in Washington. Gen. Crook is now in Washington, looking out for your interests. We want to count the Indians so as to provide them with rations, and keep them supplied.[36]

For his part, Crazy Horse expressed to Clark that he too desired to live in peace. He also informed the lieutenant about his wish that he and his people be allowed to have a place of their own in the Tongue River country.[37] In the months ahead Crazy Horse would continue to insist upon this issue, adding one more point of contention between the northern Indians and government authorities.

At the conclusion of the council the participants left for the short ride to Red Cloud Agency with Clark, Red Cloud, and the agency headmen in the lead. Clark, who continued to wear He Dog's headdress, "made an imposing appearance" according to Garnett.[38] Some of the northern Indians, however, were not so impressed. According to the Oglala Shave Elk, "he looked so comical that even we Indians laughed."[39]

In the early afternoon the procession arrived at the designated camping area at the agency. The pony herd was promptly handed over to Red Cloud and the Indian scouts for the time being. By the next day, however, most of the ponies had been returned to the northern Indians as gifts by the agency Lakotas. After the women of Crazy Horse's band set up camp the warriors turned in their firearms, which resulted in the confiscation of only 76 guns. Clark insisted that the Lakotas possessed more firearms than were retrieved. With the assistance of a small number of Indian scouts, with Garnett and Frank

Grouard as interpreters, he set about a thorough search of each lodge. When Clark completed his examination of the lodges, the camp had yielded a total of 117 firearms. Unknown to the Crazy Horse village, Clark enjoyed an added measure of security while searching the tipis, as a group of Northern Cheyenne warriors concealed themselves above the camp ready to assist Clark if the need arose. The task, however, was accomplished in a surprisingly calm atmosphere, with much credit for this feat being attributed to Clark's cool demeanor.[40]

When Clark made his report to Colonel Mackenzie on the day's events, he numbered the ponies seized at 2,000. He went on to state the total number of firearms seized as 117 and also tallied 889 individuals as composing Crazy Horse's band, 217 of which were men.[41] When Red Cloud Agency's chief clerk, Charles P. Jordan, took the official census the following day, the number of people in the band was recorded at 899. The generally accepted number of ponies taken was placed at 2,200.[42] With Crazy Horse's surrender the total number of northern Indians at both agencies, Lakotas and Northern Cheyennes, rose to over 3,400 individuals.[43]

With the arrival of Crazy Horse and his followers at Red Cloud Agency, Clark embarked upon some of the most challenging moments of his military career. The lieutenant initially exuded confidence that he could persuade the Lakota headman to become a "progressive" leader of his people. Unfortunately Clark's actions, despite his best intentions, fueled the flames of jealousy among competing factions of tribal leaders. The irony of the situation, as upcoming events at the Nebraska agencies would prove, was that instead of Clark "working" the Indians they in fact "worked" him.

✧ 6 ✥

DOG FEASTS AND FAILED DIPLOMACY

It was not by chance that Crook assigned Clark the difficult task of not only recruiting and maintaining a force of scouts at Red Cloud and Spotted Tail Agencies but also monitoring the activities of the Indians at these agencies and promptly reporting them to the brigadier general. Both Sheridan and Crook were impressed by men who could communicate effectively with Indians and gain their trust. Clark was such a man. In addition, both generals knew the value of using informants and spies within the confines of the Indian camps as an effective means of gathering intelligence.[1] The ambitious lieutenant thus set out to establish such a network. Spying became an increasingly important function of some of the scouts.

Clark's personality also suited him well for the task at hand. John W. Ford, correspondent for the *Chicago Times*, perceived something in Clark that a number of people, both Indian and white, came to know. According to the reporter, "There is a personal magnetism about the man that attaches a person to him as soon as one meets him." The correspondent went on to note: "This is used to great advantage with Indians. His Indian soldiers perfectly worship him. His word is law to them. His perfect control of them shows that Indians can easily be got along with if dealt with honestly, treated kindly, and with a firm hand."[2]

First Lieutenant Jesse M. Lee, serving as the military Indian agent at Spotted Tail Agency, further endorsed Clark: "Lieut. Clark possessed in a high degree a personal magnetism and pleasing manner that charmed everyone. His selection by Gen. Crook for this most difficult of duties, was a high compliment to his marked abilities and splendid accomplishments. He was, without a doubt, one of the most promising and talented officers in the Army."[3] Perhaps just as important, Clark quickly made a name for himself for being able to think like an Indian, for being sensitive to their plight, and for his knowledge of their culture.

As will be seen, during Crazy Horse's stay at the agency Clark sought the headman's friendship and attempted time after time to appease him. On numerous occasions Clark visited with the Oglala leader socially and officially and also tried to make Crazy Horse an integral part of his complement of Indian scouts. For his part, Crazy Horse seemed to tolerate the lieutenant but also manipulated the relationship in an effort to exert his own will and maintain some degree of power among his people.

Just days after the May 6 surrender Little Wound, an agency Oglala leader and ally of Red Cloud, held a council and feast, hosting about one hundred men. Crazy Horse and He Dog were among those attending the event. Clark and correspondent Robert E. Strahorn ("Alter Ego" of the *Chicago Tribune*) were the only two whites in attendance. Following the council a feast was held. The main dish was dog meat, an Indian favorite. Strahorn ate the dish, primarily because he did not want to offend his gracious hosts.[4] Clark probably ate it in an effort to impress Crazy Horse and the other Lakotas.

On the following day, May 12, Clark succeeded in recruiting Crazy Horse and twenty-five other northern Indians as scouts. Crazy Horse would go on to command one of the companies as its first sergeant. His headmen welcomed the opportunity to join, as it enabled them to retain ponies and to be issued carbines, pistols, and ammunition.[5] These former warriors appreciated the chance to be armed once again. An atmosphere of goodwill prevailed. Service as Indian scouts also offered the men an avenue toward some degree of prestige among their people. In speaking of the enlistment, interpreter William Garnett observed that "Clark, in the bigness of his heart, and to convince the late hostiles of his confidence in them declared that he was going to treat them all alike."[6]

Crook expressed pleasure at Clark's success in securing Indian scouts, writing on May 18: "Referring to the Indian scouts now in service in the department, I would say that they have been carefully organized and contain in their ranks some of the most influential men of their several bands, and their retention in service for some time to come is of paramount importance to the work of removing the tribes in question."[7] Crook was speaking of the upcoming removal of 13,000 to 14,000 Indians then located at Red Cloud and Spotted Tail Agencies to the Missouri River, a move that they fervently opposed.

Not everyone was enthused about Clark's actions, however. Garnett criticized the lieutenant for enlisting Crazy Horse and his men. He was especially critical of putting firearms and ammunition into their hands. Fellow interpreter Baptiste Pourier felt that it was bad policy to arm these men and joined Garnett in opposing the confidence that Clark placed in the men so recently considered enemies.[8] While he did not agree with Clark on this matter, Garnett still held the lieutenant in high esteem. According to Eli S. Ricker, the interpreter told him that "Clark had the most gratifying reputation all around, among white men and Indians, of any officer he ever knew. He was a brave, generous, and noble man and officer."[9]

In late May (probably the 24th) a small band of Northern Cheyennes under Last Bull came into Red Cloud Agency to surrender. The group consisted of sixteen men, five women, and eleven children. One of the men was Wooden Leg, a veteran of the fight at the Little Big Horn. After their surrender they met Clark, who made a favorable impression on Wooden Leg: "One of these soldier chiefs we specially liked. We learned from a Cheyenne his name among the Indians was White Hat. He could make good signtalk. It appeared he understood Indians better than any white man soldier I ever had seen. I suppose that was why we liked him."[10]

Clark informed the small band that they would have to give up their ponies and firearms. All complied with the request with the exception of Black Coyote, who informed the lieutenant that he was not giving up his gun. After a few tense moments and the intervention of Last Bull, the warrior finally turned over his firearm.

Of the men in the band only Wooden Leg owned a gun captured from the fight at the Little Big Horn. When he surrendered the piece Clark examined it closely, showed it to other officers, and finally asked where Wooden Leg got the gun. Fearful of answering, Wooden Leg remained quiet.

> He asked me again, making signs so clear that I could not help but to make some kind of answer. I told him the truth. I showed him just how I seized and wrenched it away from a soldier riding toward the river during the first part of the great battle a year before this time. The way they talked about it, it appeared the Indians had not been giving them

these guns taken from the soldiers. After a little while, White Hat shook hands again with me and made signs to me: "You are a brave man. Do not be afraid any soldier will want to kill you."[11]

On May 25 General Crook, who had arrived at Camp Robinson two days earlier, held a council with the Indians of the two agencies. Clark arranged for the general to review his scouts before the convening of the council. For two hours before Crook's arrival at the gathering, Clark drilled his men in order to perfect their maneuvers for the upcoming exhibition.[12] He took pride in his scouts and wanted them to make a lasting impression. During the demonstration Crazy Horse rode at Clark's side on the right of the line,[13] yet another example of the lieutenant's desire to draw Crazy Horse into a position of trust and friendship. At the conclusion of the review, Crook and Crazy Horse met for the first time.

The primary topic discussed during the council pertained to the future location of a new reservation. The headmen who spoke once again voiced their desire for an agency in their own country to the north and expressed their disdain for an agency on the Missouri River. Crook stated that he would help them but was not in a position to decide the matter, explaining that only the government could rule on such things. He pointed out to the members of the council that a delegation of their leaders must go to Washington, D.C., in order to discuss the situation with the president and commissioner of Indian affairs.[14]

At the conclusion of the council Crook accepted an invitation to the Oglala village for a dog feast. There the headmen continued to impress upon the general their wish to remain in their own country. Crook reiterated the need for a trip to Washington in order to settle the question. The issue of the upcoming buffalo hunt was also addressed. Crook promised that the buffalo hunt would proceed as soon as all the nonreservation Indians south of the Yellowstone River surrendered.[15] The anticipated relocation of the reservation, the promised buffalo hunt, and the projected journey to Washington became the vexing issues of the day that would continue to confound the relationship between the Lakotas and the government.

During the discussions at the Oglala camp the prized meal of dog meat made its way around to the assembled dignitaries. For reasons unknown, Clark passed on the delicacy and paid an Indian seated behind him a dollar to eat his portion. The lieutenant offered to do likewise for Crook, but the general declined the offer and eagerly consumed the canine. The Lakotas who witnessed the event were amused that the general would eat dog while Clark refused it.[16]

Two events in the days immediately following the council emboldened Crazy Horse and other northern Indians. On May 26 Lieutenant Colonel Luther P. Bradley, Ninth Infantry, replaced Mackenzie as commander at Camp Robinson. Clark took it upon himself to introduce the new commander to a number of Lakota headmen. The New England–born Bradley had served in the Civil War, advancing to the rank of brigadier general of volunteers, before joining the regular army after the conflict. He had commanded Fort C. F. Smith, Montana Territory, during the Red Cloud War. When Mackenzie left, the cavalry presence at Robinson fell to four hundred men, less than half its strength earlier that spring.[17] In the days following Mackenzie's departure Clark rapidly sensed the effect of the troop reduction on the northern Indians.

Two days after Bradley took command the Northern Cheyennes from Red Cloud Agency departed for their journey to their new permanent home, joining the Southern Cheyennes on their reservation in Indian Territory. The Northern Cheyennes, who considered themselves to have been ill treated at the hands of Crazy Horse after the attack on Dull Knife's camp, had eagerly sought to support the military at Red Cloud Agency. Their departure signaled a further easing of control at the agency. Clark, always keeping Crook apprised of Indian matters, sent a dispatch to the general, then at Fort Laramie. It stated that First Lieutenant Henry W. Lawton, escorting the Northern Cheyennes, was encamped about nine miles from Camp Robinson with 972 of these Indians, leaving about 150 still remaining at Camp Robinson.[18]

With the departure of the Northern Cheyennes, Clark found it necessary to reorganize his Indian scouts. The group had formerly consisted of Companies A, B, C, and D, containing 224 scouts. With the addition of Crazy Horse and 25 of his men the total reached 250. A new company, Company E, was created. When the Northern Cheyennes left for the south, Company A lost 30 scouts from that tribe. This prompted Clark to reorganize the companies to nearly equal strength with each other, which was accomplished by moving men from one company to another.[19]

During the final days of May Clark received reports concerning the recent attack on Lame Deer's camp of Miniconjous by soldiers under Colonel Nelson A. Miles, Fifth Infantry, and the death of Lame Deer. The camp represented the last village of nonreservation Lakotas south of the Yellowstone River. It was reported that the remnants of the band were heading to Red Cloud Agency. News of Sitting Bull's rumored location also reached the lieutenant. After careful investigation Clark concluded that the reports concerning the Lame Deer fight were accurate but that the rumors concerning Sitting Bull were false.[20]

On June 1 Clark met with a group of scouts from Crazy Horse's camp at his quarters. He subsequently dispatched some scouts from Crazy Horse's band to the vicinity of the Little Powder River to locate the Miniconjou camp, now under the leadership of Fast Bull. The scouting party returned about two weeks later, having found the trail of the camp but failed to locate the village itself.[21] A week later Clark sent out another five men under the supervision of Four Crows to go north in order to gather information on the Miniconjou camp. Finding no new trail, the party returned to Camp Robinson on July 3. Still, Clark praised his scouts to department headquarters, noting that they "have been out twelve days and have been almost constantly in the saddle, exercising great energy and activity as well as good judgement, and certainly deserves [sic] great credit."[22]

On June 9 a relatively minor yet revealing event took place at Red Cloud Agency. Crazy Horse and his warriors arrived at the agency for beef issue day. In the past his people's allotment had been thirty-one head of cattle. But this time butcher Ben Tibbetts issued only twenty-nine because the animals weighed more than usual. Crazy Horse became upset at the shortage and refused to take the reduced herd. Upon noticing a stray steer, however, the Oglala leader ordered his men to capture it. After adding the steer to the allotment in the corral, Crazy Horse and his men drove thirty cattle back to the northern village. Clark was present to witness the event but did nothing to intervene.[23] The lieutenant's reluctance to act is evidence of his continued desire to befriend and win over Crazy Horse, whom he saw as integral in his efforts to control the northern Indians and persuade them to change their ways.

Instead of chastising Crazy Horse, Clark criticized First Lieutenant Charles A. Johnson, acting Indian agent, who was in charge of the beef issue. In writing to First Lieutenant Walter S. Schuyler, Clark touched on the event: "Johnson has had some little trouble with his beef issue." He went on to state that the agent "has not the ability or force to command very much respect anywhere."[24]

The day had been a trying one for Clark. In addition to the ruckus involving the beef issue, on the same day he had to deal with another incident when a small band of twenty Northern Cheyennes came in to surrender. In the same letter to Schuyler Clark wrote that the Northern Cheyennes "were the first to show any ill temper in disarming since I have been here." He added: "One of the young bucks was a little insolent but I nipped it in the bud and would have nipped his career with a great deal of satisfaction and pleasure but he subsided and made excuses."

Clark took the Northern Cheyenne ponies away from them and explained to Schuyler that "it seems hardly fair that in view of the fact that all of the other hostiles have their ponies these should be deprived but I took them yesterday as much for a lesson to the Sioux as anything else to show them that anything bordering on insolent conduct would be quickly punished." Apparently Clark did not realize that his lack of action against Crazy Horse sent a message of weakness, which could not be compensated for by denying the Northern Cheyennes their ponies.

On the following day Clark convened a council with a group of Lakota headmen in order to discuss the apprehension of the remnants of Lame Deer's Miniconjous. Expecting at any time to hear from the first group of scouts that he had sent out, the lieutenant wanted to gauge the headmen's willingness to take action. Clark felt optimistic about a forthcoming surrender and after the council notified Schuyler that the Lakotas would help to bring the Mininconjous in, "forcibly if they find it necessary."[25]

On June 13 Clark rode out to Crazy Horse's camp after receiving an invitation from the Oglala leader. Crazy Horse wanted to meet with the lieutenant in order to discuss the promised buffalo hunt. During the council Crazy Horse indicated that the Lakotas wanted to embark upon the hunt in about twenty-five days.[26] Clark intended to ride over to Spotted Tail Agency the next day and wanted Crazy Horse to join him. It is believed that the offer was extended to Crazy Horse during Clark's visit to his camp and that the Oglala leader accepted at that time.[27] On the following morning Clark and Crazy Horse made the journey to the Brule Agency. The purpose of Clark's visit was to pay compensation money to one of the bands there for some ponies that had been confiscated. The two men spent the next three days at the agency, with Clark arriving back at Camp Robinson on June 17. Upon his return from the agency Clark reported to Schuyler that "everything going on well there."[28]

In June Clark also faced the task of providing scouts to accompany an upcoming expedition to explore the Yellowstone and Big Horn valleys headed by Generals Sheridan and Crook. The small group of Lakota scouts, joined by Frank Grouard and Baptiste Pourier, first traveled to Camp Brown, Wyoming Territory, where the various members of the party gathered before venturing into the Big Horn Mountains. In addition to gaining knowledge of the terrain, the trip included an ample amount of leisurely hunting and fishing. The group also visited the site of the Custer fight, which allowed the generals to study the battlefield firsthand. The scouts remained with the party until late July, when they embarked upon their journey home.[29]

Clark always maintained an interest in Indian culture and happenings at the agencies. Interpreter William Garnett explained that the lieutenant "was quick to observe and get onto anything brewing."[30] In late June Clark took advantage of a rare opportunity for a white man when he observed and recorded a sun dance held at Crazy Horse's village. Generally held early each summer, the annual ceremony represented the rebirth and renewal of the world as the Indians knew it, to promote the growth of new grass, lush and tall, to feed and keep healthy a greater number of buffalo with their newly born calves, thus ensuring the prosperity of the tribe. For those vowing to participate in the piercing portion of the ceremony, their actions were motivated as an expression of thanks for past good fortune or as an offering for some prayer yet unanswered. Clark understood the significance of the event and noted that the ceremony "partakes as strongly of a religious character as any custom which the Indians have preserved since the invasion of the white race."[31]

Clark paid close attention to all facets of the sun dance. The first day of the four-day ceremony commenced with the cutting down of a cottonwood tree that served as the medicine pole for the sun dance, to be placed at the center of the ceremonial arbor. The lieutenant witnessed the event, which took place about two miles from the camp, and took detailed notes on this and all other parts of the ceremony. Once felled and limbed, the pole was then transported by wagon to the ceremonial area, a modification of the traditional way of moving the pole and a change that bothered an aged Lakota man who discussed the process with the lieutenant.

Later, as the medicine pole reached the site of the sun dance arbor, the Lakotas staged a traditional sham battle. This particular one imitated the Custer fight from the preceding year. Clark viewed the spectacle from a nearby hill. As he watched the Indian veterans of the Little Big Horn, he thought of Custer and his men "surrounded by this horde."[32] The mock battle pitted the northern warriors, reprising their roles in the fight, against the agency Lakotas, playing the part of Custer's men. Instead of faking the action, however, the northern Indians struck the agency Indians aggressively. The situation became tense. The agency Lakotas became quite upset, and revolvers were fired. Clark became alarmed and hurried down from the hill. He managed to stop the gunfire and calm the potentially explosive situation.[33]

During the course of the remaining three days of the ceremony Clark continued to observe the activities of the participants and take notes. On the second day they erected the medicine pole in the center of the dance area and constructed the arbor surrounding it for the accommodation of spectators. Clark looked on during the early portion of the third day as the Indians were piercing their infants' ears or, as Clark described it, "cutting holes in the ears of the babies."[34]

Next came the most important aspect of the sun dance ceremony, the piercing and tearing away of the flesh of those who pledged to undergo the ordeal. According to Clark, ten men participated in the piercing segment of the ceremony. He watched as each dancer had two holes cut into his chest through which skewers were inserted. Ropes suspended from the top of the medicine pole were then attached to the skewers on the chest of each man. As the dancing commenced, each participant blew on an eagle bone whistle and stared upward at the medicine pole, leaning back as he moved in an effort to tear the muscles binding him to the pole. Thus the ceremony continued until the dancers succeeded in tearing their flesh and finally freeing themselves.

Clark described the ceremony as "this horrible worship called a Sun-Dance." His description exposed his ethnocentric attitude: he interpreted events and people through his perceived idea of moral superiority, a mind-set that he never overcame. Clark did much in his later writing to dispel many common myths concerning Plains Indian culture and customs. When it came to certain practices of a religious or spiritual nature, however, his ethnocentric thinking often predominated. While he viewed numerous aspects of Indian culture with an untainted eye and could even admit "that there are no people who pray more than Indians," he could also describe something as nonthreatening as a Northern Cheyenne medicine dance to promote a good hunt as a "rude, wild, savage form of worship."[35]

Gore was not the issue in labeling the sun dance as horrible. Clark played major roles in two bloody engagements the previous year and would display his courage in future conflicts. He was not a man who shied from the sight of blood. The bloodletting and mutilation associated with the sun dance appalled him because of its sheer savagery as he saw it and because it was undertaken as a religious activity. Unfortunately, only a portion of what he witnessed found its way into print with the publication of his book on sign language. He confessed to his readers: "It would take many pages to describe this horrible ceremony in detail, I have only tried to give some of the more salient points."[36]

In the days after the completion of the sun dance a group of twenty-three lodges of northern Indians from Spotted Tail Agency petitioned Red Cloud Agency's newly arrived agent, Dr. James S. Irwin, to remain at his agency. According to the new agent, the Indians claimed that they belonged to Crazy Horse's band and had come to the agency on his invitation and that the Lakota leader wished them to be transferred. The new agent sought Clark's advice on the matter and found that "Lieut. Clark is of the opinion that it would be advisable to allow them to remain here rather than refuse them which would cause confusion and much hard feeling."[37] The lieutenant's response was consistent with his continued attempts to appease Crazy Horse and his followers. What Clark failed to realize, however, was that this most recent addition to Crazy Horse's camp represented a continuation of that leader's bid to secure ever-increasing power at Red Cloud Agency. A tempest was brewing between Crazy Horse and the northern Indians on one hand and Red Cloud and the agency Indians on the other. Clark remained oblivious to the severity of the situation.

One of Clark's other efforts to befriend Crazy Horse would ultimately contribute to the turmoil at Red Cloud Agency. At some point in the summer of 1877 Clark arranged a marriage between Crazy Horse and an attractive young mixed-blood girl named Helen "Nellie" Larrabee, the daughter of a French trader and a full-blooded Southern Cheyenne woman. Clark believed that Crazy Horse would view his role as matchmaker as a favor and that the relationship would make the Lakota leader more relaxed and help to change his attitude toward whites.[38]

Just like some of Clark's other well-intentioned actions, the plan backfired. Instead of easing Crazy Horse's mind, his new wife filled his head with rumors and gossip that alienated him even further from military and government officials and increased his paranoia. For example, Nellie believed that the proposed trip to Washington, D.C., represented nothing more than a ruse to get Crazy Horse out of the country forever and drilled this and other ideas into her husband's head. Nellie was described by William Garnett as a woman "not of the best frontier variety." He clearly held her in low esteem, also calling her "insidious and evil."[39]

In her book on Crazy Horse author Mari Sandoz mentions a letter from Clark to Crook in which he expressed his satisfaction with the union between Nellie and Crazy Horse.[40] Efforts to locate the letter have unfortunately been unsuccessful. Sandoz also speculated that Clark and Nellie were romantically tied before and after Crazy Horse's death but could never prove her suspicion.[41]

Proof of any relationship between Clark and Larrabee has never been found. It appears that the rumor of the alleged affair emanated predominantly from the mixed-blood community at Red Cloud Agency and beyond via gossip and innuendo.[42] William J. Bordeaux, the son of interpreter Louis Bordeaux, reveals a certain degree of animosity toward Clark in *Custer's Conqueror*, reflecting a sentiment most likely shared by others. This sheds light upon an added source of fuel to power the rumor mills.

In the years following Crazy Horse's death some speculation arose concerning Clark's true motivation in placing Nellie in Crazy Horse's life. Rather than being seen as an act of friendship, the gesture was viewed by some as an attempt by Clark to infiltrate Crazy Horse's lodge with an informant as part of his spy network.[43] Although this may have been at least a part of the lieutenant's initial goal, it failed miserably. Nellie added to Clark's problems, and her influence increased the eventual tension that existed between the two men. Lacking an informant in the Oglala leader's lodge, the lieutenant continued to rely on others to acquire information from outside the tipi.

Clark had to contend with other rumors as well, this time from beyond the confines of the Nebraska reservations. On July 13, 1877, the lieutenant reported to department headquarters that he had just returned from Spotted Tail Agency, where he had completed the enlistment of scouts. Clark touted that the principal headmen from that place had joined the ranks of the scouts and "are beginning to appreciate the benefits that accrue to them through the enlistment." He went on to add that the rumors that small bands of Indians were fleeing the agencies were false. He reassured headquarters that through frequent census taking and other measures "I have no hesitancy in positively stating that no such parties have left." Clark concluded the report with his usual air of optimism: "Indian affairs at both agencies are in a satisfactory condition, the influence of the agency Indians over those who have recently came in from the north is particularly good."[44]

Around this same time Clark called Crazy Horse and about thirty others to his quarters for a council. Clark addressed his audience while sitting atop the back of an office chair, with his feet on the seat. The assembled Indians sat on the floor with the exception of Crazy Horse, who sat on a chair near the lieutenant, a clear indication of his stature among his people. The topic of conversation at this particular meeting concerned the continued problem of white horse thieves. The outlaws stole ponies from the Indians and drove them to the Black Hills country, where they were sold. In an effort to stop the thieves, the scouts continued to assist military personnel in apprehending the outlaws, who were then turned over to the proper authorities for prosecution.[45] These horse thieves also plagued both the Indians and whites as well in another way, as explained by Clark: "White horse-thieves on the frontier frequently disguise themselves as Indians and 'run off' stock; but, as a rule, they make a trail which can be easily detected."[46]

The next meeting between Clark and Crazy Horse took place just before Clark left on detached service at Forts Laramie and Sanders on July 16. The two men were joined by Lieutenant Colonel Bradley and a group of Lakota leaders. The time for embarking upon the promised buffalo hunt in the north country had come and gone with nothing being done to move the hunt forward. The two officers assured the Lakota headmen that the hunt would still take place and that it was simply delayed. More importantly, the two officers proposed that the hunt take place after the Washington delegation's return, thus reversing the order of events previously agreed upon. The Lakota leaders accepted the proposition.[47]

Upon his return to Camp Robinson on July 27, Clark called another council together to discuss the buffalo hunt. Seventy Lakotas attended the gathering, including Crazy Horse, Red Cloud, Little Big Man, and Young Man Afraid of His Horses. At the meeting Clark read a message from General Crook, stating that he would honor his promise of a buffalo hunt and that they would be absent for about forty nights. After the hunt, sometime in the middle of September, a delegation would journey to Washington, D.C., to discuss the matter of agency relocation to the Missouri River. Thus the earlier sequence of going out on the hunt before traveling to Washington was restored. At the time of the council the secretary of the interior had set the number of Indians in the delegation at eighteen. Clark announced this number to the headmen while reading Crook's message. More importantly, the headmen were informed that they should choose their most able leaders to join the delegation.[48]

The last order of business at this council was to determine where the feast after the meeting should be held. Young Man Afraid of His Horses recommended Crazy Horse's village. Upset by the nomination, Red Cloud and one or two other Lakotas abruptly left the room. With no formal objections being voiced, however, the council adjourned.[49] Angered by the decision to allow Crazy Horse to host the feast, Red Cloud increasingly perceived Crazy Horse as a threat to his political power at the agency. In the days and weeks following the July 27 council the gap between Crazy Horse and the northern Indians and Red Cloud and the agency Indians widened. Clark's continued favoritism toward Crazy Horse only served to make matters worse.

At about 10 on the night of the council and feast, agent James S. Irwin received a visit at his quarters by two agency Lakotas loyal to Red Cloud. They expressed their opposition to the feast at the Crazy Horse village and also warned the agent that Crazy Horse would use the upcoming buffalo hunt as an opportunity to break away and embark upon a war against the whites. The two men presented a convincing argument, for Irwin turned against Crazy Horse from that point on.[50]

On the following day General Crook issued an order authorizing the sale of arms and ammunition to all Indians planning on joining the buffalo hunt. The general's decision received some criticism from those opposed to arming Indians who had been deemed enemies until recently. Despite these concerns, it appeared at the time that the buffalo hunt would become a reality.[51]

More important to Crazy Horse than the hunt, however, was the location of the future agency for his people. The Lakota leader still insisted that a northern agency be established west of the Black Hills and wanted the matter settled before the trip to Washington. Red Cloud and other agency leaders disagreed with Crazy Horse's choice for the future site of their agency and increasingly influenced tribal opinion to favor an agency on the White River in the present reservation.[52]

From the moment the Washington trip was first mentioned Crazy Horse refused to commit to going there as a member of the delegation. His attitude continued to frustrate military authorities. He stubbornly held out on making a decision until he was granted assurances of a northern agency. Crook saw Crazy Horse's participation in the delegation as an important matter. The general became determined that the Lakota headman should be a member of the delegation. As time passed he placed increasing pressure on Clark and other officers to force the Lakota leader into a commitment.[53]

With the buffalo hunt looking more certain a lightened mood prevailed at the agency. Clark reflected the feeling of optimism, informing Crook that "Crazy Horse and his people are getting quite sociable and I reckon I shall have to be considered one of their tribe soon, as I have been invited down to three feasts." Revealing something of his sense of humor, at the end of his rather lengthy report he added: "I have now given you so much Indian that if you will just take a smoke you will have the same sensation you would have enjoyed (?) had you been at a council."[54]

In early August Clark received a telegram from Crook informing him that the Indian Office had authorized a delegation of fifteen to twenty headmen to go to Washington, D.C.[55] The lieutenant promptly called a council and read the general's message to the assembled headmen. After the council Clark met with Crazy Horse and others and explained the contents of the message "kindly and fully." In the days that followed he continued to discuss the delegation with them at their lodges and in his own quarters. In regard to his handling of Crazy Horse in the matter, Clark explained to Crook that the Lakota leader "was not pushed for a decision, hoping that the influence of his head men might be sufficient."[56] In this connection Clark wrote Lieutenant Jesse M. Lee, acting Indian agent at Spotted Tail Agency, stating that "Crazy Horse told me he wanted to do right, but needed plenty of time to consider; and so matters rest."[57]

While Clark remained steadfast in his positive opinion of Crazy Horse, agent Irwin held quite the opposite viewpoint. After Crazy Horse refused to sign receipts for his rations and also committing other defiant acts, Irwin expressed his concerns to Commissioner of Indian Affairs J. Q. Smith. "It now appears that Crazy Horse has not been acting in good faith with the Army," Irwin lamented, observing: "I think the most if not all the difficulty arose from a misconception of Crazy Horse's character."[58]

In addition to the added pressure applied to Crazy Horse by representatives of the military and government, the agency rumor mill generated further turmoil, with agency headmen doing what they could to drive a wedge between Crazy Horse and white authorities. In addition to the stress created by his rivals, Crazy Horse's new wife, Nellie, continued to fill the Lakota leader's head with gossip, feeding his fears. This was especially true for the proposed trip to Washington, which she presented as a trap to get rid of him. Other northern Indians also began to warn Crazy Horse about impending doom if he went with the delegation.[59]

Clark, however, continued to believe in the northern Indians and in his efforts to influence them into doing what he viewed as the right thing. Addressing the poisonous effects of gossip, the lieutenant wrote: "Rumors between the two Agencies have grown into such proportions, their influence is so bad and pernicious, keeping the Indians in an unsettled, restless state, I hope we can stop them. The northern Indians at both agencies have done well, and as long as they are trying to do what is right, it is not fair nor just that they should be kept constantly on nettles by stories of damage that is going to be done them."[60] These were hardly the words of a man bent on promoting jealousy and ill-will among the various Lakota factions, as some of Clark's critics at the time and some historians since have suggested.

Among the legitimate concerns at both agencies regarding the delegation was its small size. Lakota leaders at Red Cloud Agency and at Spotted Tail Agency voiced their opinions that the number of delegates should be expanded.[61] They were not alone. On August 8 Captain D. W. Burke, commanding Camp Sheridan, wrote to Clark, expressing his desire that the number of participants be enlarged. Clark himself confided to Crook: "I regret very much that the delegation is so small—there should be thirty at least. The Indians are particularly anxious to have more go, and I heartily wish it might be increased."[62] The final number of delegates would be only slightly greater than originally planned.

Near the middle of August tensions at Red Cloud Agency began to increase at an accelerated rate. The War Department set into motion this most recent downward spiral when it rescinded Crook's order to allow the sale of arms and ammunition to the Indians. Crazy Horse viewed this action as the death knell for the buffalo hunt and as a result increasingly opposed the trip to Washington, D.C. Clark extended an invitation to meet with the Oglala leader, who flatly refused the offer. Lieutenant Colonel Bradley made a similar overture that Crazy Horse accepted, which could probably be considered a personal snub of Clark. Sensing an upcoming conflict, moderate elements of Crazy Horse's camp left him in order to join agency relatives. At about this same time Crazy Horse unsuccessfully sent envoys to Spotted Tail Agency in an effort to induce Touch the Clouds and others to leave and join him at Red Cloud Agency.[63] Battle lines were being drawn. Soon Clark would finally abandon his efforts to win over Crazy Horse, thereby sealing the Oglala leader's fate.

❈ 7 ❈

DEATH OF CRAZY HORSE

On August 17 another council involving the Oglala leaders and government authorities convened at Red Cloud Agency. During the meeting Clark read a message from Crook to the assembled headmen. In the telegram the brigadier general specifically stated that he wanted Crazy Horse to join the delegation to Washington, D.C. The notion of allowing the Oglala leader to make up his own mind or be influenced by those near him had come to an end. What Crazy Horse now faced was essentially a directive from Crook to attend to tribal business in Washington. Clark met with Crazy Horse and tried to impress upon him the importance of his attendance, telling him that it was "necessary for us all to work earnestly and honestly together." At the conclusion of the council agent Irwin issued two head of beef to the Lakotas so that they could hold a feast, discuss matters, and come to a decision as to who would represent them in Washington. Clark personally added to the bounty of the feast by purchasing foodstuffs for the headmen.[1]

On the following day the northern Indian leaders met with Clark at his quarters. Crazy Horse bluntly informed the lieutenant that he was not going to Washington but had selected the men who would go. He not only told Clark who was going (predominantly leaders from the northern Indian faction) but also told him that headmen such as Red Cloud and Spotted Tail should not be included among those making the trip. Clark "kindly, but firmly" informed Crazy Horse that he could decide only for himself and his band and that representative leaders from the various bands would compose the delegation.[2]

This was a crucial and pivotal moment in the relationship between the two men and tragically, as events would later prove, in Crazy Horse's life. After this meeting Clark's attitude toward the Lakota leader soured; his patience had completely run out. From this point on Clark's willingness to befriend Crazy Horse could no longer be used as a means of manipulation. To the contrary, Clark would now allow himself to serve as a pawn for Red Cloud and the other agency leaders who desired to destroy Crazy Horse's power while at the same time they would provide the lieutenant with the means and information, both true and false, to pursue his own objectives in bringing down Crazy Horse.

When writing to General Crook on August 18 Clark made his feelings known in no uncertain terms. He explained to the general that "everything has been done that could possibly bring about the very desirable object of having Crazy Horse go." He added: "I cultivated the friendship and confidence of all the northern Indians and Crazy Horse in particular and succeeded in getting on excellent 'dog-eating' terms with them and him, but it is impossible to work him through reasoning or kindness." Clark continued: "Force is the only thing that will work out a good condition in this man's mind; kindness he only attributes to weakness." Setting forth his intentions to dismantle Crazy Horse's power and influence, Clark explained that "this power could be easily broken at the present time—and I believe it necessary. I am very reluctantly forced to this conclusion, because I have claimed and felt all along that any Indian could be 'worked' by other means; but absolute force is the only thing for him." Clark assured the general that he was "keeping a sharp watch, through some of the scouts I can fully trust, on both Agencies, and they keep me pretty well posted."[3] The lieutenant's network of spies had always been an important tool in controlling the Indians at both agencies. Once Clark's attitude toward Crazy Horse changed, the network became increasingly active and played a significant role in forthcoming events.

In speaking of promises made to Indians Clark observed: "It is a matter of vital importance to any one who wishes to gain influence over them that no mistakes should be made,—no promises made unless with the certainty of fulfilling them."[4] Yet, just a day or two after his epiphany concerning Crazy Horse, Clark announced Crook's decision to cancel the buffalo hunt.[5] By this time, however, Crazy Horse and some of the northern Indians were the only ones who still wanted to go out on the hunt. After the lieutenant's declaration Crazy Horse became increasingly belligerent and now opposed the delegation altogether. During this time the Oglala leader also became more and more alienated not only from the agency Indians but from the northern Indians as well, including Little Big Man.[6]

Tribal political jockeying predominated at Red Cloud Agency in the days that followed. Crazy Horse refused to attend the meeting when the Oglala agency Indians met to discuss the agency relocation issue. Little Big Man and other moderate northern Indians also declined to participate. Those present at the council decided that they would not support an agency in the north country as Crazy Horse wished. On August 26, just as Crazy Horse's power was waning, false rumors circulated that Sitting Bull had left Canada and was moving into the Powder River country. This news restored a large measure of political power to Crazy Horse, as the factions of the northern Indians reunited in anticipation of a possible reunion with Sitting Bull's followers on the northern hunting grounds. This information also fueled speculation among government authorities that another war would soon follow if Crazy Horse rejoined Sitting Bull.

Concerns increased as word spread throughout the agency of Crazy Horse's determination to leave for the north. To confuse matters even further, with this recent turn of events came a call from Lieutenant General Sheridan for assistance in dealing with the Nez Perces to the northwest. They had been engaged in a conflict with the army since mid-June, having refused to settle on their government appointed reservation, and were now encroaching into Montana and Wyoming Territories. Sheridan pressed for the use of Clark's Lakota and Northern Arapaho scouts against the Nez Perces.

Information received from Camp Robinson led Sheridan to believe that 200 to 250 scouts could be counted on for action against the Nez Perces. On August 30 Clark declared to his superiors: "If there is a prospect of some work with the Nez Perces, I would like very much to add a few of the head men of the Sioux to the party going out and take charge of it myself; postponing the trip to Washington till our return." Sheridan replied to Clark's request: "If Clark can go with the scouts I would be delighted, and his importance with them cannot be too highly appreciated. I do not want the trip to Washington broken up; it is fixed upon and must be carried out. Could not some other officer take them on [to Washington]?"[7]

By the following day, however, the plan to use the scouts unraveled when Clark met with Crazy Horse, Touch the Clouds, and about twenty other northern Lakota leaders in his office. Frank Grouard served as interpreter for the council. Clark informed the assemblage of his desire that they participate in the upcoming operation against the Nez Perces. Touch the Clouds then spoke on behalf of the headmen. The Miniconjou leader reminded the lieutenant that the northern Indians had done all that was asked of them since surrendering and that they had been promised peace in return. Now they were asked to go to war, which they did not want to do. But as a demonstration of their continued loyalty they would go north and fight the Nez Perces.[8]

This was not the message that Grouard relayed to Clark, however. The interpreter made a critical error in translating the words of Touch the Clouds and twisted them into a completely different meaning than intended. The information received by the lieutenant was that the northern Indians would go north and fight the whites![9]

Ignorant of the mistranslation, Crazy Horse expressed his approval of what he had heard from the Miniconjou headman by exclaiming "hau" at the conclusion of the speech. Clark now turned his attention specifically to the Oglala leader and asked him pointedly about his intentions. Crazy Horse said that he was going north to hunt with his entire band (women and children included) and that they were going to leave soon. At this point the conversation between the two men became increasingly heated. The discussion eroded into an argument. Even so, Crazy Horse did offer Clark the concession that his warriors would assist against the Nez Perces once his band arrived at the northern hunting grounds. But the lieutenant stood his ground, insisting that only scouts should go along. Crazy Horse countered that either the entire village would go or else none would go. Throughout the exchange Grouard became more and more frustrated and struggled to translate what was said accurately. Fearful at the tone that the council had taken, the interpreter left Clark's quarters.[10]

Somewhere between Camp Robinson and Red Cloud Agency Grouard met interpreter William Garnett. He informed Garnett of the events at Clark's quarters, noting that the situation was tense and that he should go there. Garnett proceeded to the council in order to resume Grouard's duties. Availed of the services of another interpreter, Clark asked Crazy Horse yet again if he would go north to fight the Nez Perces. Crazy Horse replied that he had already told Clark what he wanted to do: go north and hunt. At this point the debate became even more antagonistic. Crazy Horse ridiculed Clark: "You are too soft; you can't fight." Clark snapped back at the Lakota leader, telling him that the area was a theater of war and that he did not want Crazy Horse's camp in the middle of it. Clark's words did not matter to Crazy Horse, who once again affirmed that his people were going to go hunt. Clark then issued his final response: "You cannot go out there, I tell you." Turning to the northern headmen Crazy Horse spoke his final words on the matter: "These people can't fight; what do they want to go out there for; let's go home, this is enough of this." With this parting shot Crazy Horse and the others exited the room and left Camp Robinson.[11]

So the relationship between Clark and Crazy Horse degraded further, with the two men being furious with one another by the end of the council. Grouard had failed miserably in expressing what was said, whether by ineptitude or by malice was unimportant. It does not appear as though Clark really took the mistranslation seriously at the council, but he did use it later to serve his purposes. He held interpreters and their craft in low esteem: "The lack of honest and efficient interpreters has been one of the great causes of all our trouble with the Indians, one of the greatest obstacles to a thorough understanding of the Indian question." It also "stained the soil of every State with innocent blood, and led the race to the threshold of extermination."[12]

Clark, an expert in the use of the Indian sign language, could easily have straightened out the mistranslation of "whites" and "Nez Perces" through hand gestures, yet he chose not to do so. Clark could have asked Garnett to clarify the matter when he entered the scene but instead focused the interpreter's efforts solely toward Crazy Horse's participation against the Nez Perces. Despite the mistranslation, by the end of the council Crazy Horse had made it clear that he only intended to go north to hunt and planned to depart soon. What Clark probably found most disturbing was the tone and ferocity of Crazy Horse's insulting words, which did not go unnoticed by those in attendance.

Clark, who was charged with the task of controlling the Indian populations of two agencies, now faced the most challenging dilemma of his career. Insurrection led by Red Cloud Agency's foremost resident now threatened to undo what he had spent months working toward. Ambitious and career driven, the lieutenant found himself under extreme pressure to act. Crazy Horse's determination to leave and Frank Grouard's mistranslation provided the means by which he could maintain control over the situation and Crazy Horse himself.

Armed with Grouard's error in interpretation, Clark sounded the alarm to Captain Burke at Camp Sheridan after the council. "Crazy Horse and Touch-the-Clouds, with High Bear, came up to me and told me that they were going north on the warpath," Clark wrote to the captain.[13] This clearly was not the case, but Clark was convinced that bloodshed would be inevitable if Crazy Horse and the others left. To his way of thinking Crazy Horse's insistence on leaving was tantamount to a declaration of war. Clark's primary objective at this moment was to prevent the northern Indians from fleeing the reservation. Once the threat of them leaving had been addressed, attention could then be focused on dealing specifically with Crazy Horse. Commenting on Clark's words to Burke, Spotted Tail agent Jesse M. Lee subscribed to the idea that Clark had been motivated by Grouard's mistranslation and stated that "the resulting events show how even the most careful man might be misled as to the real intent of Indians."[14]

Despite what was said at the council, Clark still clung to the hope of departing with his scouts the following day and continued to assemble the auxiliaries, bringing together 150 scouts and an additional 100 volunteers. Messengers from Crazy Horse, however, brought orders from the Oglala leader that the scouts were to disband or face the wrath of his followers. Crazy Horse claimed that the scouts would be used against Sitting Bull's people, not the Nez Perces. In a demonstration of Crazy Horse's continued influence, the scouts did as he instructed.[15]

Clark kept Camp Robinson post commander Lieutenant Colonel Luther P. Bradley informed of the day's events. Throughout August 31 telegraph lines buzzed with activity as Sheridan, Crook, and Bradley discussed what to do about sending the scouts out against the Nez Perces. In a series of dispatches Bradley telegraphed his superiors to inform them of trouble at Camp Robinson. First, he let them know that some of the scouts did not want to go north. Later he told them that he would try to expedite the departure of the scouts but that Crazy Horse, Touch the Clouds, and others believed the scouts would be used against Sitting Bull and were going to leave the reservation with their bands. As a result, said the lieutenant colonel, he had ordered cavalry from Fort Laramie to come and surround their villages. Bradley ended by warning: "There is a good chance for trouble here and there is plenty of bad blood. I think the departure of the scouts will bring on a collision here." Sheridan subsequently ordered Crook, who was en route to Camp Brown, Wyoming Territory, to proceed to Camp Robinson instead. He then wired Bradley and instructed him to put the scout situation on hold until consulting with Crook.[16] On the following day, presumably under instructions from Crook, Clark sent forth a message to his scouts stating that their services were no longer needed in connection to the Nez Perce campaign.

When Touch the Clouds and High Bear returned to Spotted Tail Agency on September 1, they were summoned to Captain Burke's quarters. Burke and agent Jesse M. Lee had received notification that the northern Indian village at Red Cloud Agency was to be surrounded and that the same thing would take place at the northern Indian camp at Spotted Tail. Both men were quite concerned over Clark's report on what had been said at the previous day's council and wanted to meet with the two northern Indian leaders. Those assembled at the quarters included military officers, agency Brules and northern Indians, and Frank Grouard, along with a variety of other interpreters. Burke and Lee asked Touch the Clouds to reiterate all that had been said at the council.

Not long after Touch the Clouds started his reply, it became evident that Grouard had made a critical error in translating. Interpreter Louis Bordeaux and Grouard engaged in an argument as to the actual statement of Touch the Clouds concerning fighting the Nez Perces. Realizing Grouard's grave mistake for the first time, the Miniconjou leader vented his anger toward him as well. Lee, who understood the gravity of the situation, prepared to leave for Camp Robinson the next day in an attempt to avert an outbreak of hostilities.[17]

Upon reaching Camp Robinson the following day Lee met with Bradley and Crook, who had arrived at the post earlier that morning to oversee affairs there personally. Lee surmised that "Clark had suddenly lost all confidence in Crazy Horse, including Touch-the-Clouds, and all our Indians belonging to the northern bands." He informed Bradley and Crook that some mistake had been made: all of the Indians at his agency were peaceful and there was no threat of them leaving. After making this declaration, Lee stated that he "was directed to see Clark and tell him about it, which I did, but he seemed *positive* that there was no mistake." Lee then explained to Clark all that had occurred the preceding day during his meeting with Touch the Clouds, Grouard, and the others. Most importantly, he stressed to the lieutenant Grouard's error in translating the Miniconjou's words. "In the course of the discussion—which was by no means tame—I said I would guarantee that no Indian from Spotted Tail would go north, at which Clark smiled incredulously." Lee added that "it still seemed the intention of Clark to have something done to Crazy Horse and his band. Just what, I did not *then* know." Before leaving Camp Robinson, Lee did manage to get his point across to both Crook and Bradley. The two officers expressed their gratitude to him for apprising them of the true nature of the situation.[18]

Two companies of the Third Cavalry led by Major Julius W. Mason also arrived on the scene that day from Fort Laramie. At first Crook ordered Bradley to use these troops to surround the northern Indian villages at both agencies on the following morning, preventing them from fleeing to the north. After speaking with Lee, however, the general changed the order: the troops would be used only for Crazy Horse's camp.[19]

Crook's plans to surround the Crazy Horse village were derailed later that day. The remnants of Lame Deer's band of Miniconjous now under Fast Bull's leadership were coming into Spotted Tail Agency to surrender. Crook feared that some of Crazy Horse's followers might successfully escape the surround and then get mixed in among the surrendering Miniconjous, thereby inadvertently involving them in the fighting that might follow. The general found it prudent to cancel the operation for the time being and instead invited Crazy Horse to meet with him and the other Lakota leaders in council, giving Crazy Horse one last opportunity to vindicate himself.

Following Crook's wishes, Clark summoned He Dog to extend the general's invitation to Crazy Horse to meet with him at the council the following day. The lieutenant also procured a large supply of provisions so that He Dog's wife could prepare a feast that night and He Dog could discuss the council with his old friend. Crazy Horse, however, feared there would be trouble at the Crook council and refused to attend both the feast that night and the council the next day.[20]

Messengers from Crook arrived at the Crazy Horse village the following morning, extending the general's invitation to join the council later that afternoon on White Clay Creek. Crazy Horse responded that instead of attending the council he preferred to meet solely with Clark in order to explain to the lieutenant that he and his people wished to return to their homeland in the north. Despite the change in the two men's relationship over the past two weeks and perhaps unaware of the depth of Clark's new attitude toward him, Crazy Horse may have sought once again to manipulate the lieutenant.

As subsequent events unfolded, all appeals for a meeting between Crazy Horse and Crook, Clark, or anyone else for that matter proved futile. As the division between Clark and Crazy Horse widened, the lieutenant relied more and more on information provided by his network of spies. Clark reflected years later:

> In 1877 it became necessary for the military authorities to know something of the movements and plans of the great war chief of the Sioux, Crazy Horse, and to discover these one of the enlisted scouts suddenly

became smitten with the charms of a dusky maiden who lived in the tepee adjoining that of the chief, and as she reciprocated the tender feeling, the scout would stand just outside of Crazy Horse's lodge, holding the girl in a fond embrace, while his quick ears took in every word that was uttered in the lodge. He discovered a conspiracy, which, if it had not been for his cunning shrewdness and prompt and loyal action to the whites, would in all probability have terminated in the murder of a general officer, but which eventually led to the necessary killing of the chief himself.[21]

In the days following Crazy Horse's death Clark described the killing as "unavoidable" given the immediate circumstances at the time of the Oglala leader's death. Clark's later use of the word "necessary" is interesting yet understandable, given the lieutenant's knowledge of Crazy Horse's unconquerable spirit, his negative views on assimilation, and the amount of influence that he maintained over the tribe, all things that Clark viewed as fatal for the survival of the Lakotas.

The scout referred to by Clark was a Lakota named Little Wolf, who supposedly overheard Crazy Horse making plans to kill Crook and other whites at the upcoming council. The Lakota scout passed the information on to his brother, Lone Bear, who in turn relayed the story to Woman Dress, another of Clark's informants and a member of the Red Cloud faction at the agency.[22] Such news could be used to crush any hope of Crazy Horse's participation in the upcoming Washington delegation, for agency leaders feared that if he went to Washington he would be bestowed with the power that they so desperately sought to maintain.

Crook, Clark, Bourke, and a few other men boarded an ambulance on the morning of September 3 and proceeded to the council. Along the way, at Frank Yates's store, they were to pick up interpreters William Garnett and Baptiste Pourier. When the ambulance arrived at the store they saw the two interpreters with Woman Dress. When the ambulance came to a stop, Garnett told Crook that Woman Dress had just informed them of Crazy Horse's plot to kill the general. Pourier followed by vouching that Woman Dress's word could be trusted. Clark earnestly believed his informant and promptly convinced Crook that to continue on the journey would spell trouble. After persuading Crook to turn back, the lieutenant then supplied an alibi, telling Garnett to go to the council and announce that the general had received a message that prevented him from attending the gathering. Clark's final instructions to the interpreter were to tell the Lakota agency leaders at the council to go to Camp Robinson and report to him there.[23]

When Garnett arrived at the site of the council, he found a large number of agency Lakotas gathered there; but Crazy Horse and the other northern Indian leaders were not present. This in itself should have raised doubts about the veracity of Woman Dress's claims, but it did not. It was not until about ten years later that Garnett, along with Pourier, personally confronted Little Wolf and Woman Dress about the murder plot story being fabricated by the agency faction. When meeting with Crook at Pine Ridge Reservation in 1889, the two interpreters were finally able to tell him about the true nature of affairs at the time of the council. Crook responded: "I ought to have gone to that council and I should not have listened to Clark."[24]

Upon his return to Camp Robinson, Crook promptly ordered Bradley to resume preparations for the delayed "round up" of the Crazy Horse camp.[25] That afternoon the Lakota leaders summoned by Clark arrived at Bradley's quarters for their meeting with Crook. As the ranking officer at the post, the general was entitled to use the commanding officer's quarters for his purposes, so the meeting took place there. Clark and Crook were the only officers present, joined by three interpreters: Garnett, Pourier, and Grouard. The group of agency Indians included Red Cloud and Crazy Horse's old enemy No Water, among a dozen others. No Water had shot Crazy Horse in the face in 1870 due to Crazy Horse's affection for No Water's wife. Crazy Horse had been extended an invitation to attend by Crook but declined. At the meeting Crook requested the assistance of these loyal headmen in settling the Crazy Horse issue once and for all. At first the Lakota leaders called for the killing of Crazy Horse, but Crook objected on the grounds that it would amount to murder. After discussing the matter further, the Oglala leaders asserted that in their opinion it would be best for them to assemble a small war party of agency Lakota warriors to go to Crazy Horse's camp that night, surround and disarm the camp, and kill Crazy Horse if necessary to complete the task.[26]

Crook rejected the outright killing of Crazy Horse but supported his arrest and the breaking up of the entire band by the agency Lakotas, using force only if absolutely needed. The general approved the nighttime operation, stressing to the Oglalas the importance of secrecy.[27] During the meeting possible rewards for the capture of Crazy Horse were discussed as an added incentive to the men. Crook later supported conditional authorization of one such reward on the day before Crazy Horse's eventual surrender, thus dispelling any notion that a reward was offered solely for the Oglala leader's killing.[28] Feeling assured that everything at Camp Robinson was in order, the general then left the post shortly after the meeting to resume his journey to Camp Brown.

Given Clark's drive to succeed, it is believed that at some point he offered his own prized sorrel racing horse as a reward to the man arresting Crazy Horse. The chance to own Clark's horse may have been more important to the Lakotas than the reward money. Gambling represented a favorite leisure activity for these men, and horse racing ranked high among their games of chance. During his efforts to socialize with the Indians of the agencies Clark frequently participated in horse races with them. His sorrel racer gained a reputation as an outstanding running horse and became highly sought after by the Indians.[29] In the long run, the horse could potentially bring great wealth to its owner. Clark was well aware of this when he offered the animal as a reward.

In an interview a number of years after the fact interpreter William Garnett maintained that Crook and Clark not only accepted the agency Lakota plan to kill Crazy Horse on the night of September 3 but also offered Clark's horse and a $300 reward for killing him. According to Garnett, he was summoned to Bradley's quarters later on the day of Crook's council. It became clear to him that word of the plot to kill Crazy Horse was circulating. Agent Irwin and Crazy Horse's friend He Dog had become privy to the plot and had approached Bradley, who knew nothing of Crook's plan, to discuss the matter. After verifying the information that Bradley received from his visitors, the interpreter left the quarters. Garnett contended that when he was later summoned to Clark's quarters he found him incensed over the loss of secrecy. This led Clark to send Garnett to the agency Lakota camp to terminate the murder plan.[30] While Garnett's account is compelling, the portion of the interpreter's testimony supporting the rumored murder plot has to be questioned in light of the historical record.

Military authorities had focused primarily on the capture and arrest of the Lakota leader, using force only if absolutely necessary. While Crook and Clark believed that Crazy Horse's apprehension should be an Indian endeavor, Bradley still maintained that the military should undertake the task and do so the following morning. Once it became clear that the nighttime surround had been exposed and the element of surprise lost, the course of action formulated by Crook and the agency Lakotas became unworkable. Crook's previous orders to Bradley for the daylight military intervention became the plan of operation once again.[31] For his part, Clark was infuriated by the cancellation of the surround set for that night. Pacing up and down the floor of his quarters after learning that the operation had been compromised, the lieutenant complained to Garnett: "These Indians can hold nothing." He then instructed the interpreter to "go down to the Indian village right away, and stop them Indians from approaching Crazy Horse. When you go down, tell those Indians not to disturb Crazy Horse, but tell all to report to Fort [Camp] Robinson before sun-up in the morning."[32]

Clark's foremost concern remained the possible escape of Crazy Horse to the north, thereby potentially plunging the nation into yet another war on the plains. Clark was ignorant of the Oglala leader's current state of mind, and his fears proved ill founded. Previously Crazy Horse had expressed his simple wish to move away and return north. But as the day advanced the Oglala leader began rethinking his situation. After learning of the story presented to Crook by Woman Dress and hearing an ever-increasing number of rumors that included an impending attack on his camp with plans to kill him, Crazy Horse gave up on the idea of fleeing and became fatalistic. He would fight and die right where he was.[33]

As pressure mounted on Crazy Horse late into the night, Jesse M. Lee was preparing to leave Camp Robinson with Spotted Tail for their agency. Before departing Lee and Clark became entangled in another exchange of words. Lee described Clark as being "fussy and headstrong."[34] Bradley and Clark wanted Spotted Tail's participation in the surround the following day, while Lee believed that the Brule leader should be at his own agency controlling matters there. The agent won his argument. Lee made a final comment to Clark before he departed: "Don't let Crazy Horse get away; he might come to Spotted Tail Agency." According to the agent, "Clark replied, with a trace of sarcasm, 'Lee, don't you worry about that. Crazy Horse can't make a move without my knowing it, and I can have him whenever I want him. I'll send you the news of our success in writing by good courier.'"[35]

Early the next morning, September 4, while some four hundred men of the military contingent prepared for the advance on Crazy Horse's camp, Clark busied himself with issuing arms and ammunition to a similar number of Lakotas, Northern Arapahos, and Northern Cheyennes taking part in the apprehension of Crazy Horse. He then gathered the leading men and in conjunction with them determined the organization of the Indian element for the upcoming surround.[36] Clark would command his complement of scouts, and the headmen of the "friendly" Indians would all lead their warriors. The overall objective was clear, as stated by Bradley: "My orders from General Crook were to capture this chief, confine him, and send him under guard to Omaha."[37]

Once assembled, the attacking force proceeded toward the Crazy Horse camp, departing at 9 in the morning. Eight companies of the Third Cavalry under Major Mason along with the Indian contingent traveled down the White River, with roughly half of the command on each side of the river. Among the scouts riding with Clark that day were a number of Crazy Horse's former followers, including He Dog.[38]

When the advancing column reached a point about three or four miles from the Crazy Horse camp, it was approached by Crazy Horse's brother-in-law, Red Feather. He informed Clark that the camp was ready to surrender its arms and move closer to the agency. Red Feather was instructed to tell Crazy Horse that the command was on its way to his village and that he was to follow directions when it arrived. Little Big Man arrived shortly afterward, bearing contradictory news that Crazy Horse was catching his horse and would either flee or stay and fight.[39]

As the column continued on its way to the village, Looking Horse, a Miniconjou who had previously served as a scout but now remained in the Crazy Horse camp, rode up to Clark and lashed out angrily at the lieutenant. After dressing down Clark, the warrior made his way to some of the Oglala scouts and scolded them for bringing soldiers to the camp. In response, Woman Dress shot Looking Horse's horse from under him. Bull Head and other scouts then descended upon the Miniconjou and beat him to unconsciousness.[40]

Clark ordered the Indian contingent onward with strict instructions that they were not to fire upon the village unless they received fire first. As the scouts leading the command came within about a quarter-mile of the village a group of about seventy warriors could be seen gathered on a knoll. A lone rider bolted down toward Clark and his men, a sixteen–year-old Sans Arc Lakota warrior named Crayfish. The brave young Lakota was soon followed by another rider, Black Fox, one of Crazy Horse's closest allies. The warrior, dressed in full regalia with an eagle-feather headdress, charged up to the advancing attackers and began haranguing and challenging them. Clearly prepared to die, Black Fox sought a fight. About half the warriors from the knoll were positioned behind Black Fox, running their ponies back and forth in anticipation of battle. Excitement filled the air, and the two sides seemed to be on the cusp of bloodshed. In an effort to avoid confrontation, American Horse and He Dog approached Black Fox with a pipe and induced the warrior to smoke and talk with them. After a short deliberation, the two men defused the situation by convincing the northern leader that the march on the village was peaceful in nature and that they simply wanted to arrest Crazy Horse and disarm the village. Black Fox then called off his warriors. The column was allowed to proceed.⁴¹

During their discussion with Black Fox, American Horse and He Dog learned that Crazy Horse had taken his wife and fled the camp. At the conclusion of the parley the men of the command could see Crazy Horse, his wife Black Shawl, and two accomplices riding over a distant bluff to the east. Clark immediately dispatched ten scouts under No Flesh to pursue Crazy Horse and bring him back. A short time later, after learning "further particulars," the lieutenant sent an additional ten men under No Water to apprehend Crazy Horse and bring him to Clark's quarters at Camp Robinson. In all probability Clark had become aware that Crazy Horse was taking his ailing wife to her relatives at Spotted Tail Agency. As an added incentive, Clark offered No Water $200 if he was successful. Clark sounded somewhat less confident than on the previous evening: "I have great hopes that they will get him."⁴²

Attention now turned to the remnants of the village itself. Largely deserted, the camp had once consisted of some seventy lodges. Now only about forty remained. The small encampment prepared for the move to Red Cloud Agency and by 11:00 A.M. the cavalcade of soldiers and Indians started back toward the agency.⁴³

Later that day Clark's plans for the remnants of the Crazy Horse camp became quite clear. He telegraphed Crook to inform him of the $200 offer to No Water and outlined his intentions for the band: "I believe it would be best to turn over the remnant of this band to the head men I spoke to you about and not try to take any ponies."⁴⁴ Crook generally supported the lieutenant's ideas, replying: "I will authorize the payment of two hundred dollars to No Water if the Indians you speak of will go peaceably to the other bands and you think will behave themselves. You can let them keep their ponies."⁴⁵

Clark was not the only officer at Camp Robinson facing scrutiny and pressure to secure Crazy Horse and the other northern Indians who fled that day. After learning of the morning's events, Crook fired off a telegram to Bradley. The general's concerns went beyond just Crazy Horse: "By all means catch Crazy Horse and have the friendly Indians if they fail to capture the rest of Crazy Horse's band to induce them to come back for it will not do to make renegades of them and have them go on the war path which they will do if they can't be brought back."⁴⁶

Shortly after his return to Camp Robinson, Clark sent a message to Lee at Spotted Tail Agency to apprise him of the situation: "There has been no fight;

Crazy Horse's band is just going into camp, and will give up their guns without trouble, in all probability. Crazy Horse has skipped out for your place. Have sent after him. Should he reach your agency, have 'Spot' arrest him, and I will give any Indian who does this, $200."[47]

Just before Clark's message reached Lee, however, the agent heard that Crazy Horse was at his agency in the northern Indian camp. The agent and Camp Sheridan commander Captain Burke boarded an ambulance and started out for the northern village. Not long after leaving the post the two officers met Crazy Horse and approximately three hundred warriors from the northern village on their way to Camp Sheridan. The entire party then returned to the post, where they found Spotted Tail and about three hundred of his Brule warriors. After enduring some very tense moments as the two opposing factions argued and almost fought, the two officers managed to get Crazy Horse into Burke's quarters to hold a conference. Joining Burke and Lee were Crazy Horse, Touch the Clouds, Spotted Tail, and another Brule named Swift Bear. Louis Bordeaux served as interpreter. During the meeting that followed Crazy Horse recalled the various troubles that he had faced at the other agency, the illness of his wife, and his desire to be transferred to Spotted Tail Agency. Lee informed the Oglala leader that he must go to Camp Robinson and would be given an opportunity to state his case to Bradley there. Lee also pledged to Crazy Horse that he would do what he could to aid the headman's cause. With these assurances Crazy Horse then promised that he would return to Red Cloud Agency with Lee the following morning. At the conclusion of the meeting it was agreed that Crazy Horse could spend the night at Touch the Clouds' camp. The Miniconjou leader promised to return Crazy Horse back to Camp Sheridan at 9 the following morning for the trip to Camp Robinson.[48]

On the morning of September 5 Crazy Horse promptly arrived at the post at the designated time. He had undergone a change of heart over the course of the night, however, and now did not want to go to Camp Robinson, fearing that something bad might happen to him there. Lee assured him that no harm would come to him and insisted that he had to go. Crazy Horse relented once again, with certain conditions. First, the Oglala leader requested that both he and Lee should go unarmed. Next Crazy Horse wanted Lee to tell Bradley all that had transpired at Spotted Tail Agency and that he, Burke, and Spotted Tail supported Crazy Horse's desire to be transferred to that agency. Finally, he wished to inform Bradley of his desire for peace and that his true intentions had been misunderstood. While Lee and the interpreter Louis Bordeaux boarded an ambulance for the trip to Camp Robinson, Crazy Horse asked for and received permission to ride horseback. Joining Lee and Bordeaux in the ambulance were agency leaders Black Crow and Swift Bear, along with Crazy Horse's allies Touch the Clouds and High Bear. Seven mounted northern Indians accompanied the group. A small number of agency Indians also went along to escort the entourage and prevent Crazy Horse from escaping along the way.[49]

Meanwhile at Camp Robinson preparations were underway to manage Crazy Horse's incarceration. Bradley had sent a message to Burke late the night before, instructing the captain that Crazy Horse "must be held as a prisoner and must come here as such."[50] Crook had ordered Crazy Horse's arrest; now that he was apprehended, Bradley apparently could rely in part on army regulation and doctrine in order to assist him in handling the matter. Accordingly, Crazy Horse would be treated as a prisoner in compliance with those regulations. Under customary dictates, an incoming prisoner would be delivered to the officer of the day, who in turn would be responsible for confining the prisoner in the guardhouse to await the prosecution of his case.[51]

Pursuant to this course of action, Bradley issued a general order stipulating that Crazy Horse be placed in the guardhouse upon his arrival.[52] Clark kept Crook informed of events as they transpired. He telegraphed the general, stating that Burke was on his way to the post with Crazy Horse and mentioning as a matter of fact that the Oglala leader would be placed in the guardhouse. He suggested that Crazy Horse be transported that same night to Fort Laramie and then on to Omaha. The lieutenant also recommended the idea of having two or three Lakotas accompany Crazy Horse to that point so that they could return and vouch that the Oglala leader had not been killed. In closing, Clark asked Crook to send a telegram to Bradley outlining the plan for Crazy Horse's removal to Omaha.[53] Crook's subsequent telegram to Bradley contained a premature expression of congratulations for a job well done and included an endorsement of Clark's suggestions concerning Crazy Horse's removal.[54] Given the general's approval, Clark set about forming the upcoming escort for the journey to Omaha, securing the services of Little Big Man, No Neck, Plenty Wolves, and interpreter Baptiste Pourier.[55] Crook updated his superior, Sheridan: "Crazy Horse is now a prisoner and I have ordered Bradley to send him down here. I wish you would send him off where he will be out of harm's way."[56] Ultimately the plan for Crazy Horse's incarceration stipulated that he travel from Omaha to Chicago, per Sheridan's request, and then on to St. Augustine, Florida, for imprisonment.[57]

As Camp Robinson readied itself for the Oglala leader's arrival, Lee's procession continued on its trek to the post. When it reached a point about fifteen miles out from Spotted Tail Agency, the caravan was joined by a small group of Spotted Tail's scouts. A short time later another party of the Brule leader's men joined the escort. By the midway point between the two agencies a third group of agency Indians arrived, bolstering the number of scouts to more than forty, just as Lee and Burke had previously planned. After a brief stop for lunch the procession continued, as both Lee and Bordeaux fell into a light slumber. Suddenly awakened, Lee became alarmed when he could not see Crazy Horse. The agent was informed that Crazy Horse had galloped ahead of the ambulance and disappeared over the crest of a small hill just ahead. Lee ordered some of the scouts to bring the Oglala leader back to the ambulance. During his few brief moments of freedom Crazy Horse found a small party of northern Indians on the other side of the hill and obtained a pistol, which he successfully hid from Lee and the others. Upon his return to the ambulance Crazy Horse was instructed to ride immediately behind the conveyance for the remainder of the trip.[58]

When the party came to within fifteen miles of Red Cloud Agency, Lee sent a message to Clark asking if he should take Crazy Horse to the agency or to Camp Robinson. He stressed that tact rather than force had been used to bring the Oglala leader to this point. Finally, he informed Clark that Crazy Horse had been promised an opportunity to state the facts of his case as he saw them. Lee asked Clark to make arrangements so this could be done. A short while later, when the group was about four miles from Red Cloud Agency, a messenger returned with Clark's reply: "Gen. Bradley wishes you to drive direct to his office with Crazy Horse."[59] The lieutenant, who had spent the day at the agency, returned to Camp Robinson shortly after sending his reply to Lee.

After enduring some precarious moments as the procession passed through the Oglalas at Red Cloud Agency, the party finally arrived at Camp Robinson as the sun began to set. A large number of Oglala riders from the agency had joined the procession. When the ambulance pulled up to the adjutant's office, Clark and Bradley were at their respective quarters at opposite ends of the parade ground. The task at hand now devolved to the officer of the day, Captain James Kennington, who had been ordered to the adjutant's office by Bradley.[60] In an important deviation from regulations, a select group of influential Lakota scouts, handpicked by Clark,[61] were utilized along with their men as an adjunct to Kennington's guard detail. As such, they would most likely be under the command of the officer of the day; while this is speculative, it would explain Clark's absence from the scene. Maintaining the security of the post was the primary function of the guard detail, so the Lakota auxiliaries would prove useful in that capacity and in assisting with Crazy Horse's confinement.

The atmosphere at the post was filled with tension as warriors from both factions crowded the parade ground near the adjutant's office and the guardhouse next door. Soldiers from the camp manned positions around the guardhouse. As soon as Crazy Horse dismounted, Little Big Man approached him, grabbed him by the arm, and escorted him to the adjutant's office. At the doorway to the office Lee met with the adjutant, Second Lieutenant Frederic Calhoun, who informed the agent that Crazy Horse was to be turned over to the officer of the day. Wishing to honor the promise to Crazy Horse that he could state his case to Bradley, Lee asked if the Oglala leader could talk to Bradley first. Instructed by Calhoun to take the matter up with Bradley at his quarters, Lee set off for the commanding officer's quarters as Crazy Horse went into the adjutant's office with a small group of Lakotas, including Little Big Man and Touch the Clouds.[62]

Lee's meeting with Bradley did not go well, as the lieutenant colonel flatly refused to see Crazy Horse. Officially designated a prisoner, Crazy Horse would get no preferential treatment and thereby no meeting with the post commander. The only consolation given to Lee was Bradley's assurance that no harm would come to Crazy Horse. Returning to the adjutant's office, Lee feared trouble. Instead of telling Crazy Horse the truth, he told him that Bradley thought it was too late in the day to hold talks. He then gave the Oglala leader Bradley's assurance that if he would go with Captain Kennington he would not be harmed.[63]

As Crazy Horse exited the adjutant's office, his arm was held on one side by Kennington, while Little Big Man secured the other. During the short walk between the adjutant's office and guardhouse the throng of gathered Indians surged closer to Crazy Horse and his escort. Red Cloud's and American Horse's men formed a protective line in front of the buildings in an attempt to maintain a degree of order. Crazy Horse passed through the door of the guardhouse along with a small group of Lakota scouts and members of the guard. A few seconds later a loud commotion could be heard from within the building as Crazy Horse, realizing that he was about to be jailed, struggled against his captors.[64]

During his ensuing fight for freedom, as Kennington and Little Big Man tried to restrain him, Crazy Horse pulled out a knife from under the blanket he wore and cut a deep gash in Little Big Man's wrist. As the two men continued to jostle each other at the doorway, the red blanket that Crazy Horse had been wearing fell from his body, revealing a holstered pistol. The scout Plenty Wolves promptly secured it. Despite his wound, Little Big Man persisted in the struggle as the two men surged out of the building.[65]

Once outside three more Lakotas joined the fray in an attempt to restrain Crazy Horse as Little Big Man released his grip on the Oglala headman. As Crazy Horse vainly tried to free himself, his body twisted toward a sentry just as the soldier lunged at Crazy Horse with his bayonet. The blade penetrated Crazy Horse's body just above the hip on his left side. The sentry quickly removed the bayonet and delivered a second blow, this time piercing the Oglala leader's lower back on the right side. Crazy Horse, critically injured, fell to the ground in front of the guardhouse.[66]

Pressed by a multitude of Lakotas, members of the guard surrounded the wounded headman's body as soldiers poured forth from barracks and stables in response to a recently sounded alarm.[67] Having witnessed the events at the guardhouse, interpreter William Garnett rushed to Clark's quarters to inform the lieutenant that Crazy Horse had been stabbed. He Dog, after briefly ministering to his fallen friend, also proceeded to the lieutenant's quarters, located across the parade ground from the guardhouse. Furious over the course of events, He Dog scolded Clark: "You promised in a treaty that we both swore to, that nothing like this would happen again; that there would be no more blood shed." The angry Lakota headman struck Clark's face and stormed off.[68]

In the pressure of the moment as the northern Indians and agency Indians came to the brink of fighting each other, the question of what now to do with Crazy Horse came to the forefront. Captain Kennington wanted to follow orders and insisted that the Oglala leader be placed in the guardhouse. The northern Indians, brandishing their weapons, violently disagreed and thereby forced Kennington to rethink the matter. Assistant post surgeon Valentine T. McGillycuddy, after examining Crazy Horse's wounds, tried to break the impasse and hurried to Bradley's quarters to get permission to move the victim to the adjutant's office. Bradley, like Kennington, remained steadfast in following orders and refused the request. Upon returning to the scene, the surgeon found that the northern Indians still remained adamant that Crazy Horse could not be placed in the guardhouse. The doctor was forced to go to the commanding officer once again. Bradley very reluctantly agreed to grant this one solitary concession and allowed Crazy Horse to be moved to the adjutant's office.[69]

A small group of Lakotas carried Crazy Horse on his blanket and transported him into the adjutant's office, where the Lakota leader was placed on the floor at his own request. Fully understanding the severity of the internal bleeding caused by Crazy Horse's injuries, McGillycuddy declared the Lakota's situation to be hopeless and administered morphine to ease the dying man's suffering. A small group of individuals joined the doctor for the death vigil, which included interpreters Louis Bordeaux and Baptiste Pourier, Touch the Clouds, and Crazy Horse's father and stepmother.[70]

Shortly after Crazy Horse was placed inside the adjutant's office, the excited crowd that had once filled the parade ground began disbursing. As tensions eased and the vigil for Crazy Horse continued across the parade ground from his quarters, Clark composed a series of telegrams to General Crook in order to keep his superior informed of recent important developments. The first mentioned the struggle between Crazy Horse and Little Big Man, noting the wounds to the scout and a minor wound to Touch the Clouds, but nothing was said of Crazy Horse's injuries.

As for the group of scouts that he had selected to handle the Crazy Horse situation, especially Little Big Man, Clark pointed out: "The Indians I selected simply did better than I can express and deserve great credit, and I hope may get it." The next message informed the general of Crazy Horse's wound and its severity and also stated Clark's belief that it came "possibly from a bayonet, but probably from a knife" and "the latter I am trying to persuade all Indians."[71] Interestingly, both Clark and McGillycuddy made efforts to convince the Indians that it was Little Big Man or Crazy Horse himself that had inflicted the fatal wound, probably in an attempt to deflect hostile feelings toward the military.[72]

The final telegram in the series turned to administrative matters concerning Clark's scouts. He sought the general's approval in matters pertaining to the payment of the scouts and backdating Crazy Horse's discharge from the service to August 31. The lieutenant also suggested that the various leaders absorbing Crazy Horse's band could select new scouts to replace those who had their guns taken away in the recent fray. Clark closed the message by stating: "These chiefs are doing even better than I anticipated."[73] Bourke, acting on behalf of Crook, replied: "He approves your suggestions about Crazy Horse's discharge and enlistment of other Indians." The telegram also stressed the importance of capturing the remnants of Crazy Horse's band, admonishing Clark "to keep up pursuit of those Indians until the last one is captured."[74]

At the adjutant's office Crazy Horse's life continued to fade. In his final hours the Oglala leader spoke very little but made it clear that he personally held Little Big Man responsible for his stabbing. Crazy Horse's father took a broader view, blaming the jealousies of Red Cloud and Spotted Tail for his son's impending death. Touch the Clouds looked no further than Crazy Horse himself as the source of the final conflict: "He has looked for death, and it has come." As September 5 came to a close, Crazy Horse took his final breath at around 11:30. McGillycuddy pronounced him dead.[75] Crazy Horse's father took his son's body, which was eventually placed upon a burial scaffold near Camp Sheridan.

News of Crazy Horse's death reached Clark through interpreters Louis Bordeaux and Baptiste Pourier early the following morning. Clark had been out somewhere and upon his return found the two men in his quarters. When he asked about Crazy Horse's condition, Pourier informed him that the Oglala was dead. Unable or unwilling to believe what he was told, Clark asked Bordeaux if it was true. The interpreter responded in the affirmative. According to Bordeaux, "Clark, who was a man of great humanity, could not restrain the tears as he said: 'It is a shame! It is a shame! He ought not to die.' He meant that he ought not to have been killed." Clark sat down, placed his face in his hands, and cried.[76]

Clark's emotional response to hearing of Crazy Horse's passing can best be understood by considering the lieutenant's probable state of mind at the time. Despite the souring of the relationship between the two men in previous weeks, Clark had come to know Crazy Horse as something of a friend even if the Oglala leader did not share those feelings. More importantly, for weeks Clark had been under an increasing amount of pressure in dealing with Crazy Horse and trying to avert another Indian war. Crazy Horse's killing had the potential to plunge the military and the Lakotas into another full-scale conflict once again. In addition, Crook held Clark responsible for all matters pertaining to his scouts. Understanding their involvement in the attempted confinement and subsequent death of Crazy Horse only added to the amount of stress weighing on Clark's mind. Ambitious to a fault, the lieutenant may have felt that his future hung in the balance.

Reflecting upon Crazy Horse's death years later, Clark wrote:

> The Sioux chief Crazy Horse had a most remarkable dream some ten days before he was killed. While walking on the prairie near his camp one day he came across a dead eagle. He went to his tepee and gloomily

sat there for many hours afterwards. Being asked by some of his people as to what was the matter, he said 'that he had found his dead body on the prairie near by,' and a night or two after this he dreamt that he was on an elevated plateau riding a white pony. He was surrounded by his enemies and big guns (cannon), and he was killed, but not with a bullet. He had always claimed that he bore a charmed life, and could not be killed by a bullet. In putting him in the guard-house he attempted, with his knife, to cut his way to liberty though surrounded by about twenty soldiers, and was bayoneted in the attempt. A white pony was held by one of his friends just outside the circle of soldiers, and some howitzers were standing a few yards in front of the guard-house.[77]

Interestingly, whereas the Lakotas assembled at the vigil on the night of September 5 attached responsibility for Crazy Horse's death to Lakotas, a number of whites did not see it that way. Jesse M. Lee asserted in his diary on September 6 that the trouble occurred "as the result of mismanagement on the part of Philo Clark, *and mis-interpretation on the part of Grouard.*"[78] His wife, Lucy, expressed her sentiments in a more veiled manner: "All this trouble is the result of an Indian policy difficult to understand and impossible to carry out; and this present excitement was precipitated by the misunderstandings and the mismanagement of some who were entrusted with its execution."[79] McGillycuddy maintained a harsher view: "A combination of treachery, jealousy and unreliable reports simply resulted in a frame-up, *and he was railroaded to his death.*"[80]

A mood of apprehension permeated the agencies and their associated posts in the hours following Crazy Horse's death. A high degree of uncertainty existed concerning the Lakota response to the killing, especially when it came to the northern Indians. Clark spent little time mourning the Oglala's passing and on the following morning reported the news to Crook in a very detached manner, stating coldly: "The death of this man will save trouble." Despite the tension in the air, Clark reassured the general that everything was going smoothly.[81]

By September 9 the excitement had eased. Clark admitted to Crook that "we were all a little excited here and in looking back upon it I must say it is wonderful that we did not have a row. Crazy Horse's death is considered by most of the Indians as a right good thing for all concerned, though some few have stated that they were going to have revenge and state that 'White Hat' is to be their victim. Of course this is not pleasant and I hope they may change."

He continued: "From the conversations which I had with some of the head men they will always support we got C.H. here to kill him but it was really unavoidable when the time came to take his arms."[82]

On the following day Clark received a telegram from Crook, who expressed his pleasure concerning conditions at the agencies and asked Clark to "give my thanks to Little Big Man, Touch the Clouds, and others who did well." Crook then turned to administrative matters, probably referring to the previously authorized reward money for No Water: "The check will be sent as soon as I get to Omaha. Expect to reach there the afternoon of Wed. the 12th. Can't you borrow the money until the check arrives[?]"[83]

Clark's final official action concerning Crazy Horse took place when he drafted a report to the commissioner of Indian affairs dated September 10, 1877. Clark summarized Crazy Horse's disposition, his own unsuccessful efforts to win over the Oglala leader, the supposed plot to kill Crook, and the events of September 4 and 5 leading to Crazy Horse's death. He wrote that most Indians viewed his passing as "a real benefit to their people and justify the killing as he first drew his knife." Some sought vengeance, but Clark did not anticipate further trouble, as Crazy Horse's band had been broken up. Clark cast the headman in a bad light, perhaps as further rationalization for the killing: "It is claimed by the Indians that this dead chief had with his own hand killed thirty-four white men and four white women, not counting those killed in battle." Clark praised the Northern Arapaho and Lakota leaders and their young men, who "acted in the most praiseworthy manner during these troubles" and "probably prevented another war." He closed the report by relating the headmen's optimism in regard to the future of their people.[84]

With Crazy Horse's death and the subsiding of hostilities and turmoil associated with his killing, other important matters remained to be addressed. Now attention once again focused on the rapidly approaching journey by the Northern Arapaho and Lakota delegation to Washington, D.C. For Clark the most formidable episode of his career had passed, but other challenges and opportunities lay ahead.

Cadet William Philo Clark, shortly before his graduation from the United States Military Academy. This portrait is from the class of 1868 yearbook album. *Courtesy Author's Collection.*

Helen "Nellie" Larrabee, Crazy Horse's troublesome third wife, who was rumored to be romantically tied to Clark. This image was taken in the 1880s. *Courtesy National Anthropological Archives, Smithsonian Institution, 43584A.*

Opposite, top: Grand Duke Alexis of Russia buffalo hunt, 1872. This image shows a group of mounted hunters prior to leaving on a hunt from Camp Alexis, Nebraska. Clark joined a number of prominent officers, including Lieutenant Colonel George A. Custer, participating in the hunt. Photograph taken by E. L. Eaton, Omaha, Nebraska. *Courtesy Nebraska State Historical Society.*

Opposite, bottom: Brigadier General George Crook and his headquarters staff and orderlies at the conclusion of the grueling Starvation March, 1876. As an aide to Crook, Clark should be pictured here but remains unidentified. Crook is sitting on a pile of branches to the left of the headquarters flag. The photograph was taken at Whitewood Creek in the Black Hills by Stanley J. Morrow. *Courtesy United States Military Academy Library.*

First Lieutenant Clark poses with Crazy Horse's uncle, the Oglala Lakota leader Little Hawk. The image was taken by D. S. Mitchell in 1877 at Red Cloud Agency. *Courtesy National Anthropological Archives, Smithsonian Institution, 00209700.*

Opposite, top left: First Lieutenant William Philo Clark, photographed by Mathew Brady. This formal portrait was most likely made while Clark escorted the 1877 delegation to Washington, D.C. *Courtesy Library of Congress, Prints and Photographs Division.*

Opposite, top right: Brigadier General George Crook. Like the formal portrait of Clark, this Mathew Brady photograph is believed to have been taken while the 1877 delegation was in Washington, D.C. Clark worked closely with Crook during the lieutenant's challenging tenure at Camp Robinson, Nebraska. *Courtesy Library of Congress, Prints and Photographs Division.*

Lakota and Northern Arapaho delegation in Washington, D.C., 1877. Clark stands in the second row left of the center of the image, surrounded by prominent leaders of both tribes, including Red Cloud. The photograph was taken by Alexander Gardner at the Corcoran Art Gallery. *Courtesy National Anthropological Archives, Smithsonian Institution, 3179c.*

The presidential party at Upper Geyser Basin in Yellowstone National Park, 1883. President Chester A. Arthur is seated at the center, with Sheridan sitting to his right. Clark is standing in the back row at the center. Lieutenant Colonel James F. Gregory stands at the far right of the back row. *Courtesy Library of Congress, Prints and Photographs Division.*

Opposite, top: Miles-Hoyt party in Yellowstone National Park, 1878. Clark stands fourth from the left, wearing his signature white felt hat. Hattie Sanborn, Clark's future fiancée, is sitting at the far right of the front row. Colonel Nelson A. Miles sits on a rock at the center. *Courtesy Montana Historical Society Research Center—Photograph Archives.*

Opposite, bottom: Lieutenant General Philip H. Sheridan and party with Old Faithful geyser erupting in the background, 1882. Clark is sitting on the ground at far right, while Sheridan is seated in a chair at the center. This photograph was taken by Clark's friend L. A. Huffman. *Courtesy Montana Historical Society Research Center—Photograph Archives.*

Captain William Philo Clark portrait, circa 1884. This photograph shows Clark as he appeared late in his life, probably taken after he had been assigned to duty at Army Headquarters in Washington, D.C. *Courtesy United States Military Academy Library.*

❖ 8 ❖

WASHINGTON DELEGATION AND RELOCATION

Before embarking upon the trip east with the delegation, Clark attended to one other task. Believing that the Indians might be able to answer some of the questions surrounding the fight at the Little Big Horn and other engagements, Crook gave the lieutenant verbal orders to prepare a report on the "late Sioux War." Clark had been in almost constant contact with the Indians since arriving at Camp Robinson in early January. He credited his sources as "Indians who have surrendered at Red Cloud and Spotted Tail Agencies during the past eight months and information obtained from Interpreters and friendly Indians." The report did have its limitations. The lieutenant warned: "It has been a very difficult matter to get accurate information in regard to the different engagements. Not only as the Indians from Crazy Horse down have been extremely reticent, but some of the battles were on so extensive a scale that no one Indian could possibly be conversant with all the details."[1]

The report provided a brief overview of the Indians' qualities and traits as warriors then addressed the topic of leadership: "Each band having a chief but his powers and authority are in great measure limited by the will and wishes of his people." In regard to the oft-publicized roles of Crazy Horse and Sitting Bull in the late campaign Clark countered that "they are really not entitled to more credit or censure than many others so far as plans and orders were concerned." Later in the report he did concede that at the Little Big Horn Crazy Horse "gained a greater prestige than any other Indian in the camp."[2]

In his summary of the fighting Clark included information on engagements large and small, always noting Indian casualties for each event. He began with Colonel J. J. Reynolds's attack on a predominantly Northern Cheyenne village in Montana in March 1876 and concluded with Colonel Nelson A. Miles's fight against the Miniconjou leader Lame Deer and his followers in Montana in early May 1877. It was the confrontation at the Little Big Horn, however, that garnered the most attention. Given that Clark had not yet visited the battlefield, his description of the landscape is surprisingly accurate. The narrative of the battle itself provided an important account of the fight from the perspective of Indian participants. Clark included one of the earliest maps of the battlefield, attached to the report.[3] As the lieutenant explained, "The enclosed map is a fair copy of a rude sketch made for me by an Indian with a pencil on the floor of my room in giving me a description of the Custer massacre. He attempted to erase it with his moccasin but enough was left to allow me to retrace it, which I did and then copied it on paper."[4]

With the report completed, Clark made final preparations for the long-anticipated trip to Washington. The Lakota and Northern Arapaho headmen composing the delegation would finally have their opportunity to meet with the president and government officials in order to voice their opposition to their removal to the Missouri River and to settle the relocation issue. The group placed under Clark's supervision consisted of twenty-three headmen. The contingent from Red Cloud Agency included Red Cloud, Little Big Man, and He Dog. Among the representatives from Spotted Tail Agency were Spotted Tail and Touch the Clouds. The Northern Arapahos were represented by Sharp Nose, Black Coal, and Friday, who spoke English. The delegation included interpreters Leon Palladay, Antoine Janis, Jose Merrivale, and William Garnett. Agent James Irwin and his wife completed the list.[5]

The group left Camp Robinson on September 17 and traveled overland to Sidney, Nebraska, then boarded an eastbound train.[6] At Omaha the delegation encountered a minor problem when it was discovered that the Indian Department had failed to allot the money needed to pay the necessary fee for crossing the Missouri River Bridge to Council Bluffs, Iowa. Department of the Platte Headquarters promptly ordered the quartermaster's department to furnish the funds, which amounted to $5.80, reduced from $14.50 in compliance with rules for adjusting charges for transportation of troops between Omaha and Council Bluffs.[7]

On the evening of September 21 the group arrived in Chicago, met there by a large crowd that included a number of street urchins. With great difficulty

Clark led the party through the crowd to three awaiting omnibuses amid wild yells from the youngsters. The conveyances then took the group to the Sherman House Hotel to spend the night. En route to the hotel the headmen were occasionally greeted with war cries from individuals along the street, but they took it all in stride. After their arrival at the hotel the headmen went into the club room, where they sat in chairs and sofas and "tested their springing qualities to an alarming extent." Shortly afterward they enjoyed a meal, making impressive use of the utensils at their disposal. After supper the Indians amused themselves in the club room for a number of hours playing poker and other games of chance.[8]

The following day at noon the group made its way through the throng of people at the hotel and boarded carriages for an excursion through the Interstate Exposition Building on Michigan Avenue, an ornate metal and glass structure featuring prominent domes. There the Indians, protected by an ample police force, had to contend with another large crowd. After touring the building (including the conservatory) for two and a half hours, they returned to the Sherman House to enjoy another meal. At 5 the group boarded a train and continued the journey to the nation's capital.[9]

On the morning of September 24 the delegation arrived in Washington and went directly from the train station to the Continental Hotel. While a few of the headmen ventured outside, most spent the day resting after the long trip. Some who had visited Washington before had stayed at the Washington House Hotel. Spotted Tail and some of the others expressed their desire to lodge there once again. By late afternoon the change in accommodations had been arranged. The delegation walked to the Washington House. The proprietors of the Continental blamed Clark for the move, but Spotted Tail informed a newspaper reporter that they made the change because "they know this house and did not know the other." After settling into their new quarters they spent the evening at Ford's Opera House, where they attended a performance by Buffalo Bill Cody.[10]

On the following day the members of the group relaxed in their rooms, the Lakotas on the second floor and the Northern Arapahos one floor above them. A few of the headmen went outside to take short walks, only to be followed by a large group of curious boys.[11] On the next day they remained at the hotel and hosted a meeting with Brigadier General Crook along with William Welsh, former member of the Board of Indian Commissioners.[12] The conference offered the delegates and their benefactors an opportunity to plan and discuss the upcoming meeting with the president.

The following morning, September 27, adorned in various states of traditional dress, the delegates rode to the White House in two large omnibuses. They proceeded to the East Room to meet with President Rutherford B. Hayes and Carl Schurz, the secretary of the interior. Several government officials and dignitaries were also present, including Crook and the president's wife and daughter. Security at the meeting consisted of five policemen. Clark was positioned to the right of the president and began the proceedings by introducing each headman to Hayes.[13]

Once all the headmen had been introduced, the assemblage turned to the business at hand. The Oglala headmen expressed their objections to removing to the Missouri River and asserted a willingness to assimilate. Spotted Tail and the Brules deferred speaking until the following day. The Northern Arapaho leader Black Coal addressed the gathering next, stating his tribe's desire to go to the Shoshone reservation in Wyoming. At the conclusion of the speeches the council was adjourned for the day. Before leaving Lieutenant Clark introduced the delegates to the first lady and other government officials, including the attorney general and the secretaries of war, interior, and state. When all of the introductions had been completed, the delegation returned to the Washington House.[14]

The council reconvened in the East Room the following day with Spotted Tail and General Crook joining others who had already spoken. Sharp Nose addressed the assemblage as the day's representative for the Northern Arapahos. Crook spoke on behalf of the Indians and assured the president that he believed they were sincere in all that they had said. President Hayes was the last to speak at the council. He granted the Northern Arapahos their desire to move to the Shoshone reservation. Despite the best efforts of the Lakota delegates and those that supported their cause, however, the president informed them that they must go to the Missouri River because their supplies were awaiting them there. But, he assured them, they only needed to stay for the upcoming winter: they could select their own permanent homes in the spring.[15] At the conclusion of the council the delegates met with the Board of Indian Commissioners and were allowed an opportunity to express their views concerning the president's decision. The delegates made it known from the outset that they feared that they would never be able to leave the Missouri River if they went there.[16]

With the council being adjourned for the weekend, the delegates apparently set out to prove to the president that they were serious about change. It was probably at some point during the weekend that the members of the delegation accepted the suits of clothing that had been promised to them shortly after their arrival in Washington. On Sunday several of the headmen attended church services at Foundry Methodist Church, having been told that President Hayes worshipped there. A number of the delegates also took time to speak with the press in a continued effort to bolster their cause, expressing a desire to move to new agencies in the White River country immediately rather than waiting for spring.[17]

The Indians arrived at the Executive Mansion on October 1 for the final meeting with the president, dressed in their new suits and presenting a much different appearance than at the previous meetings. Spotted Tail spoke first, followed by Red Cloud. Both headmen announced the desired locations for their respective future agencies in the White River country within the Great Sioux Reservation. Among other things the two Lakota leaders requested that the government provide their people with wagons, farming implements, cattle, schools, and Catholic priests and nuns to teach their children the English language. Spotted Tail and Red Cloud requested that each delegate in attendance receive forty dollars cash to buy items for their women and children, a trunk for their clothing, and an overcoat for the upcoming winter weather.[18]

At the conclusion of Red Cloud's speech President Hayes addressed his audience. He expressed his approval of the Indians' civilian clothing and noted that it exemplified their desire to live like whites. The president did not have anything to add to what he had said before but reiterated the need to move to the Missouri River promptly, noting that the government simply did not have enough time to move their supplies from the Missouri River before the onset of winter. In regard to their requests for money, trunks, and overcoats, he explained that Congress had appropriated funds to the secretary of the interior, who would provide them with whatever he had been authorized to give. When the president concluded his speech, the delegates shook hands with him and members of his cabinet and left the Executive Mansion for their hotel.[19]

On the following afternoon the delegation held its final council in Washington, meeting with Secretary Schurz at the Interior Department. Red Cloud spoke briefly once again, stressing that his people did not want to move to the Missouri River. Spotted Tail followed and spoke at some length. He too explained that his people were against making the move, especially if forced to do so immediately, and warned that some of them might scatter. He once again pointed out that he had selected a place for his new agency and asked that his people be allowed to stay where they were until spring and then move to the new agency. When Spotted Tail had finished, Schurz issued the same response as before, once again insisting that the Lakotas must move now. He stressed again that they need only remain there for the winter and that the president would honor his promises when spring came. The secretary also assured them that General Crook would assist them with their transportation needs for the upcoming move. Schurz pledged that they would be given mills, wagons, and schools as permitted by the government. Finally, the secretary expressed his pleasure that the delegates approved of the new overcoats that he had sent them and promised that each headman would be receiving a trunk and some money that Lieutenant Clark would distribute. This concluded the meeting, and the Lakota delegates left.[20]

Attention now turned to the Northern Arapaho delegation, with President Hayes arriving and joining the council. Black Coal addressed the secretary and president first and requested that the government provide him with arms to kill game. He also asked that agent Irwin go to the Shoshone reservation to make peace between his people and the Shoshones. Sharp Nose spoke next and expressed his desire that farm implements, wagons, schoolhouses, and a Catholic priest be provided to the Northern Arapahos. Secretary Schurz promised the headmen that they would receive ammunition and that agent Irwin would go to the Shoshone Agency and make peace between the two tribes (which he did later in the month). The two sides then shook hands one final time and parted ways.[21]

Unknown to President Hayes and Secretary Schurz, the Northern Arapaho interpreter Friday attended the council in a drunken state. In an 1879 letter Clark revealed that "my Arapahoe interpreter got tight, so much so that he was of no use whatever and I interpreted the speeches of Black Coal and Sharp Nose by means of signs." Without explaining specifically how he accomplished the feat, Clark went on to boast: "and to this day the Secretary and the President, who was also present, do not suspect but what the interpreter 'Friday' did it."[22]

With the last of their official business in Washington now completed, Clark and the delegation spent a portion of October 3 at the Corcoran Art Gallery admiring works of art and posing for a group photograph. They boarded the 9:55 express train to New York City that night. The members of the delegation rode in ordinary day cars, placing mattresses along the seats and on the floors to facilitate sleep. The members of the group arrived in Jersey City at 6:30 the following morning and then traveled by ferry boat to New York City. From the ferry house they rode in coaches to the Grand Central Hotel on Broadway. After being given a brief opportunity to bathe and clean up, they enjoyed a breakfast in the hotel's dining room before spending some time lounging and resting in their seventh-floor rooms. At noon the delegates left the hotel for a thirty-minute visit to the city's aquarium followed by a ride through Central Park, which included a visit to the Museum of Natural History. By 3 that afternoon they had returned to the hotel and were met by a throng of curious people, as had become customary wherever they went.

Rain showers curtailed festivities for the remainder of the day. The headmen were scheduled to visit Gilmore's Garden, an open-air entertainment venue later renamed Madison Square Garden, but inclement weather dictated a cancellation. The delegates had also hoped to do some shopping with the thirty dollars they had each been given for that purpose, but the rain prevented them from doing so. Instead the rather tired members of the delegation had their dinner and then either lounged in their rooms or, like Spotted Tail, paced the halls. The newspaper reporters who were present took time to observe and converse with the delegation. When speaking with local reporters, Clark expressed his satisfaction with the men under his charge. According to the lieutenant, the headmen had behaved very well and in his estimation had dealt with the large throngs of onlookers with amazing composure.[23]

The next morning the delegates left their hotel for a shopping spree, making their first stop at Lyon's fancy goods store on Broadway, owned by William H. Lyon, a member of the Board of Indian Commissioners. Here the headmen spent a good portion of their money, the most popular items being satchels and a variety of trinkets. They then moved on to the store of Dunham, Buckley, and Company, where they purchased woolen shawls and comforters. When their shopping was concluded, the delegates next traveled to the Battery, a former fortress converted into a park, located on the southern tip of Manhattan.[24] Accompanied by three members of the Board of Indian Commissioners, they boarded the military steamboat *Henry Smith* for a sightseeing excursion. The secretary of war, George W. McCrary, had previously requested that the vessel be placed at the disposal of Lieutenant Clark and the delegates "in order to give them an opportunity of viewing the Harbor."[25]

A crowd of over three hundred spectators gathered to watch as Clark and the delegates embarked on their cruise. Showing an ample amount of enthusiasm and curiosity the Indians steamed away from the dock with Red Cloud and Spotted Tail in the pilot house while the remainder of the headmen gathered on the upper deck. Amid strong winds and rough waters the steamboat took the delegation first to Governors Island and then to a point near Staten Island.

From there the vessel forged its way up the East River as far as the Brooklyn Bridge, which was under construction. During the trip a bucket of salt water was procured, and the headmen were given an opportunity to taste it. Yellow Bear was the only delegate who did not spit it out in disgust. Once the steamer had turned around under the bridge, the headmen went to a cabin below deck for the return trip to the Battery, arriving there by 2 in the afternoon.

After returning to the Grand Central Hotel the delegates had their dinner and then donned their suits and went out shopping once again. At some point during the stay in New York City Clark received a $100 donation from an anonymous woman, who requested that it be spent on the women and children on the reservation. The lieutenant told reporters that the benefactor was probably unaware of the large number of women and children at the agency. He deemed it appropriate to purchase some necessary items for Indian women who did not have a man to provide for them. By 5 the headmen had completed their shopping and prepared for the long train ride home. In the evening they traveled by ferry to Jersey City and boarded the 8:25 Pacific Express for their westward journey. The headmen arranged their mattresses after boarding the train. Many had already fallen asleep by the time the train left.[26]

On the morning of October 7 the delegation arrived in Chicago. Its members ate breakfast at the Sherman House Hotel before proceeding to Mandel's dry goods store for some final shopping. The brothers who owned it had made special arrangements to open the establishment on a Sunday morning for their distinguished customers. The sibling designated to meet the delegation was late in showing up, however, and the group was met by the store's watchman, who became flustered with the headmen and yelled at them. Offended by this ill-mannered treatment, the delegates returned to the omnibuses waiting nearby. Fortunately the tardy Mandel arrived at this juncture and with Clark's influence convinced the Indians to return to the store. The headmen's remaining money was used to buy additional shawls and trinkets for family members in Nebraska. As soon as they were finished making their purchases, the delegates promptly boarded their train and continued toward their destination.[27]

On October 11 the delegation arrived home to find officials at both agencies hurriedly preparing for the move to the Missouri River while the inhabitants were reluctantly doing so. The plan for the upcoming move called for the Lakotas to travel in two separate columns. Spotted Tail's people would proceed in a general easterly direction to the recently vacated Ponca Agency on the Missouri River near the border of Nebraska and Dakota Territory. The column from Red Cloud Agency would travel in a northeasterly direction to the place where Yellow Medicine Creek empties into the Missouri River, some seventy-five miles north of the new Spotted Tail Agency. Clark would join agent Irwin and the Red Cloud column for the move east, with Captain Joseph Lawson and two companies of the Third Cavalry leading the way for the group. On October 27 the caravan from Red Cloud Agency numbering some 3,700 people set out on its journey. The cavalry contingent rode at the head of the cavalcade, with Clark's scouts on patrol along the route. Trailing behind the main body and its large pony herds were 120 freight wagons and a herd of 2,000 beef, which would feed the group for its anticipated 25-day journey.[28]

Two days later agent Lee and the Spotted Tail column embarked on the trek east, but not without difficulty. At the time of Crazy Horse's death over a thousand of his followers bolted from Red Cloud Agency to join the northern Indian village at Spotted Tail Agency. Many members of the recalcitrant northern village objected outright to any move at all when later confronted with the issue, while others expressed a desire to travel with the Red Cloud column, promising to join Spotted Tail later. The more northerly route of the Red Cloud column, however, would more easily facilitate an escape to the north country. When the date for removal arrived, the northern village (consisting of about 1,200 people) refused to join the Spotted Tail column and instead traveled a short distance to the mouth of Beaver Creek, where Captain Lawson's detachment discovered it on November 1.[29]

Lieutenant Clark and the Oglala headmen came forward and met with the leaders of the northern village in an effort to get them to join the Spotted Tail column. Clark soon found that it "was useless to try and get them to go forward, overtake Spotted Tail, and go on with him to his Agency." He observed that "if forced in this way or if we had refused to take them I was convinced they would have scattered out and gone north." The council resulted in the northern Indians joining the Red Cloud column, with Clark hoping that the new additions "will be partially absorbed in the other bands and subjected to better influences." He found them "wild, stubborn, restless, and still smarting under the bitter feelings engendered by the killing of Crazy Horse."[30] Captain Lawson maintained a similar opinion, stating that the northern Indians "seemed from the first a hard and difficult element to control."[31]

At some point during that first week of November Clark learned that Crazy Horse's family had brought his body on the journey, prompting him to inform Secretary Schurz that "even as a dead chief he exercises an influence for evil."[32]

The lieutenant's comment once again exhibited his self-righteous attitude in regard to his notions of what was best for the Indian. Yet the presence of Crazy Horse's body did in fact pose a problem, as the northern headmen attempted to use the corpse to incite anger among the peaceful faction of Oglalas. Ironically, on the same day that Clark penned his report to Schurz, Crazy Horse's family left the column to join Spotted Tail's people and buried his remains en route.[33]

Despite a clear strain on existing supplies and other possible difficulties that might arise from adding the northern Indians to the column, Clark remained confident: "I anticipate no particular trouble." The lieutenant went on to explain: "I think everything is so well organized in the different bands that no lodges will leave us en route." Unfortunately his optimism would prove meritless. In reporting the Lakota state of mind and attitude to Secretary Schurz, Clark warned that "I certainly believe there will be trouble in the spring" if the Indians were not given an agency on Tongue River. He informed Schurz that the Lakotas in general "honestly believe that they have only given away the Black Hills and that all the lands round them are still theirs." He also pointed out that the northern Indians still contested the ceding of the Black Hills because they believed that Red Cloud and others had no right or authority to give away the hills in the first place.[34]

Regarding the mass exodus itself, Clark attempted to educate the secretary about the enormity of the task at hand. The lieutenant pointed out that the column stretched for eight miles as the people and their fifteen thousand ponies trudged forward. When not on the move, the associated village encompassed an area three miles long. Again revealing his disdain for traditional Indian mores, Clark asserted that "as we camp sometimes in their midst, and listen to their infernal drumming and singing late into the night, see their painted faces looking particularly savage and wild by the light of their camp fires civilization, and gentleness, and kindness look very faint and far off." He added: "This move causes much suffering. The Indians as a rule are poorly clad, the old men and women and young children and sick people . . . make a march of this sort very trying and tedious." Clark commented on the conditions facing the column: "We have had very disagreeable weather, rain, sleet, snow, and this has of course made wretched roads."[35]

Movement was indeed slow. To exacerbate the situation, the northern Indians riding in the rear of the column continually maintained a slow pace in an effort to preserve their ponies' strength for a future break. To make matters even worse, an additional fifty lodges of northern Indians fled Spotted Tail's column during the first week of November and joined the Red Cloud group.

These recently arrived northern Indians had fired the prairies to the south, forcing the column to travel along the north side of White River.[36]

While expressing outward optimism, Clark was also practical and understood the potential for trouble. According to Captain Lawson, both Irwin and Clark urged him to remain in close proximity to the Indians. "I regulated my marches accordingly and camped each night near the Indians," Lawson said.[37] In addition to utilizing scouts in advance of the column to reconnoiter the route, Clark increasingly relied on Young Man Afraid of His Horses and other scouts to maintain a close watch on the northern village.

Clark's plan of "kindly yet firmly absorbing the different bands" did not materialize.[38] Tensions between the two factions escalated as the column slogged along White River. Ironically it was the Sans Arc headman Red Bear, a sergeant in one of Clark's scout companies and a Washington delegate, who became the most prominent leader among those advocating a break to the north. As the days passed, the call for an escape gained momentum.[39]

On November 9 the caravan arrived at the mouth of Wounded Knee Creek. Two days later the column had advanced less than six miles then halted. Fanny McGillycuddy, wife of acting assistant surgeon Valentine T. McGillycuddy, recorded the event in her diary entry for November 11: "Laid over for some reason of Mr. Clarks [sic]. Lovely day. Indians some of them dissatisfied."[40] The exact nature of the disruption remains unknown. Perhaps the lieutenant came to understand the intensity of the growing threat from the northern faction as they agitated others to join their plot and may have felt the need to council with them and attempt to calm the situation.

Another possible but less likely explanation might be found in Crazy Horse's widow, Nellie Larrabee. Mari Sandoz, a Crazy Horse biographer, apparently became privy to some hearsay information concerning Nellie and the move to the Missouri River. According to Sandoz, a number of Lakotas maintained bad feelings toward Nellie and complained about her traveling among the Lakota people during the move. Sandoz contended that Nellie might have ridden alongside Clark during the move as a protective measure if for no other reason. She added that at some point during the trip Clark became embroiled in a romantic affair with a Lakota woman, which caused him much trouble and disgrace. Nellie was suspected as the possible object of his affection.[41] Sandoz failed to verify the story, and exhaustive research has yet to uncover any documentation concerning the matter.

By November 15 the Red Cloud column had reached a point near the present town of Interior, South Dakota. Another layover was called for at this juncture in order to issue beef to the column on the following day. The situation was clearly deteriorating: Fanny McGillicuddy noted "prairie fires all around us."[42] While the beef was distributed, Clark, Irwin, and Lawson's escort forged on ahead to reconnoiter the route. Red Bear and proponents of a breakout seized upon this opportunity. Early on the morning of November 17 the faction fled into the nearby badlands to the north, despite efforts made by Oglala leaders to prevent the escape. A courier was immediately dispatched to inform Irwin and Clark of the situation. Clark responded by sending Touch the Clouds and his scouts in pursuit. The Miniconjou leader and his men intercepted the northern Indians in the badlands but failed to convince them to return.[43] "I believe every effort was made that under the circumstances could have been to prevent these people from leaving us," reported Captain Lawson,[44] thus exonerating himself, Clark, and anyone else from blame. Clark estimated that 100 of the 250 northern Indian lodges in the group had fled north.[45]

In the days following the escape the pace of the move quickened. With rations for his command dwindling, Captain Lawson and his men, joined by Irwin, pushed ahead of the column toward the new agency. Clark and twenty-five of his scouts also rode in advance, with the scouts serving as couriers and determining the route.[46] When the Lakota column arrived at the forks of the White River on November 22, its leaders were determined to go no further and declared they would make their winter camp there, about sixty-five miles from the Missouri River. On the following day a second breakout occurred. Some Lakotas fled to the north, while others moved south toward the Spotted Tail column. In all, approximately 90 additional lodges managed to escape.[47]

Traveling in advance of the column, Clark arrived at his destination on November 24, while Irwin and Lawson's military detachment came in the following day.[48] New Red Cloud Agency, located about three hundred miles from Camp Robinson, was situated along the west bank of the Missouri River on Yellow Medicine Creek. Agency buildings were located three-quarters of a mile from the military post. The agency would serve as the distribution point for annuity goods and supplies for the Lakotas during their stay in the Missouri River country. The military post at the agency, also designated by the army as New Red Cloud Agency, remained under construction. The only completed structures were quarters for one company, a hospital, a quartermaster's storehouse, and a root house.[49]

On December 1 Sheridan reported Clark's arrival at the new agency to General William T. Sherman and added that 100 of the 250 lodges of northern

Indians had fled north.[50] This figure is interesting, because it does not account for those escaping during the second breakout. Despite being at New Red Cloud Agency for a week, Clark apparently failed to inform his superiors of the most recent loss. In addition to the large number of those who fled, it was also distressing for the lieutenant to learn that the number included at least six members of the recent Washington delegation.[51]

During the month of December Clark continued his efforts to assimilate the remaining northern Indians into the agency bands. He also dedicated time to gathering intelligence, reporting to his superiors that he had interviewed two men from Sitting Bull's camp and had learned the Hunkpapa leader's current location. General Sherman revealed that he had no confidence in Clark's report: "Attaching no value whatever to this rumor—officers should be cautioned not to report the gossiping tales of vagabond Indians."[52]

Clark also attended to his duties as commander of the Lakota scouts. In addition to their service as scouts, Clark's command continued to act as couriers and also served as a police force at the new agency. When Clark arrived at New Red Cloud Agency, he commanded a contingent of 139 scouts. At the end of December all but 70 were discharged due to expiration of service.[53]

On New Year's Day in 1878 Clark and the other officers of the post attended a gathering hosted by the McGillycuddys. The fare for the celebration included cake and wine jelly that the surgeon's wife had prepared for the festivities.[54] The following day Clark received a telegram from Chicago ordering him to report to Sheridan's headquarters to consult with the lieutenant general.[55] Word of Clark's impending departure soon spread throughout the agency, much to the disappointment of numerous scouts.[56] Fanny McGillycuddy noted Clark's departure from the post on January 7: "Maj. Thornburgh, Lieut. Clark, Mr. Roberts, and Yates left for the East."[57]

Clark ventured first to New Spotted Tail Agency. He left there on January 11 and arrived in Omaha three days later. From there Clark made his way to Chicago as ordered. During his stop in Omaha Clark discussed the Lakotas and their new agencies with a reporter. He stressed to the newsman, and thereby the public, the Lakotas' deep desire to return west in the spring in order to select permanent agencies. He also pointed out once again his belief that trouble would follow if the government did not honor its promises.[58] In the end the Lakotas were allowed to leave the agencies on the Missouri, but not in the spring as promised. The Lakotas did not establish their new reservations until the fall of 1878, after a bitter struggle with the government.[59]

☆ 9 ☆

FORT KEOGH AND THE MILES-HOYT EXPEDITION

After a brief stay in Chicago to meet with Lieutenant General Philip H. Sheridan at his headquarters, Clark received a much-needed two-month leave of absence with the possibility of a one-month extension.[1] From Chicago the lieutenant ventured once again to Washington, D.C., in order to meet with the president and Secretary Schurz to discuss promises made to the Lakotas and to speak on their behalf. Following his meetings in Washington Clark wrote to Dr. McGillycuddy: "Please tell the Indians this, that they may know that even though I made them no promises I did what they asked me."[2]

Having completed his business, Clark proceeded to his hometown of Deer River, New York, to visit family and friends. The leave of absence was not entirely a time of leisure for the lieutenant, however. Clark actively pursued a promotion to the rank of captain during his stay in New York, a vacancy being available in the Commissary Department. Clark aggressively sought endorsements from both politicians and military leaders. Congressman G. A. Bagley from the 22nd District of New York assisted Clark in supporting his appointment, writing to adjutant general E. D. Townsend on his behalf. Crook also offered his aid and telegraphed President Hayes: "There is a vacant captaincy in the Commissary Dept. Please remember Lt. Clark in that connection." The president endorsed the request by recommending that "the papers of Lt. Clark be given careful consideration."[3]

In early February Clark extended his leave an additional thirty days and continued his efforts at promotion. On February 10 Representative A. G.

McCook of the 8th District of New York wrote to the president and gave a glowing endorsement: "Lt. Clark is spoken of very highly by some of my Army friends, and his appointment doubtless, would be an excellent one." Later that month Crook again came to Clark's assistance when writing to the adjutant general, stating that Clark "virtually controlled the Indians at the Spotted Tail and Red Cloud Agencies rendering valuable service to the government in that connection." Later he added: "Lt. Clark also rendered efficient services assisting the disbursing officers during the Sioux Campaign of 1876, where he showed himself to be a bright and intelligent officer, in every way fitted for the position sought."[4]

Despite his best efforts and the support he received from others, Clark failed in his bid for the appointment. He remained in Deer River through the month of March and on April 1 wrote to the adjutant general of the Department of Dakota: "I shall report to Gen. Sheridan in Chicago for duty on April 17th."[5] Three days after reporting to Chicago on the date specified, the lieutenant was ordered to proceed to Department of Dakota Headquarters in Saint Paul, Minnesota. After arriving at department headquarters on April 23, Clark was ordered to report to the commanding officer at Fort Snelling. Built in the early nineteenth century, the stone fort sat atop a bluff at the confluence of the Minnesota and Mississippi Rivers, across the Mississippi from Saint Paul. Clark joined other officers from the regiment assigned to duty with Second Cavalry recruits stationed at the post.[6]

Clark's stay at Fort Snelling was brief. On May 21 the lieutenant left the post with a detachment of recruits bound for Fort Keogh, Montana Territory.[7] Leaving the friendly surroundings of the Saint Paul area, the detachment set out for the isolated frontier post. A garrison of recent construction, Fort Keogh was situated on the Yellowstone River not far from the mouth of the Tongue River, near Miles City. Assigned to temporary duty with Company E, in early June Clark found himself in command of the company stationed at Keogh. He obtained the position because the company's captain, Elijah R. Wells, was absent on one-year sick leave. On June 21 the company was given the task of taking horses for the Second Cavalry to regimental headquarters at Fort Custer, Montana Territory, approximately one hundred miles away. Both garrisons were by-products of the recent Sioux War, established to maintain a military presence in this highly volatile region.[8]

Clark and Company E arrived at Fort Custer on June 24. At about the same time, Colonel Nelson A. Miles, commander of the Fifth Infantry and the District of the Yellowstone, had made the journey from Fort Keogh in order to examine the nearby site of Custer's 1876 fight on the Little Big Horn. According to Miles, several officers and a group of twenty-five Lakota and Northern Cheyenne participants in the fight joined him in inspecting the battlefield, but he did not mention any of them by name.[9] It is almost certain that Clark would have joined Miles on this excursion, given his fluency in sign language and the time that he had spent at the Nebraska agencies ascertaining the facts of the fight.

An astute student of the fight, Clark surely relished this opportunity to walk the battlefield for the first time. The group of officers remained at the site for several days inspecting the area. After returning to Fort Custer to rejoin his company, the lieutenant apparently made a second trip to the battlefield. On June 29 Clark left the post with Company E, taking his men to the scene of the Custer fight. They reached "Camp on Little Big Horn" near the battlefield the next day. Leaving the camp on July 1, Clark and his command arrived back at Fort Keogh four days later.[10]

Army Headquarters had accepted Clark's application for transfer to Company E during his trip to Fort Custer and the nearby battlefield, thereby ending the lieutenant's temporary status with the company. On July 23 Clark relinquished command of Company E when Colonel Miles ordered him to detached service in the field.[11] Troops stationed within the District of the Yellowstone faced the daunting task of conducting patrols and apprehending roving bands of Indians in the region who had left their reservations or had crossed south of the border from Sitting Bull's refuge in Canada. During the course of his assignment to Fort Keogh Clark would often experience both the rigors and frequent futility of this type of field service on the frontier. In this case he led a detachment of nine enlisted men on a scout in the direction of the Black Hills. When the detachment came to the Powder River, Clark went forward in an effort to locate a ford for his men. While crossing the Powder, Clark's horse suddenly stepped into a deep hole, causing it to fall backward. In the process Clark's .45 caliber Springfield rifle plunged into the river. Attempts to retrieve the rifle were unsuccessful due to the depth and swiftness of the stream.[12]

The rifle belonged to the government and was not the private property of the lieutenant, raising the question of who held responsibility for its loss. A board of survey convened months later at Fort Keogh concluded in Clark's favor, recommending that he be relieved of financial responsibility for the loss of the rifle. The recommendation then successfully made its way through the chain of command for endorsement, until it reached the Office of the Chief

Ordnance Officer at Division of the Missouri Headquarters. The chief ordnance officer ruled that according to the War Department an officer must provide his own arms and equipment, thereby making Clark financially responsible for the lost weapon.[13]

The recommendation was forwarded to General Sheridan for his comment. Sheridan's views on the matter contrasted greatly with those of the ordnance officer. In his opinion the War Department ruling referred to swords, not firearms. He believed that a sword was of no use for service on the frontier, making the use of firearms a necessity. The general further pointed out that officers were compelled to fight: just as the enlisted men and enlisted personnel did not have to purchase their firearms, so neither should officers. He did not believe that Clark should be held responsible for the expense of the lost rifle and thereby approved the findings of the board.

General William T. Sherman concurred with Sheridan, asking the secretary of war to rule favorably in this "test case." He stated: "Our officers now have to act as officers and soldiers in Indian fighting." He fully agreed that officers should not have to purchase their own weapons and recommended that current general orders governing the matter should be modified. As a result, the secretary approved orders changing the army's policy.

Clark and his small detachment returned to Fort Keogh from their scouting foray on August 7. The lieutenant stayed at the post only a week. Miles ordered Clark to join his upcoming expedition to Yellowstone National Park, located primarily in the northwest corner of Wyoming Territory. Officially Miles planned the venture in order to reconnoiter the terrain between Fort Keogh and the national park in preparation for establishing a wagon road and telegraph line west of the post. In addition, the trip offered the colonel and his fellow travelers an opportunity to visit the wonders of the reserve, established just six years earlier as America's first national park. According to Miles, he "selected a command from the most experienced veterans." The party included a dozen officers, slightly more than a hundred mounted infantry soldiers, and the eight-piece regimental band as well as a contract surgeon, two newspaper correspondents, three other civilian men, six women, and three children. Miles employed both a wagon train and pack train to haul the party's equipage.[14]

An impressive array of experienced officers from Fort Keogh and Fort Ellis joined Miles and Clark for the expedition. Major Eugene M. Baker, Major James S. Brisbin, and Captain James Egan all served in Clark's regiment, the Second Cavalry. Representing the Fifth Infantry were Captain Ezra P. Ewers, Captain

Andrew S. Bennett, First Lieutenant Frank D. Baldwin, Second Lieutenant Hobart K. Bailey, Second Lieutenant Oscar F. Long, and First Lieutenant James W. Pope. One member of the Seventh Infantry, Second Lieutenant Samuel R. Douglas, also made the journey.[15] Of the officers, Pope probably knew Clark best: the two men were classmates and had graduated together from the military academy.

Mary Miles, Alice Baldwin, and Sylvia Ewers joined their husbands on the expedition. The three children on the journey were Willie Ewers, Cecilia Miles, and Nita Baldwin. Other members of the civilian population at Fort Keogh accompanying the military contingent were Millie Baldwin, a schoolteacher at Fort Keogh not related to Lieutenant Baldwin, and Dr. Rosten G. Redd, a contract surgeon at the post who served the medical needs of the expedition.[16]

Sojourners from outside Montana Territory also ventured west for the excursion. Miles invited Colgate Hoyt, a prominent Cleveland banker who was married to Mary Miles's sister, to join the group. Hoyt in turn extended an invitation to fellow Cleveland banker Henry Clark Rouse. Both men would go on to become important railroad magnates. Hoyt's brother, the Reverend Wayland Hoyt, a Baptist minister from Brooklyn, also was in the party. Covering the expedition for the newspapers were correspondents George Wardman of the *Pittsburgh Dispatch* and Edwin Cowles, editor of the *Cleveland Leader*. The dispatches issued by these two men would inform the nation of the party's exploits.[17]

The final two members of the party were simply described by Colgate Hoyt as "two young ladies from Saint Paul."[18] The first was Rachel Rice, daughter of prominent Saint Paul politician Edmund Rice. The second, Hattie Sanborn, would prove to be an important figure in Clark's life.[19] Her father, John B. Sanborn, served with distinction during the Civil War and attained the rank of brevet major general in the Union Army. After the war he served as a member of the Indian Peace Commission that concluded the 1868 Fort Laramie Treaty, among others. Sanborn went on to enjoy a successful political career in Minnesota.[20]

It is uncertain whether Clark and Hattie Sanborn had met during the lieutenant's recent brief stay at Fort Snelling. The two undoubtedly became familiar with one another on their summer excursion to Yellowstone Park. For years Clark maintained a resolute attitude toward remaining a bachelor, once explaining to an Indian: "I have no wife, and therefore am at liberty to travel about, go to war, etc., at my pleasure and, as a consequence, can, as a chief, rise more easily."[21] Despite Clark's reservations about matrimony, the twenty-year-old Sanborn captured his heart. The young couple would eventually become engaged.[22]

Before proceeding up the Yellowstone Valley, the party first set out for a side trip to the scene of Custer's last fight. Instead of accompanying the main party, however, Clark received different instructions. On August 13 Miles ordered Clark to take a detachment of twenty men in advance of the main party and proceed early the next morning directly to Custer's battlefield, enabling Clark to visit the site yet another time within a six-week period. Mrs. Jerusha Sturgis, wife of the Seventh Cavalry's commanding colonel, Samuel D. Sturgis, along with her two daughters and a Miss Boyle had recently arrived at Fort Keogh. They were en route to the battlefield, where they hoped to locate the remains of Mrs. Sturgis's son, Second Lieutenant James G. Sturgis, who perished with his comrades during the battle. Clark and his men served as the escort for the Sturgis party to the battlefield and assisted with the grim task of locating the remains. A similar detachment was ordered to arrive at the battlefield from Fort Custer, to serve as an escort for the Sturgis party from the battlefield to that post. After returning to Fort Custer they would proceed to Terry's Landing in order to board a steamship for the journey home.[23]

Leaving Fort Keogh on August 15, the main party proceeded up the hilly badlands on the south side of the Yellowstone Valley to the mouth of Rosebud Creek. From that point Miles and a few men went off to select the best location for a wagon road and telegraph line connecting Forts Keogh and Custer. The main party traveled up the valley of the Rosebud and camped near the mouth of Muddy Creek close to the site of Miles's fight with Lame Deer's band of Miniconjou Lakotas in May 1877.[24] During that engagement a bullet barely missed Miles when a peace parley went terribly wrong. Lame Deer fired a close-range shot that missed Miles but killed the orderly positioned next to him. The headman lost his life moments later.[25] Having fought the final engagement of the Sioux War, the remnants of this band later surrendered at Spotted Tail Agency the following September during the Crazy Horse crisis.

On the morning of August 17 a portion of the party made the short ride up Muddy Creek to the site of the fight. The group picked up a number of relics, as the village of sixty-one lodges had been captured intact and its contents set ablaze. Colgate Hoyt found a German silver breastplate that was identified by etchings on the item as having belonged to Lame Deer. Hoyt later presented the object to Miles as a gift.[26]

The party left the Rosebud the following day, traveling from that stream over Tullock's Fork to the Little Big Horn and camping on the site of the 1876 Indian village. At Tullock's Fork the two newspaper correspondents encountered Clark and Lieutenant Pope, along with a scout and two Indian participants of the battle, and accompanied them for the trek from that point down a portion of Custer's trail to the battlefield. Shortly after Clark and the others arrived at the battlefield, they were joined by Miles. A brief time later the members of the main party reached the Little Big Horn, where they set up camp and enjoyed a leisurely afternoon resting.[27]

The travelers spent August 19 closely examining the scene of the fight. About thirty Indian participants in the battle, mostly Northern Cheyennes, accompanied them in going over the field as they satisfied their general curiosity and need for answers concerning the events of June 25, 1876. At some point during her time at the battlefield Mrs. Sturgis successfully located her son's remains. During the visit to the battlefield the Miles party was confronted with the spectacle of a large amount of both horse and human bones scattered about the site. The situation prompted correspondent Wardman, through one of his dispatches, to publicly call on the government to remedy the appalling condition of the burials there.[28]

Having thoroughly examined the battlefield, the party rode fifteen miles to Fort Custer. From there Miles and his group traveled a short distance from the post then made camp on the Big Horn River near a Crow village. Before leaving camp the following day, several members of the party spent their morning visiting the village. During the party's stay in the vicinity of Fort Custer, Clark and Baldwin examined a fifteen-mile portion of the terrain between that post and Fort Keogh as part of Miles's road and telegraph construction effort. The group's journey resumed as Miles and the others made their way to the Yellowstone River, using a ferry to cross the river at Baker's battlefield, where the major had faced Sitting Bull's warriors in August 1872.[29]

The members of the party then continued on their route, going up the Yellowstone River. For the next two days they rode at a leisurely pace, enjoying the fine fishing that the river had to offer. On August 24 they camped in a gorge located on Countryman's ranch, where Miles learned of the presence of warring Bannocks believed to be in the vicinity.[30] These Indians had fled their reservation in southern Idaho earlier that summer and had been fighting a series of engagements with various elements of the military in Oregon and Idaho ever since. By late August most of the fighting was over, but some small bands refused to surrender and were now fleeing to the east.[31]

Miles promptly organized an escort to take the civilians to Fort Ellis, near the town of Bozeman, while the military component of the party dealt with the Bannock danger. Miles ordered Clark to take twenty men and a nine-mule pack train to the Crow Agency in order to secure the assistance of Crow scouts in locating and fighting the Bannocks. Clark was then expected to make his way toward Yellowstone National Park via the headwaters of Clark's Fork, in search of the enemy. Miles further divided his small command by sending Lieutenant Bailey and forty men to Boulder Pass, while Miles and the remainder of the men ventured to Clark's Fork Pass.[32]

Newspaper editor and correspondent Edwin Cowles opted out of going to Fort Ellis and joined Clark on his assignment, documenting the lieutenant's endeavors for his readers. Early on the morning of August 25 Clark and his detachment left camp and proceeded up the Yellowstone River, stopping briefly at Horace Countryman's store near the mouth of the Stillwater. Countryman's business was situated on the north side of the Yellowstone, just off of Crow reservation land, where he carried on an active trade with members of that tribe. After fording the river the detachment rode on to the Crow Agency, situated near the confluence of Rosebud Creek (not to be confused with the stream of the same name in southeastern Montana) and the Stillwater River, arriving there about noon.[33]

At the agency Clark set about procuring enough supplies to last the detachment for ten to fifteen days. Through the assistance of agent George W. Frost, Clark secured the services of four Crow scouts to accompany him on his journey. An additional seventy-five warriors would later join Colonel Miles. Late in the morning of August 26 Clark and his command departed from the agency. The detachment rode out of the valley up into the scenic high country, making camp at 6 that night. The evening's supper included a doe antelope that Clark and Cowles had managed to shoot near the camp.

On the following day the route took the detachment from the grandeur of the mountain prairies into the dreary badlands at the base of the mountains. After the day's ride the men set up camp along the banks of a swift-moving stream, which offered a plentiful supply of trout.

On August 28 the command made an early departure from camp and reached the North Fork of Clark's Fork by 9 in the morning. After a brief stop to allow the animals to feed, the detachment advanced into rugged mountainous terrain. Progress became strenuous as men and animals struggled to ascend the steep slopes. After hours of hard climbing they finally reached the top.

During the expedition Clark drew a map recording his command's route. His thoughts concerning the ascent were reflected on the map, where he named the mountain "Break Your Back Mountain."[34]

Once on top of the mountain the detachment discovered signs of a military trail from the previous year's Nez Perce campaign. Continuing on their journey, the men soon found out that the only thing harder than ascending a mountain was descending one. After reaching the valley below the men pressed onward, passing a number of old Nez Perce wickiups on their way. At the end of the day's march the detachment camped in the picturesque valley of the Middle Fork, surrounded by forest but offering beautiful views of the nearby peaks.

The next day, August 29, Clark's command crossed a divide and descended into an area of very thick pine timber. The men struggled to advance as they wound their way through the hilly dense forest. In the afternoon they arrived at the North Fork and stopped for a brief lunch before resuming the march. In the late afternoon the command reached a point about ten miles east of Index Peak near the northeast corner of Yellowstone National Park in Wyoming Territory. Clark reconnoitered the area ahead of the column looking for a suitable campsite. Riding about a mile in advance of the detachment he came upon a large open park. Suddenly the lieutenant spotted a herd of about forty-five horses, ponies, and mules being driven toward him by a couple of Bannocks. Believing the rest of the Indian band to be in close proximity, Clark immediately turned his mount, rode back to his command, and ordered a charge to be made.

The command rushed forward as best it could, first through the tangle of pines and rocks and then through half a mile of boggy wetland. In the middle of this wet grassland the soldiers came upon a grove of pine trees surrounded by large boulders and discovered the enemy there. An estimated twenty-five to thirty Bannocks had just broken their camp and were commencing a night march when the attack took place. The initial charge prompted the villagers to retreat from the scene immediately, as they hurried women, children, and horses across a nearby stream and up into the rocky bank on the opposite side. The Crow scouts rode in advance of the troops, rushing forward and firing as they dashed ahead. Clark followed right behind them, "as cool as a cucumber," in advance of the charging command. As soon as Clark's men reached the bank of the stream, they began firing into the enemy on the other side. For a short time the opposing forces exchanged fire while the camp's inhabitants continued their retreat into the timber. As the last of the opponent's warriors was about to enter the protection of the tree line, one of the Crow scouts killed him and captured two ponies and a mule. Once inside the forest, the Bannocks had the advantage of being able to fire from superior cover. Clark ordered his command to take cover in the abandoned campsite. From that point only a few sporadic shots were exchanged, thus ending the engagement.

Shortly afterward the pack train arrived, and the command consumed a quick supper. The men were issued ammunition and the soldiers assigned defensive positions to guard against any nighttime incursions. During the evening the Crow scouts ventured down to the stream and held a parley with the Bannocks. When they returned to camp, they brought a boy back with them who had been sent to the camp in order to determine Clark's conditions for surrender. The youngster informed Clark that other members of the tribe were in close proximity and wanted to know what would become of his people if they surrendered. Clark promised nothing except protection and urged that they give up, as other soldiers were also in the area and that Tendoy's band of Bannocks, whom they apparently were counting on for assistance, would not help them. The boy was given a cup of coffee and allowed a few minutes to warm himself in front of a fire before being sent back to his people. The command settled in for an uncomfortable night, with cold temperatures and the sounds of wailing Bannock women.

Early the next morning the command proceeded along the side of Index Peak as its foe from the previous day slipped deeper into its mountainous refuge. About two hours into the march the advance element of the column surprised a couple of enemy warriors and succeeded in capturing one. As the command continued its progress through the rough terrain, it discovered a number of horses along the trail that had been abandoned by the fleeing Indians. Clark and his detachment pushed on until 7 that night, when they established camp on the East Fork.

Having failed to make further contact with its adversary, on the following day the detachment made its way to Baronett's Bridge on the Yellowstone River, where it anticipated rejoining the main party. Unable to find anyone in the vicinity, the command made camp. Clark sent a courier to locate Miles to inform him of recent events. Here the detachment remained, resting from its strenuous march and taking advantage of the outstanding trout fishing in the Yellowstone, which supplemented their dwindling supply of rations. A few days passed before a courier arrived, informing Clark and the others that the civilians were at Fort Ellis. Miles intended to proceed from the Crow Agency over much the same route that Clark's command had taken, and the expedition would soon reform at Mammoth Hot Springs. In one of the dispatches that Clark received while at Baronette's Bridge, Lieutenant Baldwin happily proclaimed: "You don't know how pleased we all were to learn of your success and that the General will be pleased you can well imagine."[35] The next day First Lieutenant Samuel T. Hamilton, Second Cavalry, arrived at the camp from Fort Ellis, bringing the information that Major Brisbin and a small detachment with rations were camped at Mammoth Hot Springs. Clark and his command rode off to meet Brisbin and remain at the hot springs until joined by the rest of the party.[36]

On September 3, while Clark and his men were at Baronett's Bridge, Colonel Miles discovered a band of Bannocks on Clark's Fork and quietly approached their camp during the night. At dawn the following morning the small command, supported by seventy-five Crow warriors, attacked the village. The Crow auxiliaries successfully drove off the pony herd of 250 animals while the command engaged the enemy. During the brief encounter eleven Bannocks were killed. The remaining thirty-one promptly surrendered. Miles's Crow interpreter lost his life in the fight, as did Captain Andrew S. Bennett, who was fatally shot in the chest.[37]

The next day Miles sent couriers to Fort Ellis and to Lieutenant Bailey's detachment, instructing both groups to proceed to Mammoth Hot Springs. Lieutenant Colonel George P. Buell and his command from Fort Custer arrived on the scene. Miles transferred his Bannock prisoners to Buell before setting out once again for Yellowstone National Park.[38]

At Mammoth Hot Springs Clark and his command tended to their worn-out stock and enjoyed the soothing effects of soaking in the springs. Having spent four days at Fort Ellis, the civilian contingent of the excursion advanced to the hot springs and were greeted by Clark and the others. The combined group awaited word from Miles, enduring a brief bout of snowy weather for a portion of their stay. A courier arrived from the colonel on the night of September 9, informing the group of his fight with the Bannocks. Later that same night orders were received instructing the party at the hot springs to proceed to Baronett's Bridge the next day in order to rendezvous there with Miles and his men.[39]

Leaving Lieutenant Bailey and his men along with all the wagons at Mammoth Hot Springs, the members of the party embarked upon their journey through the park on the following morning. They now had to rely solely upon mules to transport their equipage. They made their way toward Baronett's Bridge and by 3 that afternoon met Miles and his command. After reuniting the party then rode toward Mount Washburn, setting up camp on a pine-covered knoll along the Yellowstone River.[40]

After ascending Mount Washburn the party spent the next several days investigating the wonders of the national park. Clark, Miles, and the other members who succeeded in making the journey all the way to the top of Mount Washburn were rewarded for their efforts with breathtaking views of the surrounding countryside. While enjoying the scenery from the summit, they discovered a rock cairn erected there. Closer examination of the nearly six-foot-tall cairn revealed a tin can inside containing cards and sheets of paper with the signatures of such dignitaries as General Sherman and former secretary of war William W. Belknap. The members of the party added their names to the tin can. Rachel Rice and Hattie Sanborn, the only female members of the group to reach the summit, enjoyed the further distinction of being the first women to have their names included.[41] Apparently Hattie shared her future fiancé's sense of adventure.

From Mount Washburn the party continued on to the cascading waters of the upper and lower falls of the Yellowstone and the magnificence of its associated canyon. From there they advanced past Sulphur Mountain, camping near Mud Volcano, a hot spring known for its muddy eruptions. At this camp some members of the group tried their luck at fishing the Yellowstone River and nearby Yellowstone Lake but soon discovered that the fish at this locality were wormy and unfit for consumption. Other members of the party simply made the six-mile trip to the lake in order to explore its shoreline. On Sunday, September 15, the group pushed on to the East Fire Hole River in the Lower Basin. That evening, in front of the glow of a large fire, the Reverend Wayland Hoyt provided the soldiers who were escorting them with a sermon. The next morning the party continued on to the Upper Basin and camped near Bee Hive geyser about a half mile from Old Faithful. During their examination of Old Faithful several members of the group tossed sticks and logs into the mouth of the geyser just before an eruption and then watched as the wood was thrown at least one hundred feet skyward.[42]

On the morning of September 17 the party vacated its camp near Old Faithful and rode through Gibbon Canyon to a point near the Paint Pots, an area of small bubbling hot springs filled with mud of various colors. The following day the group covered the final thirty miles of its journey, from the Paint Pots back to the wagons at Mammoth Hot Springs.[43] At Mammoth the Miles party was greeted by Lieutenant Bailey and Ferdinand V. Hayden, head of the United States Geological and Geographical Survey of the Territories, and their men. Hayden's efforts in the park had been temporarily interrupted by the Bannocks.[44]

The journey through the park had been extremely enjoyable for the participants. Marches were generally made in the morning hours, allowing members of the excursion to spend their afternoons enjoying the wonders that they encountered along the way. Nights were spent around the campfire, often listening to music. While participants occasionally enjoyed fishing, hunting was not allowed while within park boundaries.[45]

Upon their return to Mammoth Hot Springs the members of the party were informed of the numerous rumors and newspaper stories announcing their demise. On September 12, 1878, newspapers reported that the Miles party had been surrounded by the Bannocks and that twenty-seven members of the escort had been killed. The erroneous information was followed the next day by dispatches relating the story of Miles's successful fight against the Bannocks, totally contradicting the previous day's news. Some members of the party quickly passed reassuring messages to loved ones via courier to Fort Ellis, where they could be sent by telegraph.[46]

Leaving Mammoth Hot Springs, the main party traveled down the Yellowstone River to Fort Ellis. At this point some members left the group. Lieutenant Pope, Colgate Hoyt, and Edwin Cowles set out from Ellis on a hunting expedition and a visit to the Crow Agency, accompanied by a ten man-escort. They would later rejoin the main party at Countryman's ranch. Miles, Lieutenant Baldwin, the Reverend Hoyt, and Henry Clark Rouse journeyed to the territorial capital, Helena. Miles attended the Territorial Fair of Montana there before reuniting with the remnants of the party. At that time politicians were clamoring for the territory to have its own military department headquartered in the capital city, with Miles as its commander. Hoyt and Rouse set out south from Helena for the Union Pacific Railroad, which would carry them east. The rest of their fellow travelers continued back to Fort Keogh along the Yellowstone River before some of them too would ultimately venture home by rail. Riding along the banks of the Yellowstone River at a leisurely pace, the party continued the journey, arriving at Fort Keogh on October 8. The remaining members of the excursion went their separate ways.[47]

⚜ 10 ⚜

LITTLE WOLF'S SURRENDER

After an absence of almost two months Clark once again assumed command of Company E upon his return to Fort Keogh. His stay at the post was once again short-lived, however. On October 14, 1878, Company E joined Companies A and I, Second Cavalry, from Fort Keogh, and Company G of the same regiment, already in the field from Fort Custer, to form a battalion under the command of Major Eugene M. Baker. The major's battalion was ordered to proceed on a scout to intercept the recently escaped Northern Cheyennes from Indian Territory (an exodus about which more will be said later), in an effort to prevent them from crossing the Yellowstone River and moving northward. Despite his appointment as a member of a general court-martial to convene on October 24 at Fort Keogh, records indicate that Clark probably remained in the field. The battalion camped in the vicinity of the head of Custer Creek, roughly fifty miles northeast of Fort Keogh, and used it as a base of operations. On November 2 Baker was ordered to return to Fort Keogh with a portion of his battalion. With Company A leaving the camp on the following day, Clark assumed command of the balance of the force. During the course of the month Clark's Company E rode an estimated 325 miles.[1]

The remaining soldiers of the battalion continued to serve in the field for a short time. Company I left the camp on Custer Creek on November 11. Company E vacated the camp on the following day, arriving at Fort Keogh on November 14.[2] Writing about the first days of this scouting foray years later, Clark recalled:

"In 1878 troops were sent out from Fort Keogh, Montana, to intercept some Cheyennes, who had been reported by an officer as crossing the Yellowstone below the post." Two days after leaving the fort Poor Elk, a Northern Cheyenne scout accompanying the column, discovered a promising trail that led to a campsite about a mile away. Poor Elk's close examination of the former camp revealed that the inhabitants "were Sioux and not Cheyennes, as stated; had recently left an agency; had not crossed the Yellowstone at the time reported, but two days previously; were evidently a party of Sioux who were on their way to join the Indians north of the British line."[3]

Less than a week after his return to the post Clark received instructions taking him into the field once again. On November 20 Colonel Miles ordered the lieutenant to the Crow camps and various white settlements along the Yellowstone River to investigate reports of depredations against local settlers by the Crows. Clark left the fort at noon and arrived at the Murphy Ranch about fifty miles from the post at 9 the next morning. Here he located a village of fifty-four lodges of Crows under the leadership of Two Belly encamped at the ranch. During the course of the next few days Clark visited the Crow camps and the ranchers located in the vicinity of Pease Bottom near present-day Hysham and Custer, Montana. Not having an interpreter, Clark relied on sign language to communicate with the Crows. His investigation revealed small offenses committed by the Crows, such as theft and running livestock, but nothing major.[4]

Clark met and counseled with both sides in an attempt to maintain the peace. He stressed to the Crow headmen at the various camps that "this was a small fire at the present time, easily put out by them, but if allowed to go on it would burn both parties." Clark encouraged the Crow headmen that he met to send runners to other Crow bands that he did not visit in order to relay his message. As for the ranchers, Clark explained: "I gave the citizens to understand that the Crow Indians had without question a right to hunt on the north side of the Yellowstone River, that the authorities would look out for the interest and welfare of both the Indians and white settlers." He went on to assure the ranchers that the Crows had been ordered to stop their depredations immediately.[5] Feeling confident that the matter had been resolved, Clark returned to Keogh in late November, where he assumed command of his company.

On December 1 the lieutenant composed an illuminating letter to his old friend Dr. Valentine McGillycuddy, reflecting his depth of trust in his former Lakota scouts. Clark had recently completed an accounting of pistols, rifles, carbines, and other ordnance used by his scouts at the Nebraska agencies. Due primarily to the hasty issue of arms on the morning of the surround of the Crazy Horse village, the lieutenant found a shortage of property amounting to just over two hundred dollars. Clark proclaimed to the doctor: "Now I worked hard, honestly and with all my ability to promote the best interests of the Red Cloud and Spotted Tail Indians and it hardly seems fair that I should have to pay this amount of money for my pains." He then asked McGillycuddy to take the matter up with the Lakotas to see if they would pay for the shortage, especially if some of them received an income from currently serving as scouts. "This to many would seem strange if not absurd to suppose Indians would club together and see a thing of this kind righted but I have a strong and abiding faith in the Oglallas and believe they will do it." Revealing a continued friendship with a Lakota comrade, Clark later instructed the doctor: "Please tell Young Man Afraid I have his glasses and will send them to him by first opportunity."[6] It remains unknown who finally paid for the shortage.

Clark remained with his company at Fort Keogh during the month of December. The routine of garrison life at Keogh took a destructive turn early that month. At 2:30 on the morning of December 12 the tranquillity of a cold winter night was shattered when Clark was awakened by the sound of gunfire. Hurrying out of his quarters, he heard a sentry call out an alarm of fire at number five quarters, inhabited by assistant surgeon Alfred C. Girard and his family. The adjoining number six quarters was the home of Captain David H. Brotherton, Fifth Infantry. Just as he had done at Fort Sanders years previously, Clark took prompt action in meeting the emergency. He and First Lieutenant Edmund Rice, Fifth Infantry, were among the first to arrive at the quarters. Upon approaching the scene, Clark could see smoke billowing from the cracks in the banking of the kitchen portion of number five quarters. Finding the kitchen door locked, he broke it open and discovered that the kitchen was filled with smoke but no flames were visible. Clark went to the adjoining number six quarters and found the same situation.

Believing that the fire most likely broke out under the kitchen, the assembled men made every effort they could to reach the source of the fire by cutting holes in the floor and tearing away the sides of the banking and building, but to no avail. Intense columns of smoke emanating from the quarters hampered all efforts to determine the exact origin of the fire. The most probable cause was determined to be either some kind of incendiary under the floor, such as burning coals, or a defective flue. Efforts were focused on saving the building rather than the personal property inside. Eventually flames burst forth. Despite the valiant efforts of the men in fighting the blaze, the quarters and their contents were completely destroyed.[7]

For Clark the excitement generated by the fire was once again followed by the routine of garrison life. While remaining within the confines of Fort Keogh during the month of January 1879, Clark took time to address the subject of the creation and organization of official Indian units within the army. This action was probably prompted by Commissioner of Indian Affairs Ezra Hayt's 1878 suggestion that a 3,000-man auxiliary Indian force, commanded by select officers, be created in order to prevent or quell future outbreaks.[8] In a letter to Brigadier General Alfred H. Terry, commander of the Department of Dakota, Clark submitted an extract from a letter outlining his plan that he had written to New York congressman Anson G. McCook, a member of the Committee on Military Affairs. Clark requested Terry's views on the matter and asked that Terry forward them to the congressman.

Clark's plan for the force envisioned battalion-sized units rather than the larger regimental bodies, considering them "too unwieldy and top heavy." He explained that at Red Cloud and Spotted Tail Agencies he had organized a battalion of five companies composed of fifty men in each and "found it to work so well that I am convinced this is the suitable organization, in fact the only one that can meet success." He did suggest, however, that the president could expand the size of each company up to one hundred men. Without specifying tribal affiliation, the lieutenant called for the creation of five of these battalions to be stationed at various departments throughout the West.[9]

Clark stipulated that each battalion would be commanded by a regular army officer with the rank of captain or first lieutenant, who would have the rank, pay, and allowances of a cavalry major while performing this duty. Companies would be commanded by lieutenants, but during this assignment they would enjoy the rank, pay, and allowances of a cavalry captain. Clark maintained that each company should have one interpreter, to be compensated at one hundred dollars per month and a ration. Each company would also have one Indian headman, who would receive seventy-five dollars monthly compensation plus a ration. The first sergeant for each company would be white, while the four sergeants and four corporals would be Indian. The remainder of each company would be composed of forty-two privates. Each Indian would receive the same pay, rations, and clothing as any other enlisted man plus forty cents a day for using his personal horse and equipment. Clark believed that the optimal enlistment period was anywhere from four months to one year.[10]

Clark's organizational plans for the auxiliary Indian battalions never materialized as he had envisioned them. The army continued to utilize Indian scouts in an informal manner for more than a decade. In 1890 it began laying the groundwork for the formation of an Indian contingent and embarked upon an experimental pilot program authorizing two units composed of one hundred men each. The following year the War Department began enlisting Indians as regular soldiers with five-year enlistments and authorized the creation of one Indian troop or company within current infantry and cavalry regiments (with some exceptions). Each company or troop was to be composed of fifty-five enlisted men. Noncommissioned officer positions would initially be filled from the existing ranks but eventually would be filled by Indians. Regimental commanders were to assign officers considered capable of performing the duty of commanding the Indian troops or companies. The venture was short-lived, however, and by 1897 the last Indian unit had been mustered out.[11]

Clark remained at Fort Keogh until January 30, when he relinquished command of his company and joined Company E's second lieutenant, Frederick W. Sibley, for detached duty north of the post at Sunday Creek. Sibley, a native Texan and fellow West Point graduate, was a veteran of the 1876 campaign. In early July of that year he and his small scouting detachment had narrowly escaped disaster when faced with a much larger force of Lakota and Northern Cheyenne warriors in the Big Horn Mountains. Clark and his junior lieutenant remained in the field only a few short days, returning to Fort Keogh on February 2.[12]

While remaining at the post, Clark turned his attention to army matters beyond the Montana frontier. In mid-December 1878 the Army Board of Equipments convened in Washington, D.C., in order to address issues surrounding possible changes to army clothing and equipment. Presided over by its president, Colonel Nelson A. Miles, the board met for the next three and a half months.[13]

As part of the process the board solicited and compiled a large number of suggestions from army personnel. In a letter dated February 20 addressed to the board's recorder, Clark outlined his recommendations. The lieutenant began by criticizing the clothing issued to enlisted men. In his opinion the material used was of inferior quality, the clothing fit badly, and it was poorly made. While he viewed all clothing in an unfavorable light, he noted that drawers and stockings were particularly poor. He saw it as an injustice to the men that they had to go to the expense of personally altering their issued clothing. Clark then turned his attention to the army's saddle, recommending that it adopt a saddle with the heavier California tree (frame), pointing out that it provided better support for firearms and also prevented sore backs for the men. He also believed that saddle girths should be wider and made of hair. The lieutenant went on to advocate other changes to curry combs, horseshoes, and saddlebags.[14] When the Army Board of Equipments completed its work and submitted its findings to General William T. Sherman, the general did not support most of the board's recommendations. But the proposals did influence eventual changes in clothing and equipment during the remainder of the century.[15]

In a different administrative matter Clark was required to submit a report to another board. One of Clark's fellow officers at Fort Keogh, the troubled captain of Company B, James T. Peale, had been recommended to be retired from the army. Clark had testified in Peale's 1876 general court-martial case. Now he and other officers were given the task of writing reports and providing relevant papers to the Army Retirement Board concerning Peale's fitness to serve. Clark wrote a highly critical assessment of the captain, clearly exposing his low opinion of Peale and his disgust at the captain's frequent drunkenness, when he often became "indecent and vulgar." Despite Clark's use of such descriptive terms as "careless, neglectful, and unreliable" to assess Peale's performance, he remained in the army.[16]

After expressing his views to the two boards Clark faced a more urgent and daunting challenge as he set out once again from Fort Keogh on yet another scout in late February. On this occasion he commanded a battalion of approximately one hundred men.[17] It consisted of his own Company E as well as Company I, Second Cavalry, under the leadership of Second Lieutenant Frederick W. Kingsbury, a midwesterner who graduated from the military academy two years after Clark. Also joining the battalion was fellow New Yorker and recent West Point graduate Second Lieutenant John C. F. Tillson, Fifth Infantry.[18] He commanded a detachment of twenty men from that regiment as well as an artillery squad composed of one noncommissioned officer and two enlisted personnel to man the accompanying Hotchkiss light mountain gun. Four Lakota scouts also augmented the battalion. The command was to proceed to the vicinity of O'Fallon's Creek, charged with the task of setting up a base camp there and intercepting a band of Northern Cheyennes believed to be in the vicinity.[19]

It will be recalled that in late May 1877 First Lieutenant Henry W. Lawton escorted 972 recently surrendered Northern Cheyennes from Camp Robinson to join their kin on the reservation at Darlington Agency in Indian Territory.

Arriving at the agency in early August, the Northern Cheyennes came to hate their new surroundings. Conflicts with their southern kin, food shortages, and disease all combined to make life in Indian Territory intolerable for the northern Indians. Early in September 1878 approximately 353 Northern Cheyennes under Dull Knife and Little Wolf took action as they fled the southern agency for their homeland. Pursued by the army from the outset, the Northern Cheyennes managed to fight and elude the military as they pushed northward. They also faced additional conflicts with ranchers and settlers. In Kansas young Northern Cheyenne warriors killed a number of them.[20]

By early October the Northern Cheyennes at last reached Nebraska's remote Sand Hills. At this point the bands of Dull Knife and Little Wolf split. Little Wolf remained steadfast in his determination to continue on to the Powder River country. Dull Knife, however, wanted to join the Oglala Lakotas at their agency near the redesignated Fort Robinson, not knowing that the Lakotas were no longer at the old Red Cloud Agency.[21] He also mistakenly believed that Clark was still there and thought that the lieutenant would look out for his interests.[22]

Consequently, on October 25 the members of Dull Knife's band surrendered to military authorities from Fort Robinson while camped on Chadron Creek. Their subsequent confinement at the fort resulted in a tragic loss of life to men, women, and children as they attempted to escape the environs of the fort in January 1879. Dull Knife and some members of his family evaded pursuit and successfully made their made their way to the Lakotas at Pine Ridge Agency.[23] The Northern Cheyenne leader would later tell Clark "of his escape from Fort Robinson, and subsequent journey of eighteen days in an arctic climate with only one blanket and a few rosebuds and snow to eat."[24]

Little Wolf, however, had decided to remain hidden in the seclusion of the Sand Hills for a portion of the winter before continuing northward. Later in the season his band resumed its trek, reaching the Black Hills and then pressing onward into the Yellowstone country. Intelligence received by military authorities that the Northern Cheyennes were now moving within possible striking distance of troops stationed at Fort Keogh prompted the orders for Clark to intercept the band.[25]

Marching out of Fort Keogh on February 22, Clark's battalion made its way down the Yellowstone River. At Sheridan Butte near the mouth of Powder River Clark ordered one noncommissioned officer and three men to remain there as a picket in order to scan the surrounding country from its heights for any sign of the enemy. Continuing down the river, the battalion established its camp near the mouth of O'Fallon's Creek at Ferry Point. From this base of operations Clark's men scouted the vicinity. He also set up an intelligence network with local ranchers and stage drivers.

On February 27 Clark was forced to move his camp to higher ground on the banks of O'Fallon's Creek. Despite a temperature of thirty-three degrees below zero on the previous two days, on the twenty-seventh the Yellowstone River rose about six feet and carried away the ice on the river. A few days later Clark moved the command back to the Powder River, where it could be resupplied with rations and forage.

The battalion was bolstered on March 7 by the arrival of two additional Lakota scouts and George Fleury, a mixed-blood interpreter at Fort Keogh. On the following day Clark ordered two Lakota auxiliaries on a lengthy scout that would take them up Powder River then eastward to the Little Missouri River and finally, if no trail had been located, down that river to scout toward Slim Buttes. When the scouts returned to camp on the morning of March 11, they reported having seen some Indians hunting approximately fifty miles up Powder River. Clark sent out three scouts to go ahead and locate the village while he collected his command and ten days' rations. By noon the command set out along the Bismarck Stage line. After riding the remainder of the day and with darkness approaching, Clark decided to press forward due to the openness of the terrain in order to conceal his command better. Marching through periodic heavy rain, the men crossed the rolling prairie toward the pine-covered ridges near the Powder River. The column continued its advance until eleven that night, when it set up camp. The night's march had been completed despite the rain and extreme darkness. Clark admitted that "but for the Indian scouts we certainly could have done nothing."[26]

The following day the soldiers of the battalion continued their march by carefully concealing themselves among the ravines until late in the afternoon, when Clark met the scouts he had sent to locate the village. After learning that the scouts had failed to discover any sign of the village, Clark decided to make camp for the night. It turned out to be a fortunate decision: the temperature plunged, and four inches of snow fell. During the evening Clark determined that the scouts must have made a mistake concerning the presence of the Indians on Powder River. As a result, he ordered the command to return to the mouth of that stream on the following morning.

While the battalion slowly retraced its trail, Clark took six scouts and thoroughly examined the area where the enemy had supposedly been observed. Finding no trace of the Northern Cheyennes, Clark sent interpreter George Fleury and two Lakotas to complete the scout that he had initially ordered to the Little Missouri River and beyond. Clark then rejoined the command, and by March 14 the battalion was back at the mouth of the Powder.

A few days after returning to camp Clark requested the assistance of Northern Cheyenne scouts from Fort Keogh. On March 19 six scouts arrived. Clark had also asked for an interpreter who knew the Cheyenne language but was informed that the only one available at Fort Keogh, a mixed-blood interpreter named Jules Seminole, had been discharged and would not be hired again. Nevertheless, Clark sent for him anyway, willing to pay for the interpreter out of his own pocket. Clark explained: "I deemed it very important and necessary that a perfect understanding should be had with these Cheyenne scouts."

When Clark met with the six Northern Cheyenne scouts he impressed upon them the key role that they would play in the anticipated subjugation of their own people. The lieutenant intended to use them to scatter the pony herd in a surprise raid, thereby making the enemy more willing to talk of surrender, or, if the element of surprise was not achieved, to have them go into the village to parley for a peaceful resolution. He stressed to the scouts that he preferred to seek a surrender without a fight. But if called on to face the Northern Cheyennes in a conflict, he needed to be able to trust them: if they felt that they could not do what was asked of them, they should return to Fort Keogh.

Clark also informed the scouts of his relationship with Little Wolf. The Northern Cheyenne leader had served under him as an enlisted scout, so Clark felt that Little Wolf "would have confidence in any message he might get from me." Knowing the Northern Cheyenne disdain for returning to the south, Clark explained to the scouts that he had recommended that Little Wolf and his people should be allowed to resettle in Wyoming Territory with the Northern Arapahos but added: "I could make no promises in regard to it."

Just as Clark finished his talk with the Northern Cheyennes, one of the Lakota scouts that had been sent to the Little Missouri River arrived in camp with the news that warriors from Little Wolf's band had captured the scouting party near the mouth of Box Elder Creek, a tributary of the Little Missouri. The Lakotas were taken to Little Wolf's camp, where they lied to their captors, making the Northern Cheyennes believe that they were on their way north to join Sitting Bull. They explained that they had stolen the government horses they were riding and offered to assist them in finding good fording locations for both the Yellowstone and Missouri Rivers and even to make it possible for them to be favorably received by Sitting Bull.

The Lakota scout who returned to Clark had made a successful escape the day after his capture when he went out hunting with one of the Northern Cheyennes and managed to get away from him, riding 125 miles in twenty-four hours. After hearing the scout's report, Clark acted quickly. The battalion left camp at 4 in the afternoon and advanced once again along the Bismarck Stage road before making camp at 11 that night. Shortly after camp was made, Fleury and the other Lakota scout arrived, having successfully escaped earlier in the morning.

Convinced that the Northern Cheyennes would know that they had been deceived, Clark again took prompt action. Eight days' worth of rations were issued, along with as much forage as could be carried on the packs. Leaving the wagons at the previous night's campsite, the battalion set out the following morning to continue its pursuit. Clark also sent three Northern Cheyenne and two Lakota scouts out in advance in order to find Little Wolf's trail or to locate the village itself.

After traveling some distance farther the following day, Clark met the two Lakota scouts, who returned to report that Little Wolf's trail had been spotted and that the three Northern Cheyenne scouts were continuing to follow it. Clark's battalion then proceeded to Hole in the Rock Creek, where it camped for the night. When Clark consulted with his auxiliaries at the camp, the scouts informed him that they believed Little Wolf was fleeing to an area of strong defense near the mouth of Box Elder Creek that was well known to both the Lakotas and Northern Cheyennes.

The following morning, March 25, the command discovered the campsite that had been used by Little Wolf's people two days before. From this point the battalion advanced a short distance then met two of the Northern Cheyenne scouts bringing with them three of Little Wolf's warriors. According to the scouts, they had entered the village the previous night and delivered Clark's terms to the Northern Cheyennes, who accepted them. The three representatives from the Little Wolf camp urged Clark to make camp where he stood and said that their village would then join him at this spot. They feared that if the soldiers advanced on their current camp the women and children might be terrified, leading to possible trouble. After considering the matter, Clark declined the suggestion and instead sent two of his Northern Cheyenne scouts, Brave Wolf and Two Moon, to go to the Northern Cheyenne camp to restate his terms and to bring Little Wolf out to meet him as the battalion approached the camp.

The column continued its march to a point about a half-mile from the Northern Cheyenne village, where Clark and Little Wolf met. During the meeting the Northern Cheyenne leader accepted the lieutenant's terms. Clark advanced his command to within one hundred yards of the camp, situated in a natural defensive fortress bolstered by breastworks. Clark placed his men in a defensive position as well and waited for about an hour to allow time for his scouts to talk with Little Wolf's people and for nerves to calm.

Clark then went into the camp and removed his firearms to exhibit his trust in Little Wolf and the others before taking a seat and holding a council with them. The lieutenant flatly told them that they must surrender their ponies and weapons as "the price of peace and they must pay it." He explained that guns would need to be given up immediately and the ponies would be taken after they arrived at Fort Keogh. Clark said that he was "truly and heartily glad we had arranged this matter without loss of life on either side."

Little Wolf responded by providing Clark with a brief summary of his people's trials and travails since leaving Camp Robinson and then stated that he refused to give up his firearms until they reached Fort Keogh. Other Northern Cheyenne leaders echoed Little Wolf's feelings on the matter. Clark decided to compromise with the headmen and to allow their warriors to keep their weapons until they reached Clark's wagons, a deal that the Northern Cheyenne leaders accepted. Clark instructed the thirty-three men and eighty-one women and children of the camp, which included a pony herd of three hundred animals, to pack their belongings.[27] They and the troops would move out that afternoon. The soldiers and Northern Cheyennes traveled about six miles from their former stronghold and made camp. Clark issued rations to his captives, while Dr. W. E. Sabin, medical officer for the command, cared for the Northern Cheyenne sick and wounded.[28]

Clark not only allowed the warriors to retain their firearms but also permitted them to hunt on their journey to the wagons. By the time the battalion and Northern Cheyennes arrived at the wagons a great deal of the Indians' anxiety and fear had evaporated. As promised, the Northern Cheyennes surrendered their firearms. Weapons of various kinds were confiscated, including four Springfield carbines, three Springfield rifles, four Sharps carbines, five Sharps rifles, one muzzle-loading rifle, three Winchester Henry repeating carbines, eight Colt revolvers, two Smith and Wesson revolvers, and one Remington revolver.

On April 1 Clark's battalion and the Northern Cheyennes reached a point just a few miles from Fort Keogh, where the lieutenant called a halt. Clark disbursed the scouts and various elements of the battalion in order to form a cordon around his captives. He then held a council with Little Wolf and all his men. Clark intended to exercise extreme caution in an effort to avoid a repetition of the carnage at Fort Robinson. Dull Knife's people had managed to smuggle some weapons when they surrendered at that post, which became a contributing factor in the subsequent killing. Clark stressed to the assemblage the importance of having surrendered all of their firearms to him. He found it hard to believe that thirty-three men would have so few firearms. Anyone who still retained weapons must give them up now. The men insisted that all arms had been surrendered, but Clark cautiously had each individual examined. The scouts also searched through all packs and bundles, but no additional firearms were found. After Clark was satisfied of a thorough disarmament, the march to the post continued. When they arrived at Fort Keogh later that morning, the lieutenant had his two cavalry companies set up a camp nearby with the Northern Cheyennes.[29]

News of Clark's bloodless victory preceded his arrival back at Fort Keogh. When the lieutenant arrived at the post, he was given something of a hero's welcome. "The troops were all out, the cannon thundered, the band played 'Hail to the Chief,' and men, women, and children crowded around him with their heartiest congratulations," reported a newsman.[30] In the weeks after his return Clark was showered with additional praise from his superiors. General Alfred H. Terry was among them, commending Clark for his "energy, skill, perseverance and excellent judgment."[31]

Just days after bringing in Little Wolf's people, Clark felt compelled to defend the band before the "proper authorities" at the Department of Dakota. The source of his angst was a passage from a report written by a board of officers at Fort Robinson that was investigating the recent events concerning the Northern Cheyennes. The report blamed Little Wolf's warriors for committing atrocities on the journey north. But Clark contended: "I am convinced when a true history of their escape and march is known, it will be redeemed from many of the dark colors which now represent it." While Clark believed that some of the young men were responsible for atrocities, he wanted to clarify the band's activities after splitting with Dull Knife's people. He pointed out that "I have no desire to shield or protect in any way, persons guilty of crime, be they black, white or red, and I think I am free from any sickly philanthropy as regards Indians." But certain facts had become known to him, and he wanted to set the record straight. He also supported the idea of involving civil authorities to investigate the allegations leveled against the Northern Cheyennes, to identify specific individuals and have them prosecuted in court.[33]

Clark went on to outline instances where the warriors had ample opportunities to kill but chose not to do so. On one occasion after the bands split a white man had been killed, Clark admitted. But he explained the circumstances surrounding the killing and thereby justified the act. As further evidence that these Indians were trying to do the right thing he cited the case in which a young man named Black Coyote had stolen some stock. Black Crane, a headman, insisted that the animals be returned. In the subsequent altercation between the two men the young warrior fatally shot Black Crane. Black Coyote and his family and friends then suffered the fate of banishment from the band.[33]

Clark also called attention to the hypocrisy of the clamor for revenge against the Northern Cheyennes by whites. Referring once again to the Fort Robinson board of officers report, the lieutenant quoted the portion that detailed the mutilation and mistreatment of Dull Knife's slain followers by civilians. This led Clark to ask: "Civilized warfare is supposed to be many removes from the savage but in all the accounts of the atrocities committed by these Cheyennes en route, is there a picture with darker or more wretched coloring than this?"[34]

The lieutenant personally vouched for the character of Little Wolf, whom he knew well from the days when the Northern Cheyenne leader had served as a scout for him at Red Cloud Agency. Clark observed that the members of Little Wolf's band "want peace and rest and a home somewhere in this country where they were born and reared." He warned that "should they be ordered back there [Indian Territory] they may seek escape by throwing themselves against the bullets and bayonets of the soldiers, or by suicide." But Clark maintained: "If allowed to remain they would be among our strongest, best, and bravest allies."

As to whether the Northern Cheyennes would be permitted to remain in the North or be returned to Indian Territory, Clark explained: "I have said nothing" and "I have made them no promises, have not even touched on the subject of their going back." He warned that if the decision was made for the Northern Cheyennes to return south it should be kept a "profound secret till everything is made ready for the movement." The men should be separated from the women and children before announcing the move. If Little Wolf's band was forced to return south, Clark trusted that he himself "may have nothing to do with it." The lieutenant once again suggested that if the band could not remain at Fort Keogh then the Northern Arapahos' agency in Wyoming Territory would be a good alternative, where they could serve as scouts and protect settlers from the Lakotas.

Clark's pleas on behalf of Little Wolf's people received favorable endorsement from Department of Dakota commander General Alfred H. Terry, who advocated that they remain at least for the time being at Fort Keogh. In forwarding his endorsement to his superiors at Division of the Missouri Headquarters, the commander emphasized the potential usefulness of the Northern Cheyennes as scouts in future activities against the Lakotas. In the end Little Wolf and his men did serve as scouts. His people remained at Keogh for the next three years, after which they were moved to a reserve in the area of Rosebud Creek and Tongue River in southeastern Montana, never to return to the South.[35]

While writing *The Indian Sign Language* years after Little Wolf's surrender, Clark took a critical tone toward the government's treatment of the Cheyenne people:

> They in their turn have been hunted like wolves, and shot down like mad dogs, until they are now only a wreck of their former greatness. Perhaps these savage and cruel wars, with their attending horrors, were but the legitimate fruit of bad policy and mismanagement of Indian affairs, or willful indifference to or misunderstandings of the conditions and circumstances of the Indians, and their relations to the Government, which in times past has too often permitted dishonest agents to be the intermediaries between the Government and them, and through weakness or cowardice has at times paid more heed to clamors of rapacious miners and settlers of the white race than to treaty obligations and plighted faith with Indians.[36]

Clark commanded his company after his return to Fort Keogh, which set up its camp near the post in order to guard the Northern Cheyenne village and to herd and guard the captured pony herd. The animals proved to be a problem for Clark from the moment he brought them to Fort Keogh. Upon his arrival the post commander, Lieutenant Colonel J. N. G. Whistler, handed Clark a telegram from E. S. Newman, a Nebraska rancher who had a number of horses stolen by Little Wolf's band. When questioned by Clark, the Northern Cheyennes admitted that they acquired the horses on the Newman Ranch.

In the days that followed other ranchers contacted Whistler, claiming that they too were victims of stolen stock. Shortly thereafter attorney Jeter Sharp, representing a number of claimants and armed with powers of attorney, arrived at Fort Keogh. The lawyer also possessed a letter from department headquarters granting him authority to retrieve some of the stolen animals.[37]

Following orders, Clark released 108 horses to the attorney in Whistler's estimation. But Sharp claimed that the owners were entitled to more animals. To settle the matter the lieutenant called for the formation of a board of officers, which convened on April 30. After considering the documents related to the case, and apparently using more exacting standards than Clark, the board decided to return 67 horses proven to be included in appropriate powers of attorney.[38]

The situation was complicated, however, because Newman had telegraphed his power of attorney to Sharp, so the rancher's paperwork had not yet passed through proper channels at department headquarters. As a result, his name was not included among the ranchers that Sharp was allowed to represent. Although, as Clark claimed, "proof of his stock was the clearest and strongest of any of the claimants," the board would not officially release Newman's stock to the attorney.[39] At Clark's request the members of the board personally examined the horses. The board's president, Captain Samuel Ovenshine, Fifth Infantry, confessed that the animals were "branded clearly" and added that "proof of ownership was entirely satisfactory to us." But Ovenshine justified the board's conclusions by explaining that, "as we were restricted to Powers of Attorney which had passed through Department Headquarters, could not take any further action on this stock."[40]

Clark decided to take matters into his own hands, keeping the post commander of Fort Keogh ignorant of his actions. Although the Company E camp was just a few hundred yards away from the post, Clark believed that as commander of the camp he had the authority to act.[41] After all, reasoned the lieutenant, his duty at the camp was officially listed as detached service, thereby freeing him to act independently. It was in his capacity as camp commander that he had requested the board's inspection of Newman's horses. "I decided it my clear duty to turn it [Newman's property] over," Clark stated, adding: "I was thoroughly convinced that a just and proper and legal claim had been made, that the proof of ownership had been ample and sufficient, clear and positive, that by further holding it a rank injustice would be done the owner as he would be subjected to trouble, expense and danger of sending some five hundred miles through a country infested with Indians and robbers, to secure his property."[42]

Newman's horses ended up leaving Fort Keogh with the rest of the stock taken by Sharp. When Clark's actions were reported to Lieutenant Colonel Whistler, after the attorney was on his way to Deadwood, the lieutenant found himself in a small amount of trouble. Whistler of course expressed his displeasure to his superiors at the Department of Dakota but tempered his views by explaining that "the error in judgment happened to be on the right side; still this fact makes it none the less an error."[43] On May 19 General Terry, who so recently had praised Clark for his capture of Little Wolf, issued a censure to the lieutenant. Clark's response was to write Terry a letter outlining the history of the matter, including supporting documents to strengthen his case. He felt assured that "on its receipt the Department Commander will withdraw his letter and not only sanction but approve my action." Clark ended his summary by stating: "I certainly feel hurt at what I consider an undeserved censure."[44] Having defended his actions as best he could, Clark soon shifted his attention to other matters in the weeks ahead, some mundane and others exhilarating.

⋆ 11 ⋆

FIGHTING SITTING BULL'S BAND

Clark and his men continued to inhabit their camp at the Northern Cheyenne village throughout the months of May and June 1879. In late May Clark became the subject of a military mix-up. Major Azor H. Nickerson apparently telegraphed Brigadier General George Crook, seeking his views on Clark's qualifications for joining the staff at West Point. Crook promptly issued a glowing recommendation favoring Clark's appointment: "His arduous and successful service entitles him to much consideration."[1] When the matter was brought to the attention of Adjutant General E. D. Townsend, he responded: "I don't understand this. Lt. Clarke [sic] has not been applied for & is not needed at West Point."[2] Evidently these words from the adjutant general ended the misunderstanding.

Taking advantage of his time in camp between forays into the Montana frontier, Clark submitted a request to the adjutant general of the Department of Dakota recommending the issue of forage biscuits for animals during field service in lieu of the customary oats and corn. In the lieutenant's opinion such biscuits would be lighter and easier to transport and would also keep for a long time in any climate: all this for the same price as traditional forage. Campaigning on the frontier required the forage to be carried by pack animals, Clark pointed out, and much of the grain transported in this manner was wasted, even if double bagged. Changing to forage biscuits would enable a pack animal to carry five times the amount of forage currently transported.[3]

Clark's request was passed along the chain of command and met with disapproval from the adjutant general, quartermaster general, and secretary of war. The quartermaster general's primary concern was the possibility for fraud on the part of contractors making the biscuits, who might use cheap fillers combined with ground grain. If post commanders on the frontier wanted their soldiers to make biscuits, however, it would be permitted.[4]

Not easily deterred, Clark made a second request three and a half months later and this time included a sample biscuit. While Colonel Miles favorably endorsed Clark's petition, the quartermaster general and secretary of war once again disapproved, largely on the same grounds as before.[5] Interestingly, in 1882 Ohio businessman George H. Crossman approached the army about manufacturing forage biscuits for its use, referring to his product by the unfortunate name "horse biscuits." Crossman's request met the same fate that Clark's had some three years earlier.[6]

In early June Clark found himself serving as a member of a general court-martial convened at Fort Keogh.[7] However, a good deal of his time during his stay at the camp near the Northern Cheyenne village was probably spent in organizing and preparing his new scouts for service in the field. According to well-known Fort Keogh photographer L. A. Huffman, "Clark had a great admiration for Little Wolf and Little Wolf for Clark, the dashing cavalryman, who was adept at sign language."[8] In addition to their friendship, the lieutenant trusted Little Wolf and appointed him as a first sergeant with his newly formed scouts.[9]

Huffman eventually became prominently known for his images of a western frontier that was quickly fading away. The photographer maintained a studio at the post, which became a favored spot for soldiers and Indians alike to lounge about and chat. On one particular day Clark and John "Big Leggins" Bruguier, a scout and interpreter at the fort, rode up to the studio, where they found Huffman and Spotted Bear, an aged Northern Cheyenne man. Clark had a sense of humor and liked to joke. In this instance he asked the interpreter Bruguier "to ask the old man if it was true that he sat down on the hill and cried the day that Custer fell."[10]

Near the end of the month Clark and Company E, and most likely the Indian scouts, moved their camp three miles away on the north side of the Yellowstone River, to join Major Eugene M. Baker and Companies A, B, and I, Second Cavalry, preparatory to taking the field.[11] The intended foe for the upcoming expedition would be Sitting Bull and his warriors. The Lakota leader and his people had been an ongoing concern for the army, and a source of unending rumors, ever since they had fled to Canada for refuge in 1877 after the Great Sioux War.

Reports of large numbers of Lakotas hunting south of the border, along with complaints of Lakota depredations from white settlers and peaceful Crows, prompted military authorities to order Colonel Miles to launch the expedition. The attacking force consisted of seven companies of the Second Cavalry, seven companies of the Fifth Infantry mounted on previously captured Indian ponies, and two more companies of the Sixth Infantry to guard the expedition's supply depot. Augmenting the command was an artillery detachment whose arsenal included a lethal 1.5-inch five-barrel Hotchkiss revolving gun. The military component of the expedition numbered 638 officers and men. Rounding out Miles's force was Clark's contingent of 72 scouts, including not only the Northern Cheyennes, but Crows, Lakotas, Bannocks, and Assiniboines as well.[12]

The command left Fort Keogh at staggered intervals, with Clark and Company E leaving the camp on the Yellowstone River on July 3 as part of Major Baker's Second Cavalry battalion. The soldiers marched north toward abandoned Fort Peck on the Missouri River, originally a trading post and then an Indian agency until flooding forced its removal to Poplar River, and arrived there on July 9. While the rest of Miles's command ferried across the Missouri that day, the Second Cavalry battalion remained on the south side of the river for the night. Clark also relinquished command of his company on that day, officially being assigned the duty of chief of scouts. At the same time Eli L. Huggins, a recent transfer from the Second Artillery newly promoted to captain, assumed command of Company E. Huggins had grown up in Minnesota Territory. He knew the Lakota language and was frequently used by Miles to pursue Lakotas.[13]

John F. Finerty, correspondent for the *Chicago Times*, joined the expedition when it arrived at the Missouri River. A veteran of Crook's 1876 Starvation March, Finerty was well acquainted with Clark. The two men were reunited at the Second Cavalry camp on the southern bluffs overlooking the river. After meeting Clark and other officers he had known during the '76 campaign, the correspondent commented that all of them, "in spite of continuous hard service, looked as well as they did three years before."[14]

The newspaper reporter camped that evening with Clark and Captain Thomas B. Dewees, who had been Clark's company captain when the young lieutenant first arrived at Fort D. A. Russell in the fall of 1868. After partaking of supper the three men sat outside the tents and reminisced about their days in the field with Crook in 1876 before retiring for the night. They slept soundly until awakened by a sudden clap of thunder, followed almost immediately by what Finerty described as a tornado, blowing away tents and leaving the men of the command drenched in a torrential rain. When the storm passed, most of the soldiers of the camp managed to get some additional sleep before morning.

The Second Cavalry battalion ferried over to the north side of the Missouri River the following day. Another Second Cavalry battalion from Fort Custer arrived on the south bank on the evening of July 11 and crossed the river the next day. The command remained encamped at the site of Fort Peck until July 15, when it marched out along the Milk River and its surrounding lush green rangeland toward Canada. The men advanced as far as Box Elder Creek (not to be confused with the stream of the same name located primarily in southeastern Montana), where they made camp and endured another rainstorm that night.

The next morning Northern Cheyenne scouts discovered pony tracks, indicating the presence of the Lakotas in the area. As a result, Clark and his scouts ventured out in advance of the command. The lieutenant and his scouts encountered a party of French mixed-bloods (Métis), who informed Clark that a large body of Lakotas had been in the vicinity of their camp the previous day. The command, meanwhile, set up its camp on Milk River near the site of an old trading station known as Campbell's Houses located near present-day Vandalia, Montana. About sundown Clark and the scouts returned to camp, bringing with them a mixed-blood prisoner.[15]

The following day, July 17, Clark and his scouts along with Company C, Second Cavalry, under Second Lieutenant Curtis B. Hoppin, and Company I, Fifth Infantry, commanded by First Lieutenant George P. Borden, were sent up Beaver Creek to look for signs of the enemy. About five miles up that stream, the detachment discovered Sitting Bull's people.[16] The presence of buffalo on the Big Bend of Milk River brought Sitting Bull and about six hundred of his followers to hunt for meat in the area. Leaving the main encampment, a hunting party had gone out to kill buffalo and finished a successful hunt later that day. While most of the Lakotas withdrew to the north, some 120 people remained at the site while the Lakota women and children finished butchering the animals. The men who stayed at the scene rested while the butchering took place. Prominent among them was the Hunkpapa Lakota leader Sitting Bull himself. It was this group that Clark encountered.[17]

Clark immediately ordered a courier back to the main command to inform Miles of his discovery and then, "with his usual dash, rushed boldly" at the

Lakotas.[18] As the Lakota women and children fled, the warriors fired upon their rapidly advancing attackers. The men retreated gradually, establishing a series of defensive firing lines as they moved.[19] Clark kept his men pressing forward, chasing the retreating Lakotas for about twelve miles between Beaver Creek and Milk River. By this time the Lakota hunters who had recently left the buffalo kill site had been informed of the fight. Approximately sixty men quickly set out to join the conflict.[20]

With the addition of these warriors, the Lakotas now had the advantage over Clark's command. The lieutenant soon found himself in the process of becoming surrounded. Clark promptly ordered another courier to the main command to inform Miles of the situation. First Lieutenant Edward J. McClernand, Second Cavalry, recalled that the courier arrived, "his pony panting and covered with foam, bearing a message from Clark saying that he was nearly surrounded and asking for speedy help." The main command quickly moved forward to the scene. McClernand, who graduated from West Point two years after Clark and had just recently been promoted to first lieutenant, noted: "Seeing our approach the Indians gave way, keeping up a running fight with Clark and Hoppin who followed close upon their heels."[21]

As the Lakotas scattered on the north side of Milk River, the artillery pieces were brought into action and fired a few shots at the fleeing enemy. In writing about the fight, former Fifth Infantry regimental adjutant George W. Baird observed: "It is doubtful whether Philo felt a qualm of fear; he could not have been blamed if he had on this occasion experienced it, for the immense host was encircling him, and but for the rapid advance of Miles and the main command, he would probably not have survived to give his graphic account of the charge that came thundering to his rescue."[22] The engagement that day resulted in the deaths of five Hunkpapa men and the loss of a large amount of their possessions, including buffalo meat and pack saddles. Two Cheyenne scouts, Medicine Stand and Shadow Come Out, along with a Crow scout named Magpie had also been killed in the affair. Two men from Company C, Second Cavalry, were wounded, as well as an Assiniboine scout.[23] The fight would prove to be the last time Sitting Bull faced the army in battle and the last armed conflict in which Clark participated.

After crossing the Milk River, the Lakotas fled in a northeasterly direction to the camps on Rock Creek in Canada.[24] Miles and his command marched back to their wagons throughout the night, enduring torrential rains and lightning. The command then remained at its camp on the Milk River until

July 21, apprehending a number of French mixed-bloods, commonly known at the time as "Red River half-breeds," and sending them to Fort Peck. These mixed-blood people were problematic to the army because they continually traded with the Lakotas and provided them with ammunition.[25] Described by Clark as "veritable gypsies," these itinerant traders generally lived in lodges and were noted for using unique carts to transport their goods and belongings.[26]

On July 22 the command crossed Frenchman's Creek, swollen from heavy recent rains. Despite a cold wind and swarms of large mosquitoes, it advanced to a point on Rock Creek a short distance south of the Canadian border and made camp. Also on that day Major Baker and four companies of the Second Cavalry were dispatched to scout along Milk River in order to capture any Red River mix-bloods they might encounter. Meanwhile the men staying at Rock Creek found themselves plagued throughout the night by rain, wind, and mosquitoes.[27]

Having forced the Lakotas back into Canada as ordered, Miles now faced the challenge of keeping them there and depriving them of their supply of ammunition. The command remained on Rock Creek near the boundary for several days. During that time Miles sent out various detachments to locate, arrest, and gather mixed-bloods in the vicinity, thus eliminating the Lakotas' main source of ammunition. Clark had been dispatched on such a mission and had succeeded in capturing a mixed-blood band. During his stay near the border Miles conferred with the Hunkpapa leader Long Dog and Major James M. Walsh of the North-West Mounted Police, a man sympathetic to the plight of the Lakotas. From the two men Miles received assurances that the Lakotas would stay north of the border and remain peaceable. The Lakota pledge fell short of Miles's intentions to force them across the border and also retrieve stolen stock and arrest Lakota men guilty of murder, but Walsh promised to investigate these matters. The colonel accepted the two men's word and considered their concessions a successful end to the campaign.[28]

In late July Clark rejoined his company. At about the same time Miles moved his men and the Red River mixed-blood captives south, making camp on the Milk River near the mouth of Frenchman's Creek. Major Baker's Second Cavalry detachment and a sizable number of captives joined the command at this camp. The column then marched out in the direction of the Missouri River and crossed the Milk River near Campbell's Houses. There the expedition's forces were disbanded and proceeded to their respective duty stations, with two exceptions. First, Miles retained a detachment from the Fifth Infantry and continued on to the Missouri River, arriving there on August 7. Second, Major Baker and most of the Second Cavalry contingent received orders to remain with the Red River mixed-bloods, guarding them until they received instructions from Washington detailing what was to be done with the captives.[29]

Clark remained with Baker's contingent of cavalrymen watching the captives, which numbered some one thousand people, along with eight hundred carts and a substantial horse herd.[30] The lieutenant and Company E left the camp on Milk River on August 2 with an unknown number of the Red River mixed-bloods and set out for Fort Peck, arriving there on August 15.[31]

Relocation of the mixed-bloods to various areas out of harm's way was determined to be the best solution for the vexing problem as to what to do with these people. As a result, Clark parted ways with his company at Fort Peck after being assigned the duty of leading a detachment to escort 340 mixed-bloods eastward to Turtle Mountain, located near the Canadian border in present north-central North Dakota. During the ensuing journey Clark's route would pass through Fort Buford, situated on the Missouri River near the confluence of the Yellowstone River. Clark and his detachment consisting of one Lakota scout, four Northern Cheyenne scouts, and sixteen soldiers from Company I, Second Cavalry, left with their wards on August 19, while Company E remained at Fort Peck until August 25 before leaving for Fort Keogh.[32]

After completing his task Clark returned to Fort Keogh on September 1. He remained there only a short time, however, before he was instructed to proceed to Lawrence, Kansas, in order to testify in a civil case as a witness in the defense of Wild Hog and other Northern Cheyenne prisoners being held there.[33] Leaving the Montana post on September 25, Clark made the trip to Lawrence for the trial, scheduled to begin on October 13.

The state of Kansas sought to prosecute the individuals responsible for the September 1878 killing of settlers there when the Northern Cheyennes were fleeing north from Indian Territory. In early February 1879 seven members of Dull Knife's band (Wild Hog, Old Crow, Tangle Hair, Noisy Walking, Strong Left Hand, Porcupine, and Blacksmith), and their families were escorted from Fort Robinson to Fort Leavenworth, Kansas, in order for the men to stand trial for murder. At Fort Leavenworth the prisoners were surrendered to Sheriff Bat Masterson and other civil authorities and transferred to Dodge City in Ford County to await trial.

The initial trial did not convene until June 24. Attorney J. G. Mohler, who was representing the Northern Cheyennes, immediately requested a change of venue away from western Kansas because he believed that his clients could not receive a fair trial there. Judge Samuel M. Peters granted the petition, thereby moving the trial to Lawrence in eastern Kansas.[34]

In July the Northern Cheyennes were moved to Lawrence, in Douglas County, to continue their wait for a trial. By the time the case reached the courtroom in October, however, the prosecution against the Indians was a total shambles. The prosecutor for the case, Ford County district attorney Mike Sutton, had married on October 1 and honeymooned until just four days before the trial was set to begin. He failed to appear in court on the opening day of the trial on October 13, and no witnesses for the prosecution were present. An official from the state attorney general's office, a Mr. Jetmore, took charge of the case and petitioned for a one-week continuance. Judge N. T. Stephens denied the motion, forcing Jetmore to file a *nolle prosequi* dismissing the charges against the Northern Cheyennes. Judge Stephens ruled in favor of the motion and dismissed all charges against the defendants. The Northern Cheyennes were then released to John D. Miles, the Cheyenne agent at the reservation in Indian Territory.[35]

In the end Clark's long journey from Montana to Kansas proved totally unnecessary. With the case being dismissed, the lieutenant made the return trip to Montana but took his time. By late October Clark had made his way as far as Saint Paul, where he spent a number of days.[36] It can be assumed that a portion of his time in the city was dedicated to wooing his fiancée, Hattie Sanborn.

✣ 12 ✣

FORT KEOGH AND THE BIG HORN MOUNTAINS

From Saint Paul Clark continued toward Fort Keogh. Traveling by way of Bismarck, he finally returned to the Montana post and rejoined his company on November 21, 1879.[1] After arriving at the garrison, Clark received a letter from Pine Ridge Reservation. The Lakotas there continued to reach out to the lieutenant for help. Young Man Afraid of His Horses, Little Big Man, and other leaders wrote to Clark expressing a variety of grievances. Not being in a position to assist them, the lieutenant forwarded the letter to Brigadier General George Crook. Unfortunately for the Lakotas, all Crook could do was suggest to the Lakotas that they take the matter up with the secretary of the interior.[2]

At this juncture of his career it appears that Clark seriously pursued the idea of writing a book on Indian sign language, having studied the subject for a considerable time. The lieutenant began to correspond with Garrick Mallery, a recently retired First Infantry captain who had become interested in Indian culture while serving in Dakota Territory in the 1870s and subsequently joined the Bureau of American Ethnology. Mallery, a Yale graduate, was currently working toward the publication of his own work on Indian sign language.[3]

The two men had their differences concerning certain aspects of the sign language, however, and Clark became openly critical of some of the signs described by Mallery.[4] The lieutenant then turned to Mallery's superior, John Wesley Powell, who was head of the bureau. Powell, who had lost his right arm during the Civil War, was a noted western explorer and earlier in 1879 had been selected to direct the Bureau of American Ethnology.[5]

In early December Clark wrote to Powell expressing the depth of his knowledge on the subject of sign language and the diversity of Indian peoples that he had communicated with. Clark boasted: "I believe I have a better practical knowledge of the language than any one white man and as good as any one Indian." He added: "I have made a study of Indian character and have at least learned enough to know how to get information from them, which I assure you is no small matter."[6]

Clark then pitched a proposal to the bureau's director. During the winter Clark could start writing his study of sign language. He would begin by working with the various tribes located at Fort Keogh and then in the spring could visit with other tribes in the region, noting any slight differences in the hand gestures. When finished, he would compare the various signs with those of other tribes in the United States. Clark pointed out that during his tour to the various tribes he could also gather information concerning their history and legends. The lieutenant emphasized that such a study must be done by personally visiting each group and noted: "I would need a 'short hand' clerk and would want actual expenses paid me." He continued: "I presume there would be no trouble in having an order issued for me to report to the Secretary of Interior or yourself for this purpose which I could probably do by letter for the present." After reading Clark's proposal, Powell replied by asking the lieutenant for a sample of his work.[7]

Determined and driven, Clark continued to pursue the project. In late January 1880 he contacted Powell and requested a map showing the Indian reservations in the states and territories and the populations of the various tribes. He also asked to be supplied with a copy of Prince Maximilian von Wied-Neuwied's work concerning sign language that he had gathered in the early 1830s when exploring the plains with artist Karl Bodmer. Clark briefly defended his criticism of the work of others, understanding that errors can take place in sign language among the best authorities. As to the request for a written sample, he replied: "I have made some notes on the customs and peculiarities of some of the northwestern tribes going as far back as possible and will send you a copy as soon as I get them in shape." With a note of sarcasm Clark added: "Facts give romance a hard rub on many of these things and it might be well to let the glamour of fiction remain." He explained a few instances where generally accepted information concerning Indians proved inaccurate.[8]

of Indians. On March 25 Company E left Fort Keogh, having been ordered to march to Rosebud Creek, where it planned to intercept a band of Lakotas that had stolen Crow ponies from Fort Custer. Captain Huggins led the command of thirty-four men, supplemented by about fifteen Northern Cheyenne scouts. Second Lieutenant Lloyd M. Brett of Company A, Second Cavalry, was also attached to Huggins's contingent.

After spending four unsuccessful days in the field, Huggins's command was joined on the Rosebud on March 29 by Company C, Second Cavalry, from Fort Custer. The force was also augmented by the addition of four Crow scouts. The soldiers then continued their search. They rode toward the Powder River, enduring snowstorms and rugged terrain during the pursuit. The horses of the combined command became exhausted, forcing Huggins to allow men mounted on weaker animals to trail behind the main column.

Huggins's depleted force, now consisting of some fifty soldiers, finally discovered the Lakota camp at the head of O'Fallon's Creek on the afternoon of April 1. After deploying Lieutenant Brett and a small detachment of soldiers and scouts to cut the warriors off from their pony herd, the two cavalry companies charged the camp, sending the Lakotas into a deep gulley for protection. During the early exchange of fire Sergeant Joseph Johnson was shot in the head and killed instantly. All attempts to drive out the Lakotas failed. The gulley offered excellent cover and allowed the warriors to defend the position against the exposed soldiers. After the initial rush the shooting became light and then halted altogether.

Huggins sent an interpreter to parley with the Lakotas to get them to surrender. Five Lakota men emerged from the gulley to confer with the captain as darkness descended on the assembled group. After issuing his terms, Huggins kept two of the men as hostages as the other three were escorted back to the gulley by an interpreter and some Northern Cheyenne scouts to discuss matters with their tribesmen. By this time it had become completely dark. When the men returned to the sanctuary, they discovered that the remaining sixteen warriors had escaped on foot into the night. Huggins deemed further pursuit to be futile and had to be content with the capture of five men from Sitting Bull's camp and the recovery of forty-five stolen ponies.[17] Years later both Huggins and Brett would receive the Medal of Honor for their actions during the April 1 encounter.

After having been informed the next day that Captain Huggins had a band of Lakotas surrounded in a gulley, Colonel John W. Davidson at Fort Custer telegraphed orders to Fort Keogh to dispatch a cavalry company and artillery piece to the scene.[18] Clark volunteered his services and was subsequently ordered to lead a detachment of fifteen soldiers, twelve Indian scouts, and a Hotchkiss gun "and proceed with all possible speed to the assistance of Captain Huggins." Leaving at 11:30 that night, the detachment marched through intense darkness and stormy weather, arriving at Powder River at 6 the following morning. At this point Clark's detachment met Company F, Fifth Infantry, commanded by First Lieutenant Edward L. Randall. He helped Clark and his men to get the Hotchkiss gun across the river and provided the detachment with extra rations and hot coffee for the men and additional forage for their horses.[19]

Captain Hamilton and Company I of the Second Cavalry, who had also been dispatched from Fort Keogh to join Huggins, arrived on the scene shortly before Clark left the Powder River. Hamilton had orders to assume command of Clark and his men. The detachment and the gun were already across the river, however, so he deemed it best that they move on immediately. Accordingly, Clark's men advanced at a rapid pace toward Huggins's supposed location. Shortly before noon Clark met Lieutenant Brett from Huggins's command, who informed him of the encounter with the Lakotas. Clark and his men therefore turned back toward the Powder River and camped that night with Huggins, Hamilton, and their commands. The various elements of the operation continued their journey back to Fort Keogh, arriving there on April 5.[20] Clark and his men had marched a total of one 130 miles, according to the lieutenant, "the first sixty-five being made in twelve hours and ten minutes after leaving Tongue River (this of course including the two hours delay at Powder River)."[21]

After returning to the post, Clark resumed the routine of garrison life at Fort Keogh for several weeks. The lieutenant was not called upon to serve in the field again until late May. On May 27 a group of five Lakotas stole four mules at Beaver Station on the Bismarck and Fort Keogh mail route, south of present-day Belfield, North Dakota, killing the station owner and another man. Reports of the attack were greatly exaggerated: rumors spread that three stations had fallen prey to the Indians. Panic soon followed as emigrants, drivers, and station managers along the route fled to safety.

Troops from Fort Keogh were called upon to investigate the matter and pursue the offenders. Major Guido Ilges, a native of Prussia and recent transfer to the Fifth Infantry, led the ensuing command, which consisted of Company G, Fifth Infantry, and Companies B, E, and I of the Second Cavalry. The force numbered 6 officers, an acting surgeon, and 115 enlisted men.

Prior to departing Fort Keogh on May 31, Major Ilges detached Clark and six men from Company E as well as six Indian scouts to proceed rapidly in advance of the main command. Four days later Clark's detachment met Ilges near Lake Station on the mail route, just west of the Montana and Dakota border. The lieutenant reported that he had been to the scene of the depredations and concluded that the situation had been blown out of proportion. Clark also informed the major that he had sent scouts out to look for signs of the fleeing Lakotas but that heavy rains had washed away all trace of the attackers. This information, coupled with the number of days that had passed since the incident, prompted Ilges to terminate the pursuit.

The major did take precautions to prevent additional attacks in the immediate future. According to Ilges, "upon the advice of Lieut. Clark in whose judgment I place great reliance, I have ordered a detachment of two noncommissioned officers and 9 privates to Little Missouri Station, to guard the mails beyond, so far as Beaver Station." Ilges also placed two soldiers at Lake Station and two more at O'Fallon's Station. In concluding his report on the affair, Ilges praised his command and added: "1st Lieut. Wm. P. Clark, 2nd Cavalry, and party of scouts and soldiers deserve special mention for rapidity of march and perseverance of scout, they having travelled over one hundred miles during [the] first 24 hours after leaving this post."[22]

General Orders No. 49, issued by adjutant general E. D. Townsend later in June, were circulated among the various posts of the army. They stipulated that on July 1 of each year commanders were to make a report of any officers under their command who exhibited a special aptitude that made them particularly well suited "for any branch of service, science, or art, either civil or military."[23] This information was considered useful to the general of the army in making selections for future duty.

In response to the orders, Captain Huggins wrote to the adjutant general and recommended Clark for active field service on the "Indian frontiers" and any duty involving Indians. Huggins wrote of Clark: "His temperament and physique are admirably adapted to these duties, and he has had long experience therein, often in an important and responsible capacity. He is personally known to leading members of most of the tribes in Montana, Wyoming and Nebraska, has a thorough knowledge of the sign language, which is the principal medium of intercommunication between different tribes."[24] Just how much influence the recommendation had on Clark's future assignment to conduct field research on Indian sign language is unknown, but it certainly may have helped.

Not long after his return to Fort Keogh from the long ride to Beaver Station Clark was ordered to lead a scouting and exploring party to the Big Horn Mountains of Wyoming Territory. Clark's detachment included Second Lieutenant Hunter Liggett, Company G, Fifth Infantry, who would serve as acting engineer officer and quartermaster for the expedition. Liggett, who had just graduated from West point the previous summer, would go on to enjoy a long military career and rise to the rank of lieutenant general before retiring in 1921.[25]

Also joining the expedition was Colonel Henry W. Farrar, an officer during the Civil War and former business manager of the *Chicago Evening Journal*. The command also included twenty enlisted men, Little Wolf and four other enlisted Northern Cheyenne scouts, and six additional Northern Cheyenne volunteers. The equipage needed for the expedition would be transported by pack mules.[26]

Liggett, as acting engineer officer, generated a map based on information gathered on the journey. He also maintained an itinerary of the route taken by the group throughout the duration of the trip through the Big Horn Mountains, using a prismatic compass and the assistance of the Indian scouts to complete the tasks. Clark was also equipped with two aneroid barometers, one furnished by the chief engineer officer of the Department of Dakota and the other by officers of the Union Pacific Railroad. The lieutenant hoped to use them to measure the altitude of various peaks and passes but later discovered that both instruments failed to work. Two of the men being utilized as packers had formerly worked as miners, so mining implements were brought on the journey as well in order to determine if the mountains might yield gold and silver.

Recent conflicts with the Ute tribe in Colorado had created a general paranoia that they might flee their homeland in an attempt to join the Lakotas in the north and possibly come into contact with Clark's group along the way. As a result, Clark was ordered to maintain communication with the Northern Arapahos on the reservation that they shared with the Shoshones to the south. If the Utes were encountered, Clark was to alarm troops and settlers in the area and engage and capture the Utes if possible.

The expedition left Fort Keogh on the afternoon of June 21 on a blistering hot day and after a ten-day march arrived at Fort McKinney in northern Wyoming Territory on the afternoon of July 1.[27] On the journey from Fort Keogh to McKinney the detachment observed some buffalo, but the immense herds formerly encountered on the plains were a thing of the past. Referring to the decimation of the herds, Clark would later write: "Though I call the wanton

The party continued to the north fork of Tongue River near the site of Second Lieutenant Frederick W. Sibley's fight with the Lakotas and Northern Cheyennes in the summer of 1876. Sibley and thirty scouts had been sent by General Crook from their camp on Goose Creek to the Crow Agency in order to acquire more Crow auxiliaries. When the small group encountered the enemy en route, a running fight ensued, forcing Sibley and his men high into the Big Horn Mountains. The men escaped calamity by abandoning their horses and evading their foe on foot. The small party managed to return to Crook, having failed to reach their destination.[33] One of the men of Clark's detachment had been with Sibley during the ordeal and went to the grove of pines where the horses had been left. There he discovered the bones of his dead horse, which he had tied to a tree. The horse had evidently been killed when the enemy fired into Sibley's former position.[34]

From this location Clark and his men followed the trail utilized by Crook and Lieutenant General Philip H. Sheridan during their reconnaissance of the area in the summer of 1877. On August 11 Clark and the others crossed the divide between the south fork of the Tongue River and Shell Creek, passing a small number of vacant mines. According to Clark, the area held some promise: the group discovered some good silver ore. In his report on the expedition Clark wrote that he still believed that the mountains held possible mineral wealth, despite their unsuccessful efforts at locating mineral resources, and recommended future investigation into the matter. After completing the search for valuable minerals, the party continued its advance in a southeasterly direction and camped on the lakes near Cloud Peak, the tallest mountain in the range.

On the morning of August 15 the detachment turned north as it followed its back trail. Upon reaching one of the forks of the Little Big Horn River the men ventured west and descended from the mountains through Pass Creek Canyon, passing small camps of the Crows along the way. Moving still further west the detachment ascended once again to the range of hills and made camp on a ridge between the Big Horn River and the headwaters of the Little Big Horn. To Clark, this spot offered the grandest views of the country to the north and west.

Having completed their examination of the high country, the men set out on August 25 to start their journey out of the mountains to Fort Custer by way of abandoned Fort C. F. Smith, located on the Big Horn River in southern Montana Territory along the Bozeman Trail. Clark had thoroughly enjoyed his time in the Big Horns and upon leaving lamented: "The invigorating atmosphere, the resinous odor of the pines, the pure cold crystal water—such as a man dying of thirst would think of—fine hunting and excellent fishing, all had taken a strong hold on us."

As the men descended from the elevated terrain the weather matched the mood of the moment: rain drizzled on the detachment. By the end of the day's march the party camped near old Fort C. F. Smith, which at this time consisted of nothing more than some adobe wall ruins and a small cemetery. The following day the detachment rode to Black Canyon and Big Horn Canyon, gazing with wonder at the grandeur of the rugged gorges. Clark noted that the party killed four bears during the examination of Big Horn Canyon. Armed with new model 1879 Springfield rifles and carbines, Clark and the members of his detachment were successful in hunting throughout the journey. Clark expressed deep criticism for the weapon's wind-gauge attachment, however, which he described as "worse than worthless" and "a simple nuisance."

On August 28 the men advanced to a tributary of Soap Creek, camping there before proceeding to the scene of Custer's 1876 fight, where Clark would have the opportunity to continue his inquiries into the battle. According to the lieutenant's report, the men moved down "Grass Lodge and Custer River for some distance" on their route to the battlefield, where they remained for a couple of days. During their stay at the battlefield the men made measurements "of some of the most disputed points." Clark noted that the bottomland that had been the site of the Indian village at the time of the battle was now utilized as a hay field to meet the needs of Fort Custer. After completing their tasks at the battlefield the men rode to Fort Custer, arriving there on September 3.

Orders awaited Clark upon his arrival. Colonel Miles instructed the lieutenant "to perform certain duties connected with the Indians in this district." This new assignment, probably associated with the Crows, kept Clark occupied for a number of days. He and the others did not arrive back at Fort Keogh until September 16. The detachment had covered approximately 780 miles during its expedition since its departure in June.[35]

✣ 13 ✣

FIELDWORK FOR
THE INDIAN SIGN LANGUAGE

Upon his return to Fort Keogh Clark rejoined his company and remained at the post. Late in September 1880 he received orders appointing him as a member of a general court-martial set to convene at the garrison in early October. After fulfilling this duty, the lieutenant was assigned once again to command Company B in place of the unfortunate Captain James T. Peale. Clark took charge of the company on October 10, shortly after it returned to Fort Keogh from detached service at Fort Buford.[1]

Clark did not remain with the company for long. He was ordered to proceed to Poplar Creek in the northern portion of the territory to assist with the management of surrendering Lakotas in the area. On October 24 Company E left Fort Keogh for the headwaters of Cherry Creek to escort Spotted Eagle's band of surrendered Sans Arc Lakotas to Fort Keogh. Among the more than five hundred individuals in the Lakota band were the noted Hunkpapa warrior Rain-in-the-Face and a small number of Hunkpapa Lakota followers. Both Spotted Eagle and Rain-in-the-Face had been allied with Sitting Bull before and during their exile in Canada. Apparently Clark accompanied his men on the trek north but continued further north in search of other surrendering Lakotas instead of returning to Keogh with the members of the escort. Clark remained in the field for several days, including a journey to Wolf Point on the Missouri River. The lieutenant, evidently empty-handed, returned to Fort Keogh on the night of November 8.[2] A major concentration of Lakotas and

Northern Cheyennes had now been assembled at the post. By the middle of November approximately two thousand surrendered Indians had been brought together at Fort Keogh, some having been there since 1877.[3]

While Clark was searching for surrendering Lakotas in northern Montana, on November 5 Lieutenant General Philip H. Sheridan issued instructions for Clark to report to him personally at division headquarters in Chicago.[4] Sheridan, a confident and unyielding man, rose to national prominence during the Civil War and afterward directed America's military activities in the West during the country's continued expansion in the region. The general would continue to play an influential role in Clark's military career.

After returning to Fort Keogh on the night of November 8, however, Clark received the distressing news that his fiancée, Hattie Sanborn, was gravely ill in Saint Paul. Wasting little time, Clark hurriedly rode out from the fort at 1 in the morning. Thirty-six hours later, at 1 in the afternoon of November 10, he reached the end of the track for the Northern Pacific Railroad at the border of Montana and Dakota Territories.[5] The westward advance of the railroad line had brought its rails to the boundary, an occasion marked on November 10 by a celebration and the driving of two silver spikes. Railroad dignitaries, military officials, newspaper correspondents, and civilians attended the event, and Clark arrived just in time to participate. A lunch featuring oysters followed the formalities of the ceremony. After the festivities Clark boarded the eastbound train and continued his journey to Saint Paul. He arrived there on the morning of November 12, a trip said to have been the fastest ever from Fort Keogh to Saint Paul.[6]

It is uncertain how long Clark remained in the city. On the afternoon of his arrival he registered his presence in the city with department headquarters. Hattie clung to life for nearly three weeks before passing away on December 5 at the age of twenty-two. Clark registered at the Metropolitan Hotel in Saint Paul that day, so he was in the city on the day of her passing. Two days later funeral services were held for her at the Sanborn residence. By December 8 Clark, certainly heartbroken, was in Chicago and residing at the Palmer House Hotel.[7]

On the following day Clark was assigned temporary duty in the Office of the Chief Engineer, Division of the Missouri, in Chicago. He reported directly to the chief engineer, Captain James F. Gregory. Clark's assignment was to assist Gregory in completing a map of Yellowstone National Park and the Big Horn Mountains, including the surrounding territory.[8] Lieutenant Liggett's map of Clark's exploration of the Big Horn Mountains the previous summer would be one of many such sources that the officers used to develop their map.[9]

Gregory, like Clark, was a New Yorker and attended West Point. The chief engineer graduated in 1865, three years before Clark. Because Gregory was in his final year at the academy when Clark was a plebe, he may have been one of the lieutenant's tormentors when he endured hazing there. After graduation Gregory served in the artillery for a little less than a year before transferring to the engineers.[10] Clark would spend much of the rest of his life in Gregory's company. If the two men had not been friends before, they became so now. Gregory's ties to the lieutenant would extend beyond Clark's death.

Just a few short days after starting his work with Gregory, Clark's friend Little Wolf, while intoxicated by whiskey, shot and killed a fellow Northern Cheyenne named Starving Elk. The incident took place at Lamphere's trading post on Two Moon Creek, not far from Fort Keogh. Little Wolf immediately went into a self-imposed exile, already aware that his people would banish him for his crime.[11] Clark detested the effects of alcohol upon Indians in general, prompting him to observe "much unnecessary bloodshed, and a great wretchedness to them have grown out of their fondness for liquor." He laid much of the blame for the problem on traders selling liquor to the Indians: "We have certainly in some cases made them savages, and then cursed and killed them for being such."[12] Knowing the customs of the Northern Cheyennes, Clark would have understood the severity of the crime for murdering a fellow tribesman and the implications of his friend's actions. He was already burdened with the loss of Hattie, and the news of Little Wolf's trouble would only have added to his misery.

After assisting Gregory with the mapping project for less than two weeks, Clark was granted a much needed two-month leave of absence.[13] Given the amount of extended duty in the field in previous months, coupled with recent events surrounding his personal life, the break would do him good. The personal time afforded would also allow him to fill his hours by continuing his work concerning the Indian sign language.

Clark apparently ventured from Chicago to his hometown of Deer River, New York, where he could spend not only Christmas but an extended visit with his family. At some point in recent weeks Clark had arranged for his prized white buffalo robe, acquired in 1879 near Fort Keogh, to be transported from that post to the Museum of the Military Service Institution of the United States in New York City as a loan to the museum.[14] Despite the relaxing surroundings of his old home, this was a hectic time for Clark. During January 1881 he focused his attention on his writing and research. Clark would present a paper on the Indian sign language in New York City for the Military Service Institution of the United States in February. As he continued the research for his book Clark wrote to John Wesley Powell at the Bureau of American Ethnology late in January, requesting a copy of Powell's book titled *Introduction to the Study of Indian Languages*.[15]

In addition to Clark's growing presence as an authority on Indian sign language, his military career was also advancing as well. On January 25 Clark received his promotion to captain, although he did not take his oath of office in Chicago until the middle of March. John Mix, captain of Company M, Second Cavalry, was promoted to major and transferred to the Ninth Cavalry, thereby creating the vacancy that Clark filled.[16] It took three years from the time Clark first sought a captaincy before he finally rose to the rank.

In February Clark journeyed to New York City in order to present his paper titled "Sign Language of the North American Indians and Some of Their Peculiar Customs" at the Military Service Institution's headquarters on Governors Island.[17] His address later appeared in the organization's quarterly publication, *Journal of the Military Service Institution of the United States*. Clark abandoned his criticism of Mallery but used the lecture in part to reinforce his basic conclusions concerning the uniformity of signs made by Indians. Clark stressed to his audience that a thorough knowledge of sign language could be a valuable asset for officers serving on the frontier.[18] When his book was later published it was intended to be utilized by army officers to learn the Indian sign language. This marvelous idea could have been more beneficial had it been realized much sooner. One of Clark's contemporaries, Hugh Lenox Scott, an officer with the Seventh Cavalry who would also become an authority on Indian sign language, noted: "The officers of our army lived with it [sign language] all about them while serving on the Plains for a hundred years, but Captain Philo Clark, Second Cavalry, was the only one I ever saw who acquired a reasonable degree of proficiency."[19] Scott also observed that "it is not until after 1880, when the works of the late Captain Philo Clark, 2nd Cavalry, U.S.A., Colonel R. I. Dodge, 11th Infantry, U.S.A., and the comparison of the sign language of foreigners, deaf mutes, and American Indians, by Colonel Garrick Mallery, of the Smithsonian Institution made their appearance that the subject can be said to have been seriously treated and discussed."[20]

While incorporating some of the material from his earlier article in the *United Service,* Clark's lecture also presented new information. The material presented in his talk once again surfaced in *The Indian Sign Language.* A good portion of his lecture centered on the notion that one must think like an Indian and know their customs to be proficient in the sign language. Therefore he provided a lengthy list of words and the concepts involved with the signs for each word. In addition Clark shared his knowledge of "peculiar manners and habits of Indians" concerning dancing, scalping, marrying, generosity, and the use of the word "medicine."[21] Due to his conviction concerning the importance of knowing something about Indian culture in order to master the sign language Clark included a large amount of ethnographic information into his later book.

Clark admitted to his audience that his opinion of the Indians differed from the negative impression held by so many. "These people are certainly savage," said Clark, "but they are just as certainly also human beings." He also discussed the Indians' plight with his audience. His description of their current condition was grim to say the least. He sadly declared that "the exterminating policy of our civilization has swept away nearly every vestige of these people who have folded and are folding their tents, and passing into total obscurity." Stressing the importance of projects such as the one he had embarked upon, he asserted that "perhaps we of the army may through this Institution save something by which future generations may learn a little of the characteristics of an extinct race."[22]

For years Clark and numerous humanitarians had championed the idea that the Indians must abandon their customs and way of life and assimilate in order to survive as a people. His dedication to this conviction guided his interaction with Indians throughout his tenure in the West. Now he sounded the death knell of an entire people. His motives for doing so remain unclear. On one hand, at the time when he composed the speech he may have given up all hope for his cause and the future of the Indian. On the other hand, perhaps he sounded the alarm in order to underscore the importance of his own work. Regardless of his motivation, it was clear that he had long been convinced of the need to destroy the traditional practices of tribal cultures that he now fought to record and preserve on paper.

After leaving New York, Clark traveled to Washington, D.C. He wrote to Sheridan on February 19 requesting an extension of his leave so that he could attend the presidential inauguration of James A. Garfield to be held on March 4.

Having no objections, Sheridan allowed Clark to remain in Washington to attend the event and extended his leave until March 10.[23] During his stay at the nation's capital city Clark boarded at the Ebbitt House, a stylish hotel used extensively by the military.

Upon his return to Chicago Clark continued to work on his sign language project. Clark's old friend First Lieutenant John G. Bourke, in Omaha, wrote to Sheridan in early March requesting to be detailed to an assignment gathering ethnological information on the North American Indians, especially the Pueblos of the Southwest. Sheridan granted initial approval and asked Bourke to come to Chicago to see him before starting on the project.[24] Bourke's request may have served as the impetus when Sheridan later assigned Clark to a similar duty.

On March 11, 1881, writing to John Wesley Powell from the Palmer House Hotel in Chicago, Clark asked him to request that the secretary of the interior arrange for a delegation of Ute Indians returning from Washington to be allowed to remain in Chicago for a day so that Clark could interview them about sign language.[25] After having been informed that he personally would have to bear the expense of the delegation's stay in Chicago, Clark once again wrote Powell. The newly appointed captain protested the decision on the grounds that "the information I desire to secure is in the interest of science and tends to promote the welfare of all Indians by a more thorough knowledge of all their customs." He pointed out that he did not expect to gain monetarily from his efforts and that "nearly all delegations remain for one day to rest at this place [Chicago]," so he considered it "strange at least" that he should be expected to pay the expense. Clark ended by simply requesting that Powell inform him of the Ute delegation's arrival time in Chicago. He would do what he could to obtain the information desired. Clark was later informed that Powell declined to assist or fund the Utes' stay in Chicago due to a misunderstanding of the request by the bureau's chief clerk, but he approved funding when the matter was clarified.[26]

When Bourke arrived at Division of the Missouri Headquarters in late March, he was greeted by Clark and several members of Sheridan's staff. After conversing with the officers briefly Bourke met with Sheridan. The general informed Bourke that he wanted him to embark upon an ethnological study of the Indians located south of the Union Pacific Railroad and that Clark would be detailed to study those tribes situated north of the rail line.[27] There would be some deviation from this general framework, as Bourke would travel to Fort Hall, Idaho Territory, and Clark would venture into Indian Territory and Utah Territory. The two soldier-scientists now had the official sanctioning of the army and the freedom to pursue their research wholeheartedly. Both men would benefit from the assignment. Clark would generate *The Indian Sign Language*, and Bourke would become a noted American ethnologist.

After the meeting Clark invited Bourke to go with him to his apartment at the Palmer House to examine his manuscript on sign language. As he admitted, Bourke probably gave the manuscript only cursory attention, "not deeming myself fit to criticize the labors of Clark, who has made this subject a profound study for years." Bourke certainly believed that Clark was a worthy colleague: "He is eminently fitted for the field now opening before him; of strong mental powers, powerful physique, indefatigable, persistent, ambitious and *magnetic*, he gets into the confidence of the Indians more quickly than any man I know excepting Genl. Crook." Clark was one of the few officers selected by Bourke to review his ethnological memoranda for "correction, sympathy, and encouragement." Later that night the two officers went to the Chicago Club, a rather exclusive social club then located across the street from the Palmer House, where they enjoyed a pleasant evening in the company of Sheridan and other army officers, along with some prominent Chicago businessmen.

On the following day Clark notified John Wesley Powell to inform him that he had been able to spend sufficient time with the Ute delegation while it was in Chicago. Rather conveniently, and hinting at possible collusion, Clark explained to Powell that Sheridan had ordered the Ute agent to consult with him about his escort and other matters that caused the group to be delayed in Chicago for a day, thereby negating the need for the bureau's reimbursement of expenses. After meeting with the Utes, Clark found them to have a "poverty of signs." This was not surprising, he concluded, because they were young men who had little interaction with other tribes and were conversant in Spanish. Clark informed Powell that he would be going to Indian Territory soon to "visit all the agencies" and "meet all the tribes." The captain then requested Powell's assistance in having the secretary of the interior provide him with a letter of introduction to present to the various Indian agents that he might encounter in order to secure their cooperation.[28]

Sheridan informed his superior, General of the Army William T. Sherman, of his plans for Clark and Bourke. Sheridan wrote that for some time he had been interested in the collection of ethnographic information concerning the Indian tribes west of the Mississippi River and endorsed Bourke and Clark as being the right men for the job. Bourke had already gathered a wealth of material, and Clark had collected an impressive amount of data on sign language. But Sheridan added that "this is only a slight item of the work contemplated in getting a thorough history of the different tribes." After outlining the scope of the project and the area of responsibility for each man, Sheridan stressed the economy of the venture, noting that it would entail "scarcely any expense to the government." Sheridan added that what little the two men required to do their work "they can get at the military posts, which will be nothing more than a horse and a man or two occasionally for escort when needed." He concluded: "They are both deeply interested in the work and I think it is due the Army that some reliable contribution on the character, habits, and history of these Indians be placed on file in the War Department especially when it can be done by such competent officers and at such slight cost to the government."[29] It is both interesting and ironic that Sheridan, who had done so much to eradicate the various traditional Indian cultures of the West, now sought to save something of them.

Clark would now realize his ambition of dedicating his time to the field of ethnology. He subscribed to the Autochthonic Theory on the origin of the Indians: they originated in North America and did not migrate to the continent from elsewhere. As to the origin of Indian sign language, the captain viewed the hand gestures as emanating from the basic need for "primitive" people to be able to communicate. Sign language, according to Clark, was then further developed and refined as tribal groups with differing vocal languages sought to communicate with one another, especially on the plains.[30]

As his book would clearly illustrate, the captain was certainly a product of his time. The Scotch Enlightenment Theory was popular among the ethnologic community during this period. This proposition held that humans are all the same but are just in different stages of progress as they evolve from savagery to civilization.[31] As Clark explained it: "The mere fact that they [Indians] had certain customs, habits, manners, and religious rites common to humanity in some other parts of the world, only shows that man in the same plane, stage, or period of savagery, barbarism, or civilization, possesses many similar traits, mentally, morally, and physically." He was greatly influenced by this theory, which led him to make statements such as this concerning the Indians: "Sickly philanthropy is too weak-eyed to see the vices which inherently belong to their stage of the development of man, and the bitter sentiments entertained by those for the position, with Clark being seen as the favorite. Unfortunately for him, Gregory received the appointment.[37]

Remaining in northern Montana, Clark continued westward and by early July was conducting his research at the Blackfeet Agency, home of the Blackfeet, Blood, and Piegan Indians. The agency was situated on Badger Creek, a tributary of Medicine Lodge River, about eighty miles north of Fort Shaw, Montana. The captain happened to be at the agency on July 4 and noted: "The Indians had been informed by the agent that it was a great 'Medicine'-day for the whites, and they commenced to gather for what they called a 'horse-and-foot' dance."[38]

From the Blackfeet Agency Clark presumably traveled south to Fort Missoula. From that post the captain continued east, visiting the capital city of Helena in the second week of July.[39] Continuing east across Montana, Clark found himself in the familiar surroundings of Fort Keogh by August. Early that same month tragedy struck the Lakotas at Rosebud Reservation. A long-standing feud between Spotted Tail and fellow tribesman Crow Dog reached a violent conclusion. Crow Dog shot and killed the Brule leader. The news of his death must have been something of a blow to Clark, who had come to know and respect Spotted Tail, stating that he was "by far the ablest Indian I have ever known."[40]

During his stay at Fort Keogh Clark decided to experience an Indian sweat bath for himself. Over the course of his career on the plains he had observed the remnants of abandoned sweat lodges and desired to learn more about them. After making the necessary arrangements with the headman of a Northern Cheyenne village located near the post, he rode out to the camp in order to join a small group of men from the camp for a sweat bath.[41]

While satisfying his own intellectual curiosity, Clark came to understand the spiritual significance of the sweat bath for the Indian participants, "as a form of worship and supplication." Without mentioning the spiritually purifying qualities associated with the sweat bath, Clark's informants appear to have stressed other aspects of the practice. Sitting Bull once used a variety of signs to describe the sweat lodge to Clark that included "making requests, hoping the Great Spirit would listen and make them live long on the earth, give them plenty to eat, furnish them all they wanted, give them success in war, and protect them in peace." Another Indian informed Clark that "the sweat-lodge is made as a 'medicine,' to ask of the Great Spirit anything we want."

Clark described the sweat lodge as being constructed of small willows set into the ground and then bent over and bound at the top forming something of an oval-shaped dome some four feet in height. This frame was covered first with buffalo hides and then with canvas and blankets. A small opening served as the entrance, with a buffalo skull positioned in front of the opening. A hole had been dug inside, about eighteen inches in diameter and twelve inches deep. This pit held the red hot stones that provided the heat source for the steam necessary for the sweat bath.

While preparations were under way for the sweat lodge, Clark went into some tall weeds and bushes and dressed for the event by stripping down and putting on a breechcloth made of a strap and towel. Emerging from concealment and approaching the sweat lodge, Clark noticed: "My appearance created some merriment on the part of the squaws." Before commencing the bath, the headman lit his pipe and offered prayers. After the headman smoked the pipe, he had Clark do the same. The two men were then joined by five other Northern Cheyenne men inside the sweat lodge. The hot stones were placed in the central pit and the entrance was closed, making the interior completely dark. The heat inside soon became overwhelming. The headman took some water in his mouth and spit it on the rocks, creating a plume of steam. "Waves of hot air and steam passed over me," Clark explained, "which seemed more like liquid fire than steam and air." When a bowl of water was passed to him, he took a drink before passing the bowl forward.

Sitting in an upright position, Clark's head touched the ceiling of the structure, giving him the full power of the heat. "My hair was so hot that I could hardly touch my hand to it. I was becoming dazed and dizzy with the heat." He continued: "I felt that I was being physically and mentally cooked." Suddenly the bottom of the sweat lodge cover was raised, allowing cool air to enter. In the light Clark noticed that his Indian counterparts were all in a bent-knee position with their heads to the ground, a configuration that prevented them from experiencing the intense heat that he had endured. Clark also discovered that the water offered him was not to be swallowed but was used by the other men to wet the hair on their heads. The captain promptly took some water and doused his scalp, providing a measure of relief.

Once again the cover of the sweat lodge was lowered. The headman spat water upon the stones. Clark assumed the position of his fellow bathers, this time experiencing much less discomfort. The raising and lowering of the cover was repeated a total of four times, then a large amount of water was poured onto the hot rocks, creating a dense steam in the sweat lodge. When finished with the sweat bath, the men plunged into the Yellowstone River, giving Clark a sense of relief and rejuvenation. The benefits were temporary, as Clark confided: "I was half ill for three or four days, and I attributed it to overheating." The experience prompted him to conclude: "I have never experienced anything like the cooking I got in that Cheyenne sweat-lodge."

Having survived his sweat bath, Clark eventually made his return to division headquarters in Chicago. On September 7 he served as a groomsman in the wedding of First Lieutenant Hayden De Lany and Georgiana Field in Chicago.[42] De Lany had attended West Point during a portion of Clark's time there and later assisted with his contingent of Indian scouts during the Powder River Expedition in 1876. The two men had clearly maintained a friendship over the intervening years. Two weeks after the wedding Clark received orders to proceed to Fort Washakie, Wyoming Territory, Fort Hall, Idaho Territory, and Fort Thornburgh, Utah Territory.[43]

After setting out on yet another research excursion, Clark arrived at Fort Washakie in late September.[44] Located on the southern edge of the Big Horn Basin, the post was originally known as Camp Brown but was subsequently renamed in honor of Washakie, the Shoshone leader and longtime army ally. On October 1 Clark was present at the Shoshone agency for the weekly issue of rations to the Indians. "Issue days are about alike at all agencies," Clark declared. He captured the scene that day in his notes so that his description of the event could be used later in his book. One aspect of issue day that did not sit well with him pertained to the butchering of the beef and the Indians' handling of the offal. "After witnessing one issue of beef," recalled the captain, "I have never wondered at the disillusioning of the young officer who had become somewhat infatuated with an Indian girl. One look at their business-like manner of handling the intestines of a freshly-killed beef would have a tendency to disenchant any one not an Indian."[45]

It was probably during this visit at Fort Washakie that Clark met with a group of Northern Arapahos, whose people shared the Wyoming reservation with the Shoshones. The captain journeyed out to a Northern Arapaho camp armed with a variety of goods, including flour, sugar, coffee, and tobacco. After his arrival a feast was prepared in a headman's lodge. During the course of his visit Sharp Nose and Wolf Moccasin provided Clark with the information he needed concerning their tribe through the use of signs.

From Fort Washakie Clark most likely ventured to Fort Hall before going south to Fort Thornburgh. At the fort located near the Snake River in southeastern Idaho the captain sought to learn more about the Bannocks, his adversary in the fight near Index Peak in the fall of 1878. One of the leading headmen of that tribe at Fort Hall, Tyhee, met with Clark and supplied him with material about his people.

At the newly established Fort Thornburgh, named after Major Thomas T. Thornburgh, who lost his life in a fight with the Utes in 1879, Clark endeavored to record information concerning that tribe. The garrison and nearby agency for the Ouray Reservation were situated at the confluence of the Green River and White River in northeastern Utah. The Ute headman named Tabby apparently served as the captain's primary source. At some point during this segment of his fieldwork Clark traversed the Uinta Mountains near the border between southwestern Wyoming and northeastern Utah. While traveling over the mountains at night during a snowstorm, Clark happened upon a Ute camp. "After some little persuasion they took me into one of the tepees, and, by the flickering light of the lodge fire, while the squaw was preparing my supper, I obtained from the chief and headmen, by means of gestures and their poorly-spoken English, a brief history of their tribe as they understood it," recalled Clark.

After completing his work in the intermountain West Clark returned to Chicago, reporting to division headquarters in early November.[46] His stay in that city was brief. Later that month he was off to complete what would be the last of his research trips. After traveling from Chicago to Saint Paul, where he remained for a couple of days, Clark's itinerary in the weeks ahead took him to various agencies in Dakota Territory. His journey, however, extended as far north as Winnipeg, Canada, where he compiled information concerning the mixed-bloods of that region.[47]

From Canada Clark traveled south to Devils Lake Reservation, now known as Spirit Lake Reservation, where he conversed with members from bands of the Eastern Dakota people. He then ventured down the Missouri River south of Bismarck to Standing Rock Agency, home of the Hunkpapas and other bands. Clark more than likely spoke with Sitting Bull during his stay at Standing Rock and obtained the information from him that he later referenced in his sign language book.[48] The Hunkpapa leader and his followers were relocated to the agency after they had given up their Canadian exile and surrendered the previous summer. Clark approached Sitting Bull's nephew, One Bull, and another Hunkpapa to draw a map for him encompassing "Indian country." The resulting map, drawn on yellow paper with lead pencil, measured five feet in length and three and a half feet wide. The map contained symbols for rivers, mountains, agencies, and other landmarks; but, perhaps most important, it identified the trail used by the Indians after their fight with Custer on the Little Big Horn.[49]

Following his visit with the Hunkpapas Clark proceeded to the agency at Cheyenne River to interview the Miniconjous and other bands located there.[50] Prior to Clark's visit a Miniconjou headman named Red Horse had given army surgeon Charles E. McChesney a series of forty-one drawings detailing the events at the Battle of the Little Big Horn. To supplement the drawings, the surgeon wished to record Red Horse's description of the battle. During his stay at the agency Clark assisted McChesney, through the use of sign language, in successfully recording the Miniconjou leader's account of the fight.[51]

Continuing down the Missouri River, the captain visited the Lakota and Dakota bands residing at Lower Brule and Crow Creek Agencies.[52] After having completed his tour of the Dakota Territory agencies, Clark returned to Chicago in late December or early January. With his fieldwork concluded, it was now time for him to incorporate his notes into the manuscript for *The Indian Sign Language*.

14

YELLOWSTONE NATIONAL PARK EXPLORATIONS

Upon returning to his office at division headquarters, Clark focused his attention on the manuscript for his upcoming book. In the middle of January 1882 he approached Dr. Philip Gillette, superintendent of what was then known as the Deaf and Dumb Institution in Jacksonville, Illinois, for his assistance. In addition to all of the information presented in his book concerning Indian hand gestures, Clark also wished to include a comparison of Indian signs with the "French system" used by the deaf.[1] When his book was published, Clark's vision became reality, as each entry included a brief description of the sign employed by the deaf.

At about this same time another map of Indian movements following the Battle of the Little Big Horn was received in Chicago. Clark had requested the map in December during his visit to the Dakota Territory agencies. The map outlined Sitting Bull's movements after the fight and was executed by Reverend John P. Williamson, a longtime missionary among the Indians in the territory. Sitting Bull verified the accuracy of the map and included a narrative of his movements after the Custer fight as well.[2]

On the afternoon of February 1 Clark met a delegation of five Northern Arapaho headmen in Chicago who were on their way to Washington, D.C., to discuss conditions on their reservation with government officials. The trip also included a brief stay in Carlisle, Pennsylvania, for the headmen to visit their own children and others of the tribe attending the Carlisle Indian School. In the weeks prior to their arrival preparations had been underway for the delegation's journey. While a number of Northern Arapahos wished to make the trip to see their children, only five individuals were permitted to travel. Prominent Northern Arapaho leaders Black Coal and Sharp Nose were among those chosen for the journey.[3]

It was also determined that an interpreter should join the group. After some discussion as to who that interpreter should be, Sharp Nose suggested that Clark escort the delegation to serve in that role. According to the tribe's agent, Charles Hatton: "The captain who has had an extensive acquaintance with these people and is certainly the best sign talker I know of, has expressed his willingness to accompany the delegation to Washington, and act in that capacity for his old friends."[4] Clark joined the group, although before leaving the Wyoming reservation the Indian Office had decided that Clark would not be needed for interpretation purposes.[5]

After almost a week of escorting the Northern Arapaho delegation to Carlisle and then to the nation's capital, on February 7 Clark made an early return to Chicago while the delegation conducted its business in Washington.[6] During the delegation's visit at Carlisle the Northern Arapaho headman Little Wolf succeeded in having his ailing son, Lincoln Little Wolf, discharged and released to his care.[7] Clark may have assisted Little Wolf in securing his son's release. After his return from detached service in the East Clark remained in Chicago, boarding at the fashionable Leland Hotel. The captain now settled into a routine at division headquarters, incorporating his field notes into the manuscript for his upcoming book.

Not limiting himself solely to his professional duties, Clark also fulfilled social obligations. On February 15 he served as an usher at the wedding of Caroline Higgins and Henry McCree of the U.S. Navy at the Trinity Episcopal Church in Chicago.[8] The joy of that event was darkened by the sad news that Clark's sister Frances died that same day. Details surrounding her death are lacking. Even the information concerning the date of her demise is contradictory, but cemetery sexton records confirm the date of death as stated here.[9]

On the last day of February Clark was called upon once again to meet with an Indian delegation in Chicago. Anthropologist Frank H. Cushing was escorting a group of six Zuni headmen on their way from the Southwest to Washington, D.C. Cushing, who was living among the Zunis at the time, became famous for his study of their culture. Clark was asked to accompany the anthropologist and the headmen to points of interest in the city. The captain's tour of Chicago's attractions included the zoo at Lincoln Park and a pier on Lake Michigan.[10]

For the next several months Clark remained at division headquarters in Chicago, drafting his manuscript. In an administrative move in early April Captain Joshua Fowler and Clark switched troop affiliations at their mutual request. Companies were now designated as troops, and the move made Clark the captain of Troop A.[11]

At some point during his assignment in Chicago Clark met and courted his future fiancée, Cornelia McAvoy. Cornelia was twenty-two or twenty-three years old at the beginning of their courtship, about fifteen years younger than her beau. She was the daughter of Irish-born John H. McAvoy, head of the Bemis and McAvoy Brewing Company, one of the most lucrative breweries in the world. In addition to his business interests, McAvoy was also an influential politician.[12] Just when the relationship began remains unknown, but the couple announced their intended wedding in the summer of 1884, to take place early in the fall of that year.[13]

After spending months at division headquarters concentrating on his manuscript, Clark was presented with an opportunity to return to the West, if only for a short time. He would join Lieutenant General Sheridan and his party in the late summer of 1882 and embark upon the general's second exploration of Yellowstone National Park. The expedition had originally been intended to be led by secretary of war Robert Todd Lincoln, son of President Abraham Lincoln, but official duties prevented his participation.[14]

Sheridan had maintained an interest in the park for years, but it was not until the summer of 1881 that he made his first personal investigation of Yellowstone. Irony once again surrounded the general who had worked so hard to bring about the opening and settlement of the American West. Now he fought vigorously to preserve a small piece of the region in its pristine natural condition and to protect the wildlife that inhabited the nation's first national park. The general made three expeditions to the park in the summers of 1881, 1882, and 1883. His parties included men of power in the realms of government and business in order to promote his efforts at preserving the park.[15]

In addition to Sheridan and Clark, the military component of the 1882 expedition consisted of the army inspector general, Delos B. Sacket; Sheridan's brother, Lieutenant Colonel Michael V. Sheridan; and Lieutenant Colonel James F. Gregory. The civilian contingent included two former Civil War generals: Anson Stager, vice president and superintendent of the Western Union Telegraph Company; and Chicago businessman William E. Strong. Others making the journey were wealthy New York banker and merchant Heber R. Bishop, Charles D. Rhodes of Chicago, and John McCullough.[16]

Sheridan and the members of his party left Chicago on August 1 and traveled by train to Green River, Wyoming Territory. On the morning of August 4 the party boarded spring wagons in Green River and started overland toward the park, camping for the night at Atlantic City. On the following day the group passed through Lander and continued the journey as far as Fort Washakie, arriving there in the afternoon.

At the fort the Sheridan party was joined by the main body of the expedition's personnel. Lieutenant Colonel Gregory, who reached the post with the exploring party's camp equipage and supplies almost two weeks before Sheridan's arrival, was there to greet his commander. Troop G, Second Cavalry, commanded by Captain James N. Wheelan, served as the escort for the journey into the park. Thomas Moore, chief packer for the Department of the Platte and a favorite of Brigadier General George Crook, supervised the party's pack train. Surgeon W. H. Forwood, medical officer for the expedition, also recorded the expedition's scientific data, including information on geology, plant species, and geyser eruptions. Shoshone Dick, a white man who had lived among the Shoshones most of his life, served as the official hunter for the expedition. Five Shoshone scouts from the Sheep Eater band and a Shoshone woman accompanied the party as well. With all of the various support personnel associated with the expedition, 129 individuals set out from Fort Washakie.

The next day, August 6, the party remained at its camp near the post and made final preparations for the journey. In the morning Sheridan went to the trader's store at the post and met with the Shoshone leader Washakie. During the day some members of the expedition visited the fort and a nearby petroleum spring, while others enjoyed soaking in the hot spring located near their camp. In the evening the party hosted some officers from the fort and also a number of Northern Arapaho headmen, including Black Coal and Sharp Nose.

At 6:15 the following morning, the usual departure time throughout the journey, the expeditionary caravan left Fort Washakie and traveled north before setting up camp on the Wind River. Sheridan customarily named each camp after a member of the party or other associate. Over the course of the next few days the party endured particularly hot weather as it advanced in a northwesterly direction along the drainage of the Wind River. The members of the party enjoyed fishing when the opportunity availed itself, along with some hunting. Sheridan allowed hunting during the entire journey but limited the hunts to what the expedition could consume. On August 12 the party found relief from the heat as it ascended the Wind River Mountains into alpine terrain, exceeding elevations of nine thousand feet before camping near the summit of the range. Sheridan named the pass utilized by the party Lincoln Pass in honor of the secretary of war. Today it is known as Sheridan Pass.

Clark, Strong, McCullough, and a Shoshone guide named Tosar left camp to go hunting early in the morning on August 13. The rest of the party descended the steep western slope down to the Gros Ventre River Valley. During the march that day the main party killed a number of antelope and one bear, while Clark and the other hunters succeeded in bringing in a single large elk to camp later that night. The fare that evening was supplemented by a large amount of trout from the Gros Ventre River.

The members of the party continued their march down the Gros Ventre River Valley the following day. Shortly before going into camp along the Gros Ventre they ascended a ridge, giving them their first view of the magnificent Teton Mountains. During the day Clark and Strong killed a number of antelope for the party to eat and in the evening other members of the group provided elk, antelope, deer, and trout. Strong winds that night caused the canvas of the tents to flap continually, preventing a good night's sleep.

From this location the expedition turned north and traveled up the valley of the Snake River to Jackson Lake. Continuing north along the Snake River, the party camped near the south boundary of the national park on August 17, about four miles downstream from the mouth of the Lewis River. At this point confusion as to which direction to take caused Sheridan to order the party to remain in camp for a day while the scouts and guides reconnoitered the area to determine a trail forward.

While some members of the party blazed the trail forward through thick timber, the remainder enjoyed a day of rest and relaxation. The newly cleared route became known as the Sheridan Trail and for years served visitors as a southern entrance into the park.[17] On August 19 the column resumed its advance as the trailblazers continued to cut the trail ahead of the main body. Clark, Rhodes, Tosar, and a small number of soldiers left the command and went out hunting toward Mount Sheridan. They returned to the camp on Lewis Lake that night with one young elk.[18]

The following day the members of the party continued in a northerly direction, passing Shoshone Lake and then advancing to the Upper Geyser Basin. At the end of the day's march they set up camp near Old Faithful and were met by Jack Baronett, the owner of the bridge over the Yellowstone River carrying his name. The Sheep Eater Shoshone scouts had no knowledge of the country yet to be passed, so Baronett would now serve as the party's guide. They remained at this camp August 21 for the men to observe not only Old Faithful but the other geysers in the vicinity as well. During the stay at Old Faithful they met a group of tourists, primarily from Salt Lake City. Lieutenant Colonel Gregory expressed alarm at the vandalism plaguing the geyser, noting that the top of the geyser's crater "has been broken down almost out of all recognition."

On August 22 the party traveled along the Firehole River to the Lower Geyser Basin, visiting the Paint Pots and other features along the route before establishing camp on Alum Creek. In the afternoon Clark and Rhodes went fishing in the stream and brought forty-five trout back to camp. During the march that day the party encountered Captain Francis M. Gibson, Seventh Cavalry, and his troop. The soldiers were escorting a government surveyor who was checking the boundary line between Wyoming and Montana. Gibson and his officers paid the Sheridan party a social visit at camp later that evening.

On the following morning Shoshone Dick and the Sheep Eater Shoshone scouts were discharged and set off for their return to Fort Washakie. The rest of Sheridan's group proceeded to Sulphur Mountain and from there to the Lower Falls of the Yellowstone, where they set up camp. During the remainder of the day various members of the party investigated both the Lower and Upper Falls. In the evening Sheridan and the others were joined once again by the group of tourists that they had first met just days before. Former Illinois congressman Greenbury L. Fort, his son, and a companion not only shared Sheridan's camp that night but also traveled with him as far as Baronett's Bridge.

On the morning of August 24 the expedition advanced along Yellowstone Canyon and then passed the eastern edge of Mount Washburn to its next campsite near Baronett's Bridge, arriving there in the early afternoon. During the day's march the column met Captain Robert P. Hughes of Brigadier General Alfred H. Terry's staff and First Lieutenant John H. Coale, Second Cavalry, escorting the founder of the Hampton Institute, Samuel C. Armstrong, on his visit to the national park. While the rest of the group settled into camp near the bridge, Clark, Rhodes, Strong, and Bishop, under the guidance of Baronett, ventured out on a hunting trip in the vicinity of Slough and Hell Roaring Creeks, intending to remain away from the main column for one or two nights.

Early the next morning John McCullough, who had been with the expedition from the beginning, left for Fort Ellis to meet prior obligations elsewhere. Sheridan and the others also parted company with Fort and those traveling with him before proceeding up the east fork of the Yellowstone River. The command then advanced up Soda Butte Creek and camped there for the night at a location approximately eleven miles from Cooke City, Montana.

On August 26 the members of the command passed the national park's boundary near the northeast corner of the park and made a brief stop in Cooke City, a mining community of about a hundred houses, before continuing to the summit of the divide between Soda Butte Creek and Clark's Fork. At this point they met a local rancher named Geer, who offered to lead them across the Bear Tooth Mountains and then down to the Yellowstone River. Forest fires, still burning, hampered travel along the Clark's Fork Trail and traversing the Bear Tooth Mountains would shorten the trip by an estimated three days, so Sheridan decided to take on Geer as his guide.[19]

From the divide the expedition advanced to the base of Index Peak, where it remained for the night. Sheridan dubbed the camp "Camp Clark" in honor of the captain, who had fought the Bannocks in 1878 in the vicinity of the site. Interestingly, in naming the camp Sheridan referred to Clark as "our Indian interpreter."[20] That evening Clark and the other hunters rejoined the command, exhausted. Although successful in their hunt, they had followed the command's trail for forty-eight miles before reuniting with their comrades.

Over the course of the next two days the command crossed the Bear Tooth Mountains, a feat previously considered impossible. The journey on the first day began with an ascent that at times passed through dense timber. By the end of the first day's march the column had reached the south side of Clay Mountain, where camp was made. Resuming their advance the next day, Sheridan and the others continued their ascent until arriving at the high point of the climb, about three miles from the head of Little Rocky Creek Canyon. From this point they began a rather treacherous descent toward the Clark's Fork Valley. Clark and a small group of hunters spent the day in search of game and did not rejoin the command until later that day after camp had been established on Little Rocky Creek. Clark and Rhodes were the only successful hunters, bringing in an elk for the party to consume.

On August 29 the expedition made its way to the valley of Clark's Fork and camped on that stream after enduring a tiresome march through a section of badlands. The following day it continued down the valley, located on the Crow Reservation. Shortly after the men left camp calamity struck. Sheridan's horse struggled in some quicksand and tossed the general into the bank of Clark's Fork, dislocating his arm. After Doctor Forwood tended to the injury, Sheridan remained with the command, although suffering in pain. During the march that day the men were joined by a number of Crow Indians who were camped nearby. The Crows accompanied the party to the campsite for that night on Rocky Fork.

On the morning of August 31 the expedition crossed the Yellowstone River near the mouth of Clark's Fork and proceeded down that river a short distance before meeting construction crews from the Northern Pacific Railroad. The superintendent of the crews offered Sheridan and his immediate entourage (including Clark) the use of a caboose to travel to Billings Station. The general gladly accepted, leaving Captain Wheelan in command, charged with the task of getting the column to Billings. Upon reaching the town in the early afternoon Sheridan and his traveling companions transferred onto the luxurious railcars that Heber R. Bishop had arranged for the party's return trip to the East. Wheelan and his men arrived at Billings two and a half hours after Sheridan and were ordered to Fort Custer.

The expedition was now completed after making a total of twenty-two camps and covering a distance of 592 miles from Green River, Wyoming, to Billings, Montana. Sheridan and the other members of his group left Billings later that evening for the rail trip to division headquarters. On the morning of September 2 they arrived at Fargo, Dakota Territory, and later that night reached Saint Paul. By the afternoon of September 3 the Sheridan party had arrived safely back in Chicago after an absence of a little over one month.

According to Gregory, the expedition proved the practical use of the southern route utilized by the party from Fort Washakie into the park. It also demonstrated that the Bear Tooth Range could in fact be crossed on horseback. In 1878 Clark had wanted to cross the range and questioned a number of Crows about a possible route. They all assured him that the trip was not possible.

In writing his report on the expedition, Sheridan expressed deep concern about the commercialization of Yellowstone National Park and urged that the federal government, and not private business, should control the park. The general also lamented the slaughter of game within the park and endorsed a plan to expand the boundaries of the park and to use troops from nearby posts to enforce game laws. Sheridan would continue to fight for his cause in the years to come.

After returning to Chicago Clark busied himself on his manuscript once again. During the course of his research he not only relied on his years of experience on the frontier and the people he encountered there but also obtained information from some of the leading scholars of the time who had studied the American Indian, either directly or through their works. Foremost among them were ethnologists such as Hubert Howe Bancroft and Henry R. Schoolcraft.

Clark continued to fulfill social obligations as well. Near the middle of September he journeyed to Fond du Lac, Wisconsin, in order to attend the wedding of Ensign Francis H. Sherman, U.S. Navy, to Margaret Bragg. The bride was the daughter of Brigadier General Edward S. Bragg, who had served during the Civil War. Bragg was not in attendance at his daughter's wedding, so Colonel John Gibbon, commander of the Seventh Infantry, gave the bride away.[21]

Other duties briefly took Clark away from his writing in late October. He was called on to serve as a member of a board of survey to convene at the Depot Commissary storehouse in Chicago. The board had the rather mundane chore of examining and reporting upon damaged subsistence goods.[22] After completing the task, Clark was able to focus once again on his manuscript.

Clark continued to enjoy the social benefits of his current assignment. During the Christmas season of 1882 he remained in Chicago. On the night of December 23 he attended a reception held at Sheridan's home. Many of the leading business and military men of the city went to the event. The list of attendees also included individuals who had participated in the recent Yellowstone expedition. Clark's friend newspaperman John F. Finerty was present as well. The special guest for the affair, John Schuyler Crosby, served as Sheridan's aide-de-camp at one time and had recently been named as the governor of Montana Territory.[23]

On March 21, 1883, Clark received a fifteen-day leave of absence to travel to northern New York. During his leave he enjoyed visiting with family and friends in Deer River. He also traveled to nearby Lowville and attended the first annual Campfire at the G. D. Bailey Grand Army of the Republic Post. Clark not only attended the event but joined the list of speakers and delivered a presentation on his experiences with Indians on the frontier as part of the night's program.[24]

Campfire events were very popular among the Union Civil War veterans who belonged to the organization commonly known as the G.A.R. (Grand Army of the Republic). These social gatherings provided opportunities to hear war stories, listen to talks concerning other historical events, and sing songs and enjoy music, patriotic and otherwise.

At the end of his leave Clark returned to Chicago to continue his work. In late May a reporter from the *Daily Inter Ocean*, a Chicago newspaper, called upon Clark at his home to interview him about his impressions of General George Crook, then engaged in a struggle with the Apaches in the Southwest. Unfortunately, the reporter insisted on asking questions about the brigadier that predated Clark's association with him beginning in the late summer of 1876. Rather than asking the captain about the tumultuous campaign that fall and subsequent events at Camp Robinson the following year, Clark had to field such questions as "What do you know of General Crook's movements from '67 to '73?" and "Can you remember anything about the Arizona expedition of '73?" The only meaningful information Clark could give was to praise Crook for his ability to gain the confidence of Indian allies through his fair treatment of them and to utilize their talents as scouts.[25] Crook was liberally using Indian scouts in his current campaign as he had done in the past.

Clark toiled with his manuscript through the early summer of 1883 until taking yet another opportunity to journey west once again. Sheridan began planning another trip to Yellowstone National Park during the previous winter. The expedition would be a continuation of his fight to protect the park. Sheridan was ably assisted by Senator George G. Vest of Missouri, who also championed the cause and would accompany the general to the park. Another political figure supportive of Sheridan's vision, Montana's territorial governor John Schuyler Crosby, added his name to the list. The most important participant, however, was President Chester A. Arthur, who decided to participate in the expedition after being persuaded to do so by Sheridan and Vest.[26] Arthur, a Republican from New York, had ascended to the presidency when President James A. Garfield was assassinated in 1881.

Robert Todd Lincoln, who had canceled on the previous year's journey, would now take part in the 1883 expedition. The final politician making the trip was Judge Daniel G. Rollins, surrogate of New York, a close personal friend of Arthur's who participated as the personal guest of the president. Vest also was allowed to invite someone and selected his son, George G. Vest, Jr., of

Saint Louis. In order to document the expedition, which marked the first time an American president visited the national park, Sheridan enlisted the services of photographer Frank Jay Haynes of Fargo, Dakota Territory.[27] Arthur insisted that no members of the press should accompany the excursion. Sheridan endorsed the idea wholeheartedly: "If we have a newspaper man along our pleasures will be destroyed."[28]

The only civilian from last year's journey to make a return appearance was Anson Stager of the Western Union Telegraph Company, who joined the group when Senator John A. Logan of Illinois was forced to cancel due to illness. In addition to Clark, who would serve as an acting aide-de-camp, other returning army officers included Lieutenant Colonel James F. Gregory, aide-de camp; Surgeon W. H. Forwood; and the general's brother, Lieutenant Colonel Michael V. Sheridan, military secretary. Thomas Moore would once again supervise the pack train for the expedition, overseeing 175 mules and horses.[29]

In preparation for the expedition's departure, in early July Sheridan ordered Clark to proceed from Chicago via Fort Custer to Fort McKinney and then on to Fort Washakie, where the various elements for the expedition would assemble. At McKinney Clark was charged with selecting the best horses from the fort for the upcoming journey and obtaining a small number of enlisted men to serve as orderlies during the excursion. At Clark's discretion, he could appoint an officer to head the detachment.[30]

At Fort Custer Clark was joined by scout James A. Campbell, a veteran of the 1882 expedition to the park. They arrived at Fort McKinney in the middle of July. During his stay there Clark acquired the horses as ordered and selected a detachment of twenty-eight enlisted men to be commanded by First Lieutenant Edwin P. Andrus, a New Yorker educated at West Point. The detachment left the garrison on July 15 and arrived at Fort Washakie ten days later. Of the enlisted men chosen by Clark, only fifteen would accompany the expedition beyond that point. Lieutenant Colonel Gregory and expedition photographer Frank Jay Haynes, in advance of the main party, reached Fort Washakie on July 27.[31] Two days later Sheridan sent word to the lieutenant colonel that he wanted Clark "to mess and tent at Headquarters" during the expedition.[32]

Sheridan and the presidential party left Chicago at noon on August 3. They traveled by train to Omaha and Cheyenne before reaching Green River, Wyoming Territory, on the morning of August 5, where Governor Crosby joined his comrades for the expedition. They remained on the train for the rest of the day. The following morning the members of the group set out for Fort

Washakie aboard three spring wagons, advancing 101 miles to the Sweetwater River. There they found their camp that had been set up for them by Captain James H. Lord, the Cheyenne Depot quartermaster.[33]

The next morning the presidential party resumed its journey and embarked upon the remaining 55 miles to Fort Washakie. As the president and those accompanying him approached their destination, they were greeted by many Shoshones and Northern Arapahos. Again they arrived to find tents that had already been set up for them, this time at the hot springs near the post.[34] There Sheridan was reunited with Clark and Gregory.

The following day, August 8, the party remained at Fort Washakie, making final preparations for the upcoming journey. Sheridan succeeded in recruiting a number of Shoshone and Northern Arapaho guides for the trip. Shoshone Dick, a member of the previous year's expedition, joined the general once again. In the afternoon President Arthur met with Washakie and other Shoshone headmen as well as Northern Arapaho leaders, including Black Coal. The Northern Arapaho interpreter struggled so much with his translations that Clark was called upon to assist by using his skills in sign language. At the end of the conference gifts were presented to Arthur and members of his party. Afterward a group of Shoshone men performed a dance for the president.

After the dance Captain Edward M. Hayes and the seventy-five men of Troop G, Fifth Cavalry (who would be serving as the escort for the upcoming expedition) provided Arthur with a demonstration of their mastery of mounted and unmounted drill. The military exhibition was followed by the performance of a sham battle by about 250 Shoshones and Northern Arapahos for the president's entertainment.[35]

No member of the press was allowed on the expedition, so Sheridan assigned his brother the duty of composing and issuing dispatches for the Associated Press throughout the journey. In order to maintain communication between the president and the outside world, Troop A, Fifth Cavalry, would serve courier duty between the presidential party and Fort Washakie during the early portion of the trip. The previous year's escort, Troop G, Second Cavalry from Fort Custer, would now provide another courier line that ran from within the national park to Fort Ellis, Montana.[36]

The presidential party left Fort Washakie on the morning of August 9, 1883, and thereafter traveled exclusively on horseback. The members of the expedition generally would awaken very early each day, leave camp between 6:30 and 7:00 A.M., and then ride until around noon. Afternoons were usually spent hunting, fishing, or relaxing. President Arthur greatly enjoyed fishing, which proved to be the predominant activity of the entire expedition. Along the route to the park Sheridan permitted hunting solely to provide food for the party. Once inside the park's boundaries, however, killing game was forbidden.[37]

Starting from Fort Washakie the expedition took the same general route to the park taken by Sheridan the previous summer. Moving north from the garrison, the party advanced up the Wind River drainage, reaching Lincoln Pass on August 15. The following morning Clark and Secretary Lincoln set out on an elk hunt, accompanied by two Indian guides. The small group of hunters was expected back in camp later that night but did not rejoin the party until the following evening along the Gros Ventre River, returning empty-handed.[38]

The party continued along the Gros Ventre to the Teton Basin before advancing up the Snake River Valley and establishing camp about two miles south of the park boundary. On August 23, two weeks after leaving Fort Washakie, the members of the presidential party entered Yellowstone Park and advanced as far as Lewis Lake. On the following day they rode to the Upper Geyser Basin and made camp near Old Faithful. The men spent the afternoon relaxing, bathing, and tending to their stock and provisions. They had intended to lay over for two days near Old Faithful, but a scarcity of forage for the animals allowed only one day to visit the wonders of the area.

From its camp near Old Faithful the members of the party retraced their trail to Shoshone Lake and proceeded east to a point on the western side of Yellowstone Lake now known as the West Thumb Bay. The following day they continued their march, passing near the edge of the lake, then made camp next to the outlet of the Yellowstone River at the foot of the lake. While the rest of the party chose to relax for the afternoon, President Arthur and Clark went fishing together. No mention was made concerning the captain's luck, but the president netted thirty-five fish.

The next morning the expedition proceeded down the Yellowstone River to a location on the edge of Yellowstone Canyon between the Upper and Lower Falls, where camp was made. During their two-day stay at this camp the men of the expedition encountered curious tourists who seemed to be more interested in the president than in the natural surroundings. The members of the party spent the following day exploring the area and enjoying a variety of outstanding views of the Upper and Lower Falls.

Leaving the camp between the falls on the morning of August 30, the presidential party continued north, passing the western side of Mount Washburn then spent the night at Baronett's Bridge. The next day they rode to Mammoth Hot Springs and set up camp near the park superintendent's home. Just three hundred yards away from their camp was the newly opened National Hotel. Some members of the party enjoyed a hot bath shortly after their arrival, while others went to visit the hotel.

The presidential party gathered around a large bonfire at camp that evening. A group of about fifty tourists from the hotel came to the president's camp to pay their respects to Arthur. During their visit the tourists entertained the members of the party with songs. When the serenading was over, the president and the men of his party were invited to the hotel for a reception given by Rufus Hatch, a major proponent of park commercialization and president of the Yellowstone National Park Improvement Company, which had constructed the hotel. While Sheridan wanted to convince Arthur of the need to preserve the park, Hatch wanted to sway both the president and Senator Vest to favor its commercial development. He had in fact scheduled his presence at Mammoth Hot Springs, in which he was accompanied by his own party of journalists and dignitaries, to coincide with the president's visit there.

Accepting the invitation, the president and the rest of his party went to the hotel for a night of champagne, cigars, and music. Although Sheridan, who represented park conservation, and Hatch, who supported commercialization, were in attendance at the same event, no mention was made of any tension between the two factions. But the reception did take an ugly turn. Apparently the only member of the president's party who did not go to the gathering with the rest of the group was Michael V. Sheridan. He arrived later, however, in a state of drunkenness. Upon seeing the lieutenant colonel in his current condition, the president excused himself from the room. As Arthur exited, the intoxicated Sheridan reportedly made a derogatory comment about the president. The party quickly broke up, ending the evening and the final day of the expedition.

The next day, September 1, 1883, Arthur and the members of his party exited the park at the north entrance and traveled the short distance to the community of Cinnabar, Montana Territory, the terminus of a recently completed spur line off the main line of the Northern Pacific Railroad. The journey from Green River, Wyoming Territory, to that location had covered approximately 500 miles. From Cinnabar the group traveled by rail to the main line at Livingston. Governor Crosby then returned to Helena, while Senator Vest remained behind in order to attend to Senate Committee on Indian Affairs business in the West.

The presidential train proceeded east, passing Billings in the afternoon before arriving at Fort Keogh that night.[39]

The party paid a visit to the fort. A number of Clark's old friends still resided at the post and enjoyed seeing him once again. Among them was fourteen-year-old Grace Logan, daughter of Captain Thomas H. Logan, Fifth Infantry. She knew Clark from his days at Fort Keogh and was glad to see him when he returned with the presidential party. In later years she remembered Clark as a "most charming and loveable man" and recalled that the captain was a favorite among the children of the garrison.[40]

After visiting Fort Keogh the presidential party continued its return trip to Chicago and Washington. President Arthur and the others participated in some of the activities held in Saint Paul to celebrate the completion of the transcontinental Northern Pacific Railroad, which now connected the Pacific Northwest with the rest of America. They then pressed on to Chicago, arriving on the afternoon of September 4. Arthur and Lincoln remained in the city and participated in a small number of festivities, including a luncheon sponsored by the Military Order of the Loyal Legion of Illinois, a patriotic organization composed of current and former military officers. Clark and members of Sheridan's staff attended the event, but Sheridan suffered from a malarial fever and was absent. The president and secretary of war then boarded their train on the night of September 5 and embarked upon the final leg of the journey to Washington.[41] The 1883 expedition marked the first time a president visited the nation's first national park, but for Clark it was the last time he would ever venture west.

⋆ 15 ⋆

FINAL MONTHS IN WASHINGTON, D.C.

Upon his return to Chicago Clark resumed his work at division headquarters. On October 22, 1883, the captain served as a member of a board of survey at headquarters in Chicago. During the Yellowstone expedition a pair of binoculars and a pocket compass issued to Lieutenant Colonel Gregory apparently had been lost. The board was assigned the task of reporting on the matter and assigning responsibility for the loss.[1] While the work at headquarters continued unabated, drastic changes in Chicago were rapidly approaching.

November 1, 1883, was a momentous day in army circles: General of the Army William T. Sherman relinquished his command to Lieutenant General Sheridan. At the same time, Sheridan assigned his former position as commander of the Division of the Missouri to Major General John M. Schofield. Sheridan and members of his staff left Chicago and arrived in Washington, D.C., that first day of November. Clark remained behind in Chicago, however, continuing to serve on special duty at division headquarters.[2]

Clark pursued other interests as well. That fall the captain sought to purchase a new horse. Clark had expressed an interest in buying a particular government horse. On November 2 a board of officers convened in Chicago in order to appraise the animal. The board set a price of $138 for the horse, a strawberry roan estimated to be ten or eleven years old named Telegraph.[3]

Clark's time in Chicago soon drew to a close. On November 26 Sheridan ordered him to proceed to Washington, D.C., and report to him in person. The captain was attached to his Washington staff as an aide-de-camp. Just a few days later Lieutenant Colonel Michael V. Sheridan, serving as military secretary for his brother, wrote to the adjutant general requesting that a special order be issued assigning Clark to duty at the Headquarters of the Army in Washington, under special instruction from General Sheridan. Clark wasted little time in responding to Sheridan's order, for the lieutenant colonel ended his letter by stating that "Capt. Clark has already reported to Lieut. General Sheridan."[4] Clark established residence at the popular Ebbitt House in Washington.[5]

Just weeks after settling into his new surroundings in Washington, Clark took advantage of the social benefits of his position at his new duty station. The captain and Sheridan became active members of the Army and Navy German and Assembly Club, a social organization dedicated to gatherings for dancing and entertainment during the city's winter social season. "German" in this case referred to a sophisticated group dance popular at the time. Sheridan became the organization's president, while Clark served on the executive committee.[6]

In early January 1884 Clark became the beneficiary of a financial windfall. At some point in 1882 he joined a large number of military officers, both retired and active, who submitted a claim to the Treasury Department for payment of salary in arrears. A recent U.S. Supreme Court decision in the case of *United States v. Tyler* caused the flood of claims to the nation's treasury. A portion of the case dealt with the method by which longevity pay was calculated. According to the Tyler decision, the 10 percent increase received by officers each five years for longevity pay should have been compounded rather than being calculated each time using the same standard pay grade. As a result of the decision large numbers of officers were owed money for past service. Congress soon passed legislation to rectify the matter and ensure that future increases would be based on a set pay grade amount. Despite the new legislation, claims submitted after the court's ruling had to be adjudicated. It took years for the Treasury Department to evaluate each claim. Clark's claim was passed by the Second Comptroller of the Treasury in late 1883 or very early in January 1884.[7]

Over the course of the next several months Clark labored at Army Headquarters, finalizing his manuscript on Indian sign language. He did not neglect his personal life, continuing to pursue outside interests and enjoy his social standing. Clark, Sheridan, and Gregory traveled to Chicago in late June to join the city's social elite for the inauguration of the Washington Park Club racetrack and the running of the American Derby. Sheridan served as president of the club and played a leading role in the track's creation. The general's wife accompanied her husband to the event, while Clark escorted his fiancée, Cornelia McAvoy, to the track. The two couples arrived at the event in grand fashion aboard a tally-ho coach (an elegant four-horse carriage) with Gregory and other friends and family.[8] From the comfort of the clubhouse Sheridan and his guests, along with an estimated crowd of ten thousand spectators, viewed the derby and lesser races held that day. For Clark the journey to Chicago represented something much more important than horse racing. He and Cornelia announced their engagement during his visit to the city.[9]

After this brief trip Clark returned to Washington, D.C. He had finally completed his manuscript after years of hard work. On July 7 he submitted the finished product to Sheridan at Army Headquarters, hoping that it would be published by the Government Printing Office. The following day Sheridan forwarded the manuscript to Secretary Lincoln and gave Clark's work a glowing endorsement: "The matters of which this report treats are of great interest to the public now, and as the savage condition of the Indians recedes from us this interest will increase. All that is of historic value regarding this wonderful people should be put in shape for the future, and as one of the best means for doing this I recommend the publication of Capt. Clark's excellent work." On July 12 Lincoln responded: "Under existing laws the Secy of War could only agree to purchase a definite number of copies. As he cannot make a requisition for printing the work at the Gov't. Printing Office, he is willing to consider a proposition for taking a reasonable number of copies upon being informed of the price at which they will be furnished."[10] Clark now faced the challenge of locating a publisher for his work.

At about this same time rumors concerning Clark's military career were circulating around Washington. The U.S. Senate was considering a House bill to increase the number of personnel in the Inspector General's Department. Gossip in the capital city suggested that Clark was an applicant for a future appointment to the department. When asked directly about the situation, Clark denied the rumors and stated that he "has not the slightest idea that it will be tendered him, if the bill should pass."[11] Speculation about the captain's future arose again later. Talk began to spread that Clark might be a potential replacement for Delos B. Sacket in the position of inspector general the following year due to Sacket's age and Clark's friendship with President Arthur.[12]

Not long after receiving the disheartening news concerning the publication of his manuscript Clark journeyed to his hometown of Deer River, New York. The purpose of the trip was purely social: the captain wished to spend some time simply visiting friends and family. He remained in the small community until August 5, when he set out for his return to Washington, D.C.[13] The time spent with loved ones proved especially fortuitous, as it was the last time they would see Clark alive.

At some point during the course of the following few weeks Clark's literary fortunes improved. He successfully reached an agreement with L. R. Hamersly and Company of Philadelphia to publish *The Indian Sign Language*. Final arrangements for the book's publication apparently were completed around the middle of September.[14] The enterprising captain's literary ambitions were about to be realized after years of labor.

Unfortunately, the sense of achievement that Clark surely felt was soon overshadowed by health concerns. On September 18 he did not go to his office and informed headquarters that he was "slightly indisposed" and would remain at his residence for the day. Clark remained at his home the following day but reported feeling better and anticipated being in his office the next day. In reality, however, he was getting progressively worse. A telegram was received by Clark's family in Deer River on the afternoon of September 20 telling them that Clark was suffering from inflammation of the bowels. John W. Clark rushed to board the evening train for Washington and arrived there at midnight the following night. He promptly made his way to his brother's home at 826 14th Street NW and was there for less than six hours before witnessing Clark's last breath at 6 on the morning of September 22. Others present at Clark's home when he died included Lieutenant Colonel Gregory, army surgeon Basil Norris, who signed Clark's death certificate and reported his death to the adjutant general, possibly one or more other physicians, and a number of members from the Washington Metropolitan Club, an exclusive private social club that Clark had recently joined.[15]

William Philo Clark lived a relatively short life. He was only thirty-nine years old at the time of his passing. The official cause of his death was identified as gastroenteritis or stomach flu, an inflammation of the lining of the stomach and intestines. The malady was also referred to at that time as trail colic.[16] Clark's fiancée, Cornelia McAvoy, had been informed of his condition; despite making the journey to Washington to be with him, she did not arrive in the city in time to see her loved one alive. On the evening of Clark's death his body was taken to the railroad depot by a local undertaker, escorted by a small number of his army friends. Later that same night Cornelia and Clark's brother left Washington with his body, bound for Deer River, where Clark would be laid to rest two days later.[17]

Clark's office at Army Headquarters, located in a room adjoining Sheridan's office, now sat vacant on the day following his death. His carved square-top mahogany desk appeared just as it had the last day he had worked there. Under the desk a package could be seen, addressed to L. R. Hamersly and ready for mailing. The package contained the final pages of his manuscript, a work reported to have been 1,500 pages long in its entirety. Later many flowers arrived at the office and were piled on the desktop, almost covering it. Accompanying the flowers was a card that read simply: "From officers of 2d Cavalry."[18]

On September 24 Clark's friends and family gathered at a church in Deer River for his funeral. The services were conducted by the Reverend George B. Rowley, a pastor with the Congregational church. Two other local clergymen, one a Baptist and the other a Methodist, assisted Rowley. Apparently out of respect for his parents' wishes, the event was a quiet affair with none of the usual military ceremony associated with an army officer's funeral. In addition to a number of friends and relatives from Deer River and surrounding communities, other attendees included Cornelia McAvoy and her brother Charles, Lieutenant Colonel Gregory, and Inspector General Sacket. General Sheridan did not attend the funeral but sent a rather long telegram of condolence to Clark's mother. In closing he wrote: "I highly appreciated your son, not only for his ability, but for his valuable services to me and to his country. I am sure there is not an officer of the army who does not join with me in extending his condolence in your present bereavement."[19] Following the funeral service Clark's body was taken to nearby Swinburne Cemetery for burial.

In the years after Clark's death Cornelia McAvoy successfully moved on with her life. She dedicated much of her remaining life to nursing after studying in Boston and London. She started the Visiting Nurses program in Winchester, Massachusetts, and played a prominent role in creating the Visiting Nurses Association. Cornelia married Henry L. Houghton, a Harvard-educated Boston doctor several years younger than herself. The couple wed in 1897 and raised two children together, living in both Winchester and Boston. Cornelia passed away at the age of sixty-eight in January 1929 at her Winchester home after suffering a long illness.[20]

Word of Clark's demise spread rapidly across the country. Many of the nation's newspapers carried the news. Just as quickly, it seemed, the sad tidings of White Hat's passing swept across remote areas of the plains among the Indians living there. The sign language that had been such a large part of Clark's life was now employed by the various tribes to announce his death. In a review of Clark's book Colonel John Gibbon, who had commanded the Montana Column during the Great Sioux War, recounted a related story. While riding some distance from Fort Washakie, the interpreter there met an Indian who told him by use of sign talk that Clark was dead. A few days later this same interpreter, who also served as a mail courier, delivered the mail containing a letter announcing Clark's death to officers at the garrison. Interestingly, Gibbon was not so much impressed by the rapidity with which the Indians received the information as he was by the accuracy of the news being carried simply by the use of sign language. He added: "The distinguished officer whose death was in this way spread amongst the people who held him in such high regard, left behind him a lasting monument of his skill, industry and untiring energy."[21]

After Clark's death attention turned toward settling his affairs and caring for his personal effects. Sheridan instructed Gregory to take charge of Clark's belongings and to ensure that they were sent to his father, William D. Clark. Gregory pointed out to the general that Clark brought only items that could be carried free on the railroad as personal baggage when ordered to Chicago and then to Washington, D.C. His other personal belongings, probably including his extensive collection of American Indian objects, were left in storage at Fort Keogh. Gregory asked that the expense of transporting Clark's belongings from Montana to Deer River be covered by the Quartermaster's Department. His request was approved. The commanding officer at Keogh was directed to ship Clark's belongings to his father.[22]

Gregory also found himself deeply involved in Clark's book project. Being named as Clark's literary executor, he was charged with the responsibility of supervising the publication. On October 17 L. R. Hamersly and Company sent a circular to the adjutant general announcing the anticipated publication of *The Indian Sign Language*. The company believed that the work would be completed around November 1. But the book was not published until early 1885. In the cover letter accompanying the circular the company extended a fine sales pitch to the adjutant general. "Relating as it does to a subject of great interest and no little practical concern to army officers and being the work of an army officer, it is in a double sense, and eminently, an army book. We trust that you will see your way to giving us a liberal order for this valuable work which we are sure will prove a most acceptable and instructive issue to the officers of your corps."[23]

Clark identified his numerous sources throughout the book, but his acknowledgments at the end of the introductory portion of the book recognized only four individuals. Two of them, Dr. Philip Gillette and Ezra G. Valentine, were educators of the deaf in Illinois and assisted Clark with his descriptions of the signs used by the deaf. The other two individuals were military men. "I am indebted to [Adjutant] General Robert Williams, U.S. Army, for advice and suggestions, and to Lieutenant-Colonel James F. Gregory, A.D.C., for much healthy criticism and material assistance running through the preparation of the entire work."[24]

Shortly after the book's release the *Journal of the Military Service Institution of the United States* printed a review written by Colonel John Gibbon. The colonel noted that the book exhibited "deep and careful research" and found it "exceedingly interesting reading." He believed that Clark's work would "add very much to the popular information regarding a race not well understood."[25]

A less flattering, highly critical review appeared in *The Nation*. The unnamed reviewer lambasted Clark's book while touting the work of Garrick Mallery, who was highly criticized by Clark. The reviewer faulted Clark for not making mention of the existing literature concerning sign language in general and for failing to acknowledge previous works specifically concerning North American Indian sign language. He also alleged that Clark copied the arrangement of his book from one of Mallery's previous works but did not claim any plagiarism in describing individual signs. Although Clark made it clear that his study was based predominantly on his personal observations during the course of his experiences on the western frontier and thereby was not a comprehensive study for all of North America, his work was critically judged as such. Even Clark's descriptions for deaf signs described in his book came under attack as being too simplistic and limited in scope. As for his Indian signs, the reviewer contended: "The signs, as described, have become his own signs, not the genuine signs of any Indian." Clark's work "will not contribute to science until it has been analyzed by scholars experienced in this branch of study. Nor will it be of much value to travelers or other persons desirous to learn sign language for their personal use." *The Nation* viewed Clark's efforts as amateurish and unprofessional when compared to the work of Mallery and the Bureau of American Ethnology. Interestingly, the reviewer felt it appropriate to end the piece with "an expression of sorrow" over Clark's death.[26]

The harsh criticism of the review in *The Nation* proved meritless. Over the years Clark's work served as an important reference for the study of Indian sign language, the Plains Indians, and the Indian Wars. In 1918 Ernest Thompson Seton published *Sign Talk*, a work completed with the aid of Hugh Lenox Scott, the Seventh Cavalry officer who shared Clark's keen interest in Indian sign language. In his preface Seton referred to Clark's work as "quite the best book on the subject, giving over 1,000 signs with photographic exactness; it is also one of the best early encyclopedic books on Indians in general." He went on: "This is practically the only publication quoted in preparing this work. I have referred to it continually as a standard—as the highest available authority."[27]

In the days and months following Clark's death a number of his superiors paused to remember him. General Sheridan recalled that the captain

> was not only a brave soldier but an officer who was competent to perform any sort of duty. There was nothing he would shrink from and he never failed in anything he undertook. It is seldom that the same man combines military skill and scholarly attainments, but Clark had both. He could lead a column of cavalry in battle one day, and the next would devote to the studying of the use of a diphthong in the Indian tongue. He could drive a mule team as skillfully as he could write an essay, and his taste was as wide as his versatility.[28]

Brigadier General George Crook paid tribute to his former aide, referencing the tumultuous time that Clark spent at Camp Robinson: "My estimate of his character and abilities could not have been more emphatically and distinctly outlined than by the responsibilities confided to him during the times when the firmest and yet most judicious behavior was an indispensable adjunct of the officers selected." Colonel Luther P. Bradley, referring to that same period, reflected that "Captain Clark rendered very valuable service at that time, and by his courage, energy and skill contributed as much as any one man to the controlling [of] the hostile elements in the bands of Minnecoujou, Ogalalla and Brule Sioux. I say here what I have said before that I regard him as a soldier of ability of the first order."[29]

Brigadier General Alfred H. Terry recalled: "Captain Clark served for years in this department; he was often intrusted with important duties and responsibilities; he never failed to fulfill both to the high satisfaction of his superiors and to his own credit and distinction. He was one of the best officers of his grade in the army." Brigadier General Nelson A. Miles added: "Captain Clark in the ordinary requirements of service discharged his duties with commendable fidelity, zeal and intelligence. In the more difficult service in the field, his career has been conspicuous for most energetic and zealous efforts accompanied with marked success."

In private life Clark was described as "a peculiarly lovable man" and "brave, gentle, and generous to a fault, full of sympathy for the misfortunes of others." His old friend newspaper reporter and later congressman John F. Finerty recalled that Clark "made friends with every one with whom he came in contact, and was a noble soldier in every respect. We have been together all over the plains, and I always found him a perfect gentleman, generous to a fault, always ready to share his last rations with his friends, and he was as happy when hungry as when feasting."[30]

After a distinguished military career and a life prematurely ended, William Philo Clark gave the world two lasting legacies and possibly someday another as well. First, he left his informative book *The Indian Sign Language*, which remains readily available to readers today and is marketed as a classic. Second, and much less well known, he gathered a collection of Plains Indian artifacts during his years on the frontier. After remaining in the family's possession for many years the collection was donated to the Morris Museum in Morristown, New Jersey, where it is being preserved for future generations.[31] Last, and potentially not least, Clark's diary (if it resurfaces) could undoubtedly prove to be an important addition to the historiography of the Indian Wars. It could add greatly to our knowledge of the events that Clark witnessed and of the man himself.

NOTES

ABBREVIATIONS

AAG	Assistant Adjutant General
ACP	Appointment, Commission, and Personal
AG	Adjutant General
AGO	Adjutant General's Office
BAE	Bureau of American Ethnology
BIA	Bureau of Indian Affairs
DD	Department of Dakota
DP	Department of the Platte
DY	District of the Yellowstone
LR	Letters Received
LS	Letters Sent
MDM	Military Division of the Missouri
NAA	National Anthropological Archives
NAMP	National Archives Microfilm Publications
NARA	National Archives and Records Administration
PR	Post Return
RG	Record Group
RR	Regimental Return
SF	Special Files
SO	Special Orders
USMA	United States Military Academy

CHAPTER 1

1. William Richard Cutter, *Genealogical and Family History of Northern New York*, vol. 3 (New York: Lewis Historical Publishing Co., 1910), 1042–43, 1227; "Death of William Durant Clark," *Journal and Republican* (Lowville, NY), August 9, 1888; Bruce Rohr, "The Glorious Past of Deer River," *Carthage* (NY) *Republican Tribune*, April 26 and May 3, 1978.
2. "Death of William Durant Clark."
3. Ibid.; "Swinburne Cemetery," Cemetery Records, Deer River, Town of Denmark, NY, Lewis County Historical Society, Lyons Falls, NY.
4. New York Secretary of State, New York State Census, 1865 (Albany, State Library).
5. Hamilton Child, *Gazetteer and Business Directory of Lewis County, N.Y. for 1872–3* (Syracuse, NY: Hamilton Child, 1872), 88; Laura Prievo, Carthage Village, NY, historian, to the author, September 13, 1996; Rohr, "The Glorious Past of Deer River."
6. Rohr, "The Glorious Past of Deer River"; Child, *Gazetteer*, 88; New York Secretary of State, New York State Census, 1865.
7. Rohr, "The Glorious Past of Deer River."
8. New York Secretary of State, New York State Census, 1865.
9. "John W. Clark Fifty Years in Business Here Passes Away," *Carthage* (NY) *Republican Tribune*, December 24, 1925.
10. "Death of Captain William Clark of Gen. Sheridan's Staff," *Journal and Republican* (Lowville, NY), September 25, 1884.
11. "The Late Capt. Clark," *Carthage* (NY) *Republican*, September 30, 1884.
12. Dave Jones, Swinburne Cemetery sexton, telephone interview with author, March 11, 2014.
13. "John W. Clark Fifty Years in Business Here Passes Away."
14. A. W. Clark to E. M. Stanton, Secretary of War, March 2, 1864, Records Relating to the USMA, USMA Application Papers, 1864, no. 25, RG 94, Records of the AGO, 1780s–1917, NARA, Washington, DC.
15. William D. Clark to Edwin M. Stanton, Secretary of War, March 3, 1864; William Philo Clark to Stanton, March 11, 1864, ibid.
16. William P. Clark, USMA Medical Cards, March 10 and 18 and April 18, 1864, File 330 ACP 1877, RG 94, Entry 297, LR 1863–94, ACP Branch Records, NARA, Washington, DC.
17. "The Late Capt. Clark."
18. Stephen E. Ambrose, *Duty, Honor, Country: A History of West Point* (Baltimore: Johns Hopkins University Press, 1966), 71–72, 77, 87.
19. "John C. Tidball," *Wikipedia*, last modified January 5, 2014, https://en.wikipedia.org/wiki/John_C._Tidball; "Henry M. Black," *Wikipedia*, last modified June 12, 2014, https://en.wikipedia.org/wiki/Henry_M._Black.
20. "The Late Capt. Clark."
21. Ambrose, *Duty, Honor, Country*, 222.
22. Ibid., 39, 63, 126–27.

23. "Superintendent of the United States Military Academy," *Wikipedia,* last modified June 19, 2014, https://en.wikipedia.org/wiki/Superintendent_of_the_United_States_Military_Academy.
24. Ambrose, *Duty, Honor, Country*, 93–94, 100.
25. Ibid., 147, 151–52.
26. Ibid., 72.
27. USMA, *Official Register of the Officers and Cadets of the U.S. Military Academy, West Point, New York,* vols. 1865–67 (New York: Baldwin and Jones, Printers, 1865–67), 1865:15.
28. 1864–65 Conduct Rolls, Records Relating to the USMA, Rolls, Registers, and Reports, RG 94, Entry 232, Monthly Class Reports and Conduct Rolls, 1831–66, Box 4, NARA, Washington, DC
29. Brevet Col. Henry M. Black Testimony, Proceedings of a General Court-Martial, Court-Martial Case Files, 1809–94, Box 2264, File 00-2531, RG 153, Records of the Judge Advocate General—Army, NARA, Washington, DC (hereafter cited as General Court-Martial proceedings); USMA, *Official Register*, 1866:13.
30. 1865–66 Conduct Rolls, Records Relating to the USMA, Rolls, Registers, and Reports, RG 94, Entry 232, Monthly Class Reports and Conduct Rolls, 1831–66, Box 4, NARA, Washington, DC.
31. Brevet Col. Henry M. Black Testimony, General Court-Martial proceedings; William P. Clark, USMA Medical Card, September 16, 1866, File 330 ACP 1877.
32. USMA, *Official Register*, 1867:11.
33. 1866–67 Conduct Rolls, Records Relating to the USMA, Rolls, Registers, and Reports, RG 94, Entry 232, Monthly Class Reports and Conduct Rolls, 1831–66, Box 4, NARA, Washington, DC.
34. Brevet Col. Henry M. Black Testimony, General Court-Martial proceedings.
35. General Court-Martial proceedings. The following discussion of the court-martial is all based on this source.
36. Defense statement of Cadet William P. Clark attached to General Court-Martial proceedings.
37. General Court-Martial proceedings.
38. Judge Advocate General Joseph Holt to AG, October 23, 1867, Court Martial Case Files, 1809–94, Box 2264, File 00-2531, RG 153, Records of the Judge Advocate General-Army, NARA, Washington, DC. The following citations from correspondence concerning Clark's reinstatement to the academy are also from this source.
39. William P. Clark to Gen. Ulysses S. Grant, November 1867.
40. Clark to President Andrew Johnson, November 8, 1867.
41. Holt to President Johnson, November 9, 1867.
42. Executive Memorandum, President Andrew Johnson, December 4, 1867.
43. Clark to Secretary of War E. D. Townsend, December 5, 1867.
44. Inspector General Edmund Schriver to AG, December 5, 1867.
45. USMA, *United States Military Academy, West Point: Register of the Officers and Cadets and Report of the Board of Visitors, 1868* (Washington, DC: Government Printing Office, 1868), 10.

46. NAMP, *List of the Graduating Class with Arm of Service for Which Each Member Is Recommended,* Publication No. M1064, June 23, 1868, File M337, RG 94, *LR by the Commission Branch of the AGO, 1863–70,* 1868.

CHAPTER 2

1. Francis B. Heitman, *Historical Register and Dictionary of the United States Army, from Its Organization September 29, 1789 to March 2, 1903,* vol. 1 (Washington, DC: Government Printing Office, 1903), 306; August 1868 RR, Second Cavalry, Roll 18, NAMP, *Returns from Regular Army Cavalry Regiments,* Publication No. M744, RG 94, Records of the AGO, 1780s–1917; William P. Clark, Oath of Office, August 10, 1868, File 330 ACP 1877, RG 94, Entry 297, LR 1863–94, ACP Branch Records, NARA, Washington, DC.
2. October 1868 RR, Second Cavalry, Roll 18, NAMP, *Returns from Regular Army Cavalry Regiments.*
3. "A Noble Soldier," *Journal and Republican* (Lowville, NY), October 9, 1884.
4. Robert W. Frazer, *Forts of the West* (Norman: University of Oklahoma Press, 1965), 184; John S. Billings, *Circular No. 4: Report on Barracks and Hospitals with Descriptions of Military Posts* (1870; reprint New York: Sol Lewis, 1974), 340.
5. Billings, *Circular No. 4,* 342; "Thomas Bull Dewees," http://www.arlingtoncemetery.net/tbdewees.htm.
6. File P16 CB 1869, Henry S. Pearce, NAMP, *LR by the Commission Branch of the AGO, 1863–70,* Publication No. M1064, Roll 442, RG 94; General Court Martial Orders No. 80, Headquarters of the Army, Washington, DC, December 3, 1868, File P313 CB 1868, *LR by the Commission Branch of the AGO, 1863–70,* Roll 412.
7. March 1869 PR, Fort D. A. Russell, WY, Roll 1050, NAMP, *Returns from U.S. Military Posts,* Publication No. M617, RG 94.
8. Heitman, *Historical Register and Dictionary,* 984.
9. SO 30, February 22, 1869, and SO 60, April 6, 1869, SO, DP, vol. 447, 1869, Entry 44, RG 94.
10. Thomas Wilhelm, *A Military Dictionary and Gazetteer,* rev. ed. (1881; facsimile: War College Series, Charleston, SC: BiblioLife, 2015), 255–56.
11. Billings, *Circular No. 4,* 329–31.
12. April 1869 PR, Fort D. A. Russell, WY, Roll 1050; June 1869 PR, Fort Sanders, WY, Roll 1094; June 1869 PR, Omaha Barracks, NE, Roll 879, NAMP, *Returns from U.S. Military Posts.*
13. July 1869 RR, Second Cavalry, Roll 18, NAMP, *Returns from Regular Army Cavalry Regiments.*
14. NAMP, File C157, *LR by the Commission Branch of the AGO, 1863–70.*
15. Heitman, *Historical Register and Dictionary,* 767.
16. Wilhelm, *A Military Dictionary and Gazetteer,* 12.
17. Charles King, *Trials of a Staff-Officer* (1891; facsimile: London: FB &c, 2015), 12.
18. SO, DP, vols. 447–48, 1869–71.
19. SO 1, January 3, 1871, SO, DP, vol. 448.

20. SO 84, May 18, 1871, SO, DP, vol. 448.
21. Douglas D. Scott, Peter Bleed, and Stephen Damm, *Custer, Cody, and Grand Duke Alexis: Historical Archaeology of the Royal Buffalo Hunt* (Norman: University of Oklahoma Press, 2013), 31–32; William Warren Tucker, *His Imperial Highness the Grand Duke Alexis in the United States of America during the Winter of 1871–1872* (Cambridge, MA: Riverside Press, 1872), 152.
22. Scott, Bleed, and Damm, *Custer, Cody, and Grand Duke Alexis*, 5, 11–12, 55–57.
23. Ibid., 56.
24. Ibid., 5, 52, 56; Tucker, *His Imperial Highness*, 154, 160.
25. Scott, Bleed, and Damm, *Custer, Cody, and Grand Duke Alexis*, 58–59; Jerome Washington Goodspeed, *Life of Col. James Fisk, Jr.* (Chicago: J. W. Goodspeed, 1872), 157–58.
26. Scott, Bleed, and Damm, *Custer, Cody, and Grand Duke Alexis*, 40–44, 59–60; Tucker, *His Imperial Highness*, 158, 171.
27. Scott, Bleed, and Damm, *Custer, Cody, and Grand Duke Alexis*, 60; Tucker, *His Imperial Highness*, 167.
28. "Bos Americanus! The Imperial Sporting Party at Camp Alexis," *New York Herald*, January 18, 1872.
29. Scott, Bleed, and Damm, *Custer, Cody, and Grand Duke Alexis*, 66; Tucker, *His Imperial Highness*, 177.
30. June 1872 PR, Omaha Barracks, NE, Roll 879, NAMP, *Returns from U.S. Military Posts*; June and July 1872 RR, Second Cavalry, Roll 19, NAMP, *Returns from Regular Army Cavalry Regiments*; W. P. Clark to AG, June 26, 1872, and E. D. Townsend, AG, to Clark, July 8, 1872, William P. Clark, File 330 ACP 1877, RG 94.
31. September and October 1872 PR, Omaha Barracks, NE, Roll 879; October 1872 PR, Fort Sanders, WY, Roll 1094, NAMP, *Returns from U.S. Military Posts*.
32. Frazer, *Forts of the West*, 185; Billings, *Circular No. 4*, 353–56.
33. Billings, *Circular No. 4*, 356.
34. April 1873 PR, Fort Sanders, WY, Roll 1094, NAMP, *Returns from U.S. Military Posts*.
35. U.S. Congress, House, Clothing to Certain Enlisted Men of the Army, 43rd Cong., 1st sess., 1873–74, vol. 8, Ex. Doc, 18.
36. File 1452 AGO 1874, NAMP, *LR by the Office of the AG, 1871–1880*, Publication No. M666, RG 94, Roll 149, 1874.
37. Ibid.
38. March and June 1874 PR, Fort Sanders, WY, Roll 1094, NAMP, *Returns from U.S. Military Posts*; SO 87, June 27, 1874, SO, DP, vol. 450.
39. July and October PR, Fort Sanders, WY, Roll 1094, NAMP, *Returns from U.S. Military Posts*; SO 152, October 14, 1874, SO, DP, vol. 450.
40. November 1874 PR, Fort Sanders, WY, Roll 1094, NAMP, *Returns from U.S. Military Posts*; SO 168, November 10, 1874, SO, DP, vol. 450; SO 100, December 23, 1874, SO, MDM, vol. 341, Entry 44, RG 94.
41. January and March 1875 PR, Fort Sanders, WY, Roll 1094, NAMP, *Returns from U.S. Military Posts*.

42. Charles M. Robinson III, ed., *The Diaries of John Gregory Bourke*, vol. 1 (Denton: University of North Texas Press, 2003), 156.
43. June and July 1875 PR, Fort Sanders, WY, Roll 1094, NAMP, *Returns from U.S. Military Posts*; "Bartlett Family History from France to England to America: Information about Ellis [sic] B. Carling," http://www.genealogy.com/ftm/w/a/t/Lisa-K-Waterman-FLORIDA/WEBSITE-0001/UHP-0117.html (updated June 27, 2009); "Suicide of an Army Officer," *Republican Daily Journal* (Lawrence, KS), July 2, 1875.
44. Sir Rose Lambart Price, *The Two Americas: An Account of Sport and Travel* (Philadelphia: J. B. Lippincott and Co., 1877), 281.
45. Ibid., 280–83.
46. Ibid., 283–88 (quotation on 288).
47. Ibid., 289.
48. Ibid., 289–92, 308–11; Robinson, *The Diaries of John Gregory Bourke*, 3:213.
49. Price, *The Two Americas*, 310–15.
50. October and November 1875 PR, Fort Sanders, WY, Roll 1094, NAMP, *Returns from U.S. Military Posts*.
51. April–June 1876 PR, Fort Sanders, WY, Roll 1094, NAMP, *Returns from U.S. Military Posts*; SO 45, April 26, 1876, Headquarters, Fort Sanders, Wyoming Territory, SO, vol. 5, 1876, Entry 7, RG 393, Part 5, Records of United States Army Continental Commands, 1821–1920: Records of Districts, 1841–1920, Washington, DC; Wilhelm, *A Military Dictionary and Gazetteer*, 468.
52. Robinson, *The Diaries of John Gregory Bourke*, 1:219.

CHAPTER 3

1. William P. Clark, File 3407 ACP 1876, RG 94, Records of the AGO, 1780s–1917, Entry 297, LR 1863–94, ACP Branch Records, NARA, Washington, DC.
2. July 1876 PR, Fort Sanders, WY, Roll 1094; July 1876 PR, Fort Ellis, MT, Roll 347, NAMP, *Returns from U.S. Military Posts*.
3. Palmer to Adjutant General, August 3, 1876, William P. Clark, File 4199 ACP 1876, RG 94.
4. August 1876 PR, Fort Ellis, MT, Roll 347, NAMP, *Returns from U.S. Military Posts*; William P. Clark, "Memo: Of a Voyage from Benson's Landing on the Yellowstone, 27 Miles from Fort Ellis, to the Mouth of Powder River," Helena, Montana Historical Society.
5. Clark, "Memo"; "The Sioux War," *New York Herald*, August 24, 1876; John S. Gray, *Centennial Campaign: The Sioux War of 1876* (Norman: University of Oklahoma Press, 1988), 222.
6. Clark, "Memo"; Gray, *Centennial Campaign*, 222; Paul L. Hedren, *Great Sioux War Orders of Battle: How the United States Army Waged War on the Northern Plains, 1876–1877* (Norman: University of Oklahoma Press, 2011), 59, 117–18.
7. Gray, *Centennial Campaign*, 223; "The Sioux War," *New York Herald*, August 24, 1876.
8. Gray, *Centennial Campaign*, 223–24; Clark, "Memo."

9. Clark, "Memo."
10. Ibid.
11. Gray, *Centennial Campaign*, 220; Robinson, *The Diaries of John Gregory Bourke* 2:72.
12. Robinson, *The Diaries of John Gregory Bourke*, 2:72.
13. Ibid., 2:72–73; Gray, *Centennial Campaign*, 220.
14. Robinson, *The Diaries of John Gregory Bourke*, 2:72–73.
15. Ibid., 2:80, 82.
16. Jerome A. Greene, *Slim Buttes, 1876: An Episode of the Great Sioux War* (Norman: University of Oklahoma Press, 1982), 15–17; Charles M. Robinson III, *A Good Year to Die: The Story of the Great Sioux War* (New York: Random House, 1995), 56–57.
17. Robinson, *The Diaries of John Gregory Bourke*, 2:85.
18. Greene, *Slim Buttes*, 13–31.
19. Ibid., 31–37; Thaddeus Hurlbut Capron, *Marching with General Crook*, ed. Ray Meketa (Douglas, AK: Cheechako Press, 1983), 52–59; Jerome A. Greene, *Yellowstone Command: Colonel Nelson A. Miles and the Great Sioux War, 1876–77* (Lincoln: University of Nebraska Press, 1991), 53–55, 61–63.
20. Greene, *Slim Buttes*, 39–42; "An Old Campaigner," *Daily Inter Ocean* (Chicago), May 6, 1883.
21. "An Old Campaigner."
22. W. P. Clark, *The Indian Sign Language* (Lincoln: University of Nebraska Press, 1982), 186.
23. Greene, *Slim Buttes*, 44–48; Capron, *Marching with General Crook*, 59.
24. Greene, *Slim Buttes*, 66–68. The following description of the attack on Slim Buttes is also from this source (51, 56–68).
25. Ibid., 68–70; Capron, *Marching with General Crook*, 60.
26. Greene, *Slim Buttes*, 71–75.
27. Ibid., 75–76; Gray, *Centennial Campaign*, 248.
28. Fred A. Hunt, "A Purposeful Picnic," *Pacific Monthly* 19, no. 3 (March 1908): 236–37.
29. Greene, *Slim Buttes*, 76.
30. Ibid., 77–80.
31. Charles King, *Campaigning with Crook* (Norman: University of Oklahoma Press, 1964), 113.
32. Ibid., 81–88; Capron, *Marching with General Crook*, 60.
33. Greene, *Slim Buttes*, 88–90.
34. "An Old Campaigner."
35. Greene, *Slim Buttes*, 93–97, 99–102; Capron, *Marching with General Crook*, 60–61.
36. John F. Finerty, *War-Path and Bivouac: The Big Horn and Yellowstone Expedition*, ed. Milo Milton Quaife (Lincoln: University of Nebraska Press, 1966), 308.
37. Capron, *Marching with General Crook*, 60–61; Greene, *Slim Buttes*, 102–3.
38. Capron, *Marching with General Crook*, 61; Greene, *Slim Buttes*, 103–5.
39. Capron, *Marching with General Crook*, 61–62.
40. Greene, *Slim Buttes*, 107–8; Robinson, *The Diaries of John Gregory Bourke*, 2:130.
41. Greene, *Slim Buttes*, 108–9; Robinson, *The Diaries of John Gregory Bourke*, 2:130–36.

42. Finerty, *War-path and Bivouac: The Big Horn*, 325.
43. Greene, *Slim Buttes*, 109.
44. Finerty, *War-path and Bivouac: The Big Horn*, 333.
45. Robinson, *The Diaries of John Gregory Bourke*, 2:144.
46. Greene, *Slim Buttes*, 111.

CHAPTER 4

1. Joe De Barthe, *Life and Adventures of Frank Grouard*, ed. Edgar I. Stewart (Norman: University of Oklahoma Press, 1958), 163–64.
2. Robinson, *The Diaries of John Gregory Bourke*, 2:152–54.
3. Dan L. Thrapp, *Encyclopedia of Frontier Biography*, 4 vols. (Glendale, CA: Arthur H. Clark Co., 1988, 1994), 1:387; Heitman, *Historical Register and Dictionary*, 1:365.
4. Hedren, *Great Sioux War Orders of Battle*, 141.
5. Donald F. Danker, ed., *Man of the Plains: Recollections of Luther North, 1856–1882* (Lincoln: University of Nebraska Press, 1961), 207.
6. Ibid., 208–10.
7. Wayne R. Kime, ed., *The Powder River Expedition Journals of Colonel Richard Irving Dodge* (Norman: University of Oklahoma Press, 1997), 4–5, 8, 13.
8. Robinson, *The Diaries of John Gregory Bourke*, 2:151, 168–170; Danker, *Man of the Plains*, 210–11.
9. Robinson, *The Diaries of John Gregory Bourke*, 2:175–79.
10. Ibid., 2:180–81; Cyrus Townsend Brady, *Indian Fights and Fighters* (Lincoln: University of Nebraska Press, 1971), 313.
11. Danker, *Man of the Plains*, 211.
12. Richard E. Jensen, ed., *Voices of the American West*, vol. 1, *The Indian Interviews of Eli S. Ricker, 1903–1919* (Lincoln: University of Nebraska Press, 2005), 27.
13. Danker, *Man of the Plains*, 212; Kime, *The Powder River Expedition Journals*, 20; Robinson, *The Diaries of John Gregory Bourke*, 2:182, 187, 196.
14. Clark, *The Indian Sign Language*, 5.
15. Robinson, *The Diaries of John Gregory Bourke*, 2:182.
16. Clark, *The Indian Sign Language*, 82.
17. Robinson, *The Diaries of John Gregory Bourke*, 2:182–85; Danker, *Man of the Plains*, 212–17; Jensen, *The Indian Interviews of Eli S. Ricker*, 30–33.
18. Robinson, *The Diaries of John Gregory Bourke*, 2:186–90; Jensen, *The Indian Interviews of Eli S. Ricker*, 33.
19. Thomas R. Buecker, *Fort Robinson and the American West, 1874–1899* (Lincoln: Nebraska State Historical Society, 1999), 72.
20. Robinson, *The Diaries of John Gregory Bourke*, 2:186, 186n8, 187; Danker, *Man of the Plains*, 217n16; Jensen, *The Indian Interviews of Eli S. Ricker*, 32.
21. Robinson, *The Diaries of John Gregory Bourke*, 2:186, 188–91.
22. Ibid., 2:196–200.
23. Clark, *The Indian Sign Language*, 421.

24. Robinson, *The Diaries of John Gregory Bourke*, 2:198, 201–7; Kime, *The Powder River Expedition Journals*, 23.
25. Robinson, *The Diaries of John Gregory Bourke*, 2:207–27; Kime, *The Powder River Expedition Journals*, 25.
26. Jensen, *The Indian Interviews of Eli S. Ricker*, 44.
27. Robinson, *The Diaries of John Gregory Bourke*, 2:220–23.
28. Clark, *The Indian Sign Language*, 423.
29. Clark to Mason, December 21, 1876, Box A-351, General Correspondence, Rosebud Agency, RG 75, Records of the BIA, NARA, Kansas City, MO.
30. Robinson, *The Diaries of John Gregory Bourke*, 2:216.
31. Ibid., 2:227–36; Jensen, *The Indian Interviews of Eli S. Ricker*, 44–45; January 1877 PR, Fort Robinson, NE, Roll 1028, NAMP, *Returns from U.S. Military Posts*.
32. Clark, *The Indian Sign Language*, 5.

CHAPTER 5

1. Buecker, *Fort Robinson and the American West*, 14–16, 20–24.
2. Robinson, *The Diaries of John Gregory Bourke*, 2:245.
3. Thomas Powers, *The Killing of Crazy Horse* (New York: Vintage Books, 2011), 250–51; Jensen, *The Indian Interviews of Eli S. Ricker*, 45.
4. Clark to Bourke, March 3, 8, and 9, 1877, NAMP, *SF, MDM*, Publication No. M1495, Roll 4, RG 393, Records of United States Army Continental Commands, 1821–1920.
5. Powers, *The Killing of Crazy Horse*, 250–53.
6. Robinson, *The Diaries of John Gregory Bourke*, 2:241–45; George E. Hyde, *Red Cloud's Folk: A History of the Oglala Sioux Indians* (Norman: University of Oklahoma Press, 1975), 289.
7. George E. Hyde, *Spotted Tail's Folk: A History of the Brule Sioux* (Norman: University of Oklahoma Press, 1974), 267–68.
8. Clark to Bourke, March 3, 8, and 9, 1877, NAMP, *SF, MDM*; Clark to Bourke, February 24, 1877, Box 49, DP, Entry 3731, LR, 1877, RG 393, Part 1, NARA, Washington, DC.
9. Clark to Bourke, March 13, 1877, ibid.
10. Clark to Bourke, March 13 and 14, 1877, ibid.
11. Jensen, *The Indian Interviews of Eli S. Ricker*, 46–47. The following discussion of Clark's meeting with Red Cloud is also from this source.
12. Ibid., 46.
13. Robinson, *The Diaries of John Gregory Bourke*, 2:251.
14. Clark to Bourke, March 28, 1877, Box 49, DP, Entry 3731, LR, 1877, RG 393.
15. Robinson, *The Diaries of John Gregory Bourke*, 2:266.
16. Clark to Bourke, April 2, 1877, Box 49, DP, Entry 3731, LR, 1877, RG 393.
17. Buecker, *Fort Robinson and the American West*, 99.
18. Clark to Bourke, April 2, 1877.
19. Robinson, *The Diaries of John Gregory Bourke*, 2:253.
20. Clark, *The Indian Sign Language*, 154.

21. Hyde, *Red Cloud's Folk*, 291; Robinson, *The Diaries of John Gregory Bourke*, 2:255–61.
22. Herman J. Viola, "Reily's Ring," in *Little Bighorn Remembered: The Untold Indian Story of Custer's Last Stand* (New York: Times Books, 1999), 182–85.
23. Robinson, *The Diaries of John Gregory Bourke*, 2:254; 4:107–8.
24. William Van Wyck Reily, File 4087 ACP 1875, NAMP, *LR by the ACP Branch, 1871–1894*, Publication No. M1395, RG 94, Records of the AGO, 1780s–1917.
25. Viola, *Little Bighorn Remembered*, 182–85; William Van Wyck Reily, File 4087 ACP 1875.
26. Endorsement by Clark, AAG, MDM to Clark, April 14, 1877, William Van Wyck Reily, File 4087 ACP 1875.
27. Robinson, *The Diaries of John Gregory Bourke*, 2:265–66.
28. Buecker, *Fort Robinson and the American West*, 93; Crook to Sheridan, telegram, April 21, 1877, DP, Telegrams Sent by Gen. George Crook's ADC, 1877–78, Entry 3727, RG 393, Part 1; Clark to Bourke, April 21, 1877, Box 49, DP, Entry 3731, LR, 1877, RG 393.
29. Robinson, *The Diaries of John Gregory Bourke*, 2:274.
30. Clark to Bourke, April 21, 1877.
31. Robinson, *The Diaries of John Gregory Bourke*, 2:277–79; Crook to Sheridan, telegram, April 27, 1877, DP, Telegrams Sent by Gen. George Crook's ADC, 1877–78.
32. Powers, *The Killing of Crazy Horse*, 261.
33. Clark, *The Indian Sign Language*, 295.
34. Ibid., 295–96.
35. Richard G. Hardorff, ed., *The Death of Crazy Horse: A Tragic Episode in Lakota History* (Lincoln: University of Nebraska Press, 2001), 139.
36. "Crazy Horse with Us," *Chicago Times*, May 7, 1877, ibid., 201.
37. Powers, *The Killing of Crazy Horse*, 263.
38. Jensen, *The Indian Interviews of Eli S. Ricker*, 47.
39. Bruce R. Liddic and Paul Harbaugh, eds., *Custer & Company: Walter Camp's Notes on the Custer Fight* (Lincoln: University of Nebraska Press, 1998), 126.
40. Kingsley M. Bray, *Crazy Horse: A Lakota Life* (Norman: University of Oklahoma Press, 2006), 281–84; Buecker, *Fort Robinson and the American West*, 94–95; Robinson, *The Diaries of John Gregory Bourke*, 2:297–98.
41. R. Williams, AAG, DP to AAG, MDM, telegram, May 7, 1877, NAMP, *SF, MDM*.
42. Thomas R. Buecker and R. Eli Paul, eds., *The Crazy Horse Surrender Ledger* (Lincoln: Nebraska State Historical Society, 1994), 14.
43. Kingsley M. Bray, "We Belong to the North: The Flights of the Northern Indians from the White River Agencies, 1877–1878," *Montana The Magazine of Western History* 55, no. 2 (Summer 2005): 31.

CHAPTER 6

1. Paul Andrew Hutton, *Phil Sheridan and His Army* (Lincoln: University of Nebraska Press, 1985), 35, 254.

2. "Crazy Horse with Us," *Chicago Times*, May 7, 1877, reprinted in Hardorff, *The Death of Crazy Horse*, 202.
3. "Gen. Jesse M. Lee's Account of the Killing of Chief Crazy Horse at Fort Robinson, Nebr.," in E. A. Brininstool, ed., *Crazy Horse: The Invincible Ogalalla Sioux Chief* (Los Angeles: Wetzel Publishing Co., 1949), 16–17.
4. "Incidents of the Surrender," *Denver Daily* Tribune, May 18, 1877, in Hardorff, *The Death of Crazy Horse*, 216.
5. Buecker, *Fort Robinson and the American West*, 99.
6. Jensen, *The Indian Interviews of Eli S. Ricker*, 49.
7. Crook to AAG, MDM, May 18, 1877, NAMP, *LR by the Office of the AG, 1871–1880*, File 1929 AGO 1876, Roll 259, 1876.
8. Jensen, *The Indian Interviews of Eli S. Ricker*, 49; Hardorff, *The Death of Crazy Horse*, 94.
9. Jensen, *The Indian Interviews of Eli S. Ricker*, 49.
10. Thomas B. Marquis, *Wooden Leg: A Warrior Who Fought Custer* (Lincoln: University of Nebraska Press, 1962), 299–304 (quotation on 304).
11. Ibid., 305–6.
12. Buecker, *Fort Robinson and the American West*, 98–99; Jensen, *The Indian Interviews of Eli S. Ricker*, 51–52.
13. Bray, *Crazy Horse*, 302–3.
14. Ibid., 303–4; Powers, *The Killing of Crazy Horse*, 274–76.
15. Bray, *Crazy Horse*, 303–4.
16. Ibid., 304; Jensen, *The Indian Interviews of Eli S. Ricker*, 53.
17. Bray, *Crazy Horse*, 306–7; Thrapp, *Encyclopedia of Frontier Biography*, 1:157.
18. Crook to Sheridan, telegram, May 29, 1877, NAMP, SF, MDM.
19. Endorsement by Clark, AAG, DP, to Clark, June 25, 1877, Box 51, DP, LR, June–July 1877, Entry 3731, RG 393, Part 1.
20. Crook to Sheridan, telegrams, May 29 and 30, 1877, NAMP, SF, MDM.
21. Powers, *The Killing of Crazy Horse*, 343; W. P. Clark to W. S. Schuyler, telegram, June 13, 1877, NAMP, SF, MDM.
22. Clark to AG, DP, July 3, 1877, Document 3668, LR, DP, 1877.
23. Bray, *Crazy Horse*, 308–9.
24. Clark to Schuyler, June 10, 1877, NAMP, SF, MDM. The following quotations from Clark to Schuyler are also from this source.
25. Clark to Schuyler, June 11, 1877, ibid.
26. Clark to Schuyler, telegram, June 13, 1877, ibid.
27. Bray, *Crazy Horse*, 310.
28. Clark to Schuyler, telegram, June 17, 1877, NAMP, SF, MDM.
29. Powers, *The Killing of Crazy Horse*, 289–300; Robinson, *The Diaries of John Gregory Bourke*, 2:311–43.
30. Jensen, *The Indian Interviews of Eli S. Ricker*, 55.
31. Clark, *The Indian Sign Language*, 361. The following description of the sun dance is also from this source (361–62).

32. Ibid., 362.
33. Jensen, *The Indian Interviews of Eli S. Ricker*, 55.
34. Clark, *The Indian Sign Language*, 362. The following outline of the elements of the sun dance is from this same source (362–63).
35. Ibid., 362, 309, 249.
36. Ibid., 363.
37. Irwin to Acting Indian Agent, Spotted Tail Agency, July 7, 1877, Box A-351, RG 75, Records of the BIA, Rosebud Agency, General Correspondence, NARA, Kansas City.
38. Hardorff, *The Death of Crazy Horse*, 26n1, 94.
39. Jensen, *The Indian Interviews of Eli S. Ricker*, 58–59.
40. Mari Sandoz, *Crazy Horse: The Strange Man of the Oglalas* (Lincoln: University of Nebraska Press, 1961), 428.
41. Hardorff, *The Death of Crazy Horse*, 30n8.
42. Bray, *Crazy Horse*, 326.
43. Mari Sandoz to Eleanor Hinman, Thanksgiving [November 27], December 10, 1947; Hinman to Sandoz, December 7, 1947, Mari Sandoz Collection (MS 080), Archives and Special Collections, University of Nebraska–Lincoln Libraries.
44. Clark to AG, DP, July 13, 1877, Box 51, DP, LR, June–July 1877, RG 393, Part 1.
45. Powers, *The Killing of Crazy Horse*, 278; "Pictures of the Sioux Chiefs," *New York Tribune*, September 7, 1877, in Hardorff, *The Death of Crazy Horse*, 232.
46. Clark, *The Indian Sign Language*, 382.
47. Bray, *Crazy Horse*, 317; Bradley to Crook, July 16, 1877, Box 41, MDM, LR, 1866–91, Entry 2546, RG 393, Part 1.
48. Bray, *Crazy Horse*, 320–21; Shopp to Smith, August 15, 1877, in Hardorff, *The Death of Crazy* Horse, 169; Powers, *The Killing of Crazy Horse*, 344.
49. Bray, *Crazy Horse*, 321.
50. Ibid., 321–22; Shopp to Smith, August 15, 1877, in Hardorff, *The Death of Crazy Horse*, 169–70.
51. Powers, *The Killing of Crazy Horse*, 344–45.
52. Bray, *Crazy Horse*, 317–18.
53. Buecker, *Fort Robinson and the American West*, 107–8.
54. Clark to Crook, August 1, 1877 Box 41, MDM, LR.
55. Bray, *Crazy Horse*, 323.
56. Clark to Crook, August 18, 1877, in Hardorff, *The Death of Crazy Horse*, 172.
57. "Lee's Account," 18.
58. Irwin to Smith, August 4, 1877, in Hardorff, *The Death of Crazy Horse*, 167.
59. Bray, *Crazy Horse*, 326.
60. "Lee's Account," 19.
61. Bray, *Crazy Horse*, 323; Burke to Clark, August 8, 1877, in Hardorff, *The Death of Crazy Horse*, 168.
62. Burke to Clark, August 8, 1877, and Clark to Crook, August 18, 1877, in Hardorff, *The Death of Crazy Horse*, 168, 173.
63. Bray, *Crazy Horse*, 326–28.

CHAPTER 7

1. Clark to Crook, August 18, 1877, in Hardorff, *The Death of Crazy Horse*, 172.
2. Ibid.
3. Ibid., 172–73.
4. Clark, *The Indian Sign Language*, 234.
5. Robinson, *The Diaries of John Gregory Bourke*, 3:69–70, 504; Bray, *Crazy Horse*, 331.
6. Bray, *Crazy Horse*, 330–32. The following information on this dispute is also from this source (332–36).
7. Lt. Col. R. Williams, AAG, to Crook and Sheridan to Williams, telegrams, August 30, 1877, File 4163 AGO 1876, NAMP, *LR by the Office of the AG, 1871–1880*, Roll 282, 1876.
8. Bray, *Crazy Horse*, 338–39.
9. Powers, *The Killing of Crazy Horse*, 360–63.
10. Bray, *Crazy Horse*, 339–41.
11. Hardorff, *The Death of Crazy Horse*, 30–32.
12. Clark, *Indian Sign Language*, 223.
13. Clark to Burke, August 31, 1877, in "Lee's Account," 19–20.
14. "Lee's Account," 20.
15. Bray, *Crazy Horse*, 343.
16. Telegrams, August 31 and September 1, 1877, File 4163 AGO 1876, NAMP, *LR by the Office of the AG, 1871–1880*, Roll 282.
17. "Lee's Account," 20–22.
18. Ibid., 22–23.
19. Bray, *Crazy Horse*, 347.
20. Ibid., 351. The following information on the proposed meeting with Crazy Horse is also from this source (353–54).
21. Clark, *Indian Sign Language*, 130.
22. Jensen, *The Indian Interviews of Eli S. Ricker*, 66.
23. Ibid., 61; Robert A. Clark, ed., *The Killing of Chief Crazy Horse* (Lincoln: University of Nebraska Press, 1988), 77–78.
24. Clark, *The Killing of Chief Crazy Horse*, 78, 96–99.
25. Robinson, *The Diaries of John Gregory Bourke*, 3:74.
26. Jensen, *The Indian Interviews of Eli S. Ricker*, 61–62; John G. Bourke, *On the Border with Crook* (Lincoln: University of Nebraska Press, 1971), 420.
27. Bourke, *On the Border with Crook*, 420; Bray, *Crazy Horse*, 355.
28. Powers, *The Killing of Crazy Horse*, 387–88; Crook to Clark, telegram, September 4, 1877, DP, Entry 3727, Telegrams Sent by Gen. George Crook's ADC, 1877–78.
29. Powers, *The Killing of Crazy Horse*, 338.
30. Clark, *The Killing of Chief Crazy Horse*, 79–81.
31. Bray, *Crazy Horse*, 358.
32. Clark, *The Killing of Chief Crazy Horse*, 81.
33. Powers, *The Killing of Crazy Horse*, 378; Bray, *Crazy Horse*, 357, 359.
34. Powers, *The Killing of Crazy Horse*, 381.
35. Bray, *Crazy Horse*, 358; "Lee's Account," 24 (quotations).

36. Bray, *Crazy Horse*, 361–62.
37. E. A. Brininstool, ed., "Chief Crazy Horse, His Career and Death," *Nebraska History* 12, no. 1 (January–March 1929): 50.
38. Bray, *Crazy Horse*, 361–62; Powers, *The Killing of Crazy Horse*, 382.
39. Bray, *Crazy Horse*, 362–63.
40. Ibid., 363; Powers, *The Killing of Crazy Horse*, 385.
41. Bray, *Crazy Horse*, 364–65; Powers, *The Killing of Crazy Horse*, 386–87.
42. Bray, *Crazy Horse*, 365; Clark to Crook, September 4, 1877, in Hardorff, *The Death of Crazy Horse*, 177.
43. Bray, *Crazy Horse*, 365.
44. Clark to Crook, September 4, 1877, in Hardorff, *The Death of Crazy Horse*, 177.
45. Crook to Clark, telegram, September 4, 1877, Entry 3727, RG 393, Part 1.
46. Crook to Bradley, telegram, September 4, 1877, Entry 3727, RG 393, Part 1.
47. Clark to Lee, n.d., in "Lee's Account," 28.
48. Bray, *Crazy Horse*, 366–72.
49. "Lee's Account," 29.
50. Bray, *Crazy Horse*, 374.
51. James Regan, *Manual of Guard Duty and Kindred Subjects for the Regular Army, Volunteers and Militia of the United States: Being a Thorough Compilation of Rules, Regulations, and Principles, Collected from the Most Authentic Sources* (New York: Harper and Brothers, 1883), 61.
52. Bray, *Crazy Horse*, 379.
53. Clark to Crook, September 5, 1877, in Hardorff, *The Death of Crazy Horse*, 179.
54. Crook to Bradley, September 5, 1877, in Hardorff, *The Death of Crazy Horse*, 180.
55. Bray, *Crazy Horse*, 379.
56. Crook to Sheridan, September 5, 1877, in Hardorff, *The Death of Crazy Horse*, 180.
57. Buecker, *Fort Robinson and the American West*, 115–16.
58. Bray, *Crazy Horse*, 377–78; "Lee's Account," 29–30.
59. Clark to Lee, n.d., in "Lee's Account," 30.
60. Bray, *Crazy Horse*, 380.
61. Clark to Crook, September 5, 1877, in Hardorff, *The Death of Crazy Horse*, 181.
62. Bray, *Crazy Horse*, 381; Powers, *The Killing of Crazy Horse*, 407.
63. Bray, *Crazy Horse*, 381; "Lee's Account," 31–32.
64. Bray, *Crazy Horse*, 382–84.
65. Powers, *The Killing of Crazy Horse*, 412.
66. Ibid., 415–16; Bray, *Crazy Horse*, 385.
67. Powers, *The Killing of Crazy Horse*, 417; Bray, *Crazy Horse*, 385–86.
68. Clark, *The Killing of Chief Crazy Horse*, 66, 95.
69. Powers, *The Killing of Crazy Horse*, 417–19; Bray, *Crazy Horse*, 386–87.
70. Bray, *Crazy Horse*, 388–89.
71. Clark to Crook, September 5, 1877, in Hardorff, *The Death of Crazy Horse*, 181.
72. Bray, *Crazy Horse*, 389.
73. Clark to Crook, September 5, 1877, 182.

74. Bourke to Clark, telegram, n.d., Entry 3727, RG 393, Part 1.
75. Powers, *The Killing of Crazy Horse*, 422–26; Bradley to AG, DP, September 7, 1877, in Hardorff, *The Death of Crazy Horse*, 184 (quotation).
76. Jensen, *The Indian Interviews of Eli S. Ricker*, 300–301 (quotation); Liddic and Harbaugh, *Custer & Company*, 135, 150.
77. Clark, *Indian Sign Language*, 155.
78. Jesse M. Lee, diary entry for September 6, 1877, in Brininstool, *Crazy Horse*, 39.
79. "Newspaper Account of the Murder of Chief Crazy Horse, Written by Mrs. Lucy W. Lee, Wife of General Lee, from Camp Sheridan," September 18, 1877, in Brininstool, *Crazy Horse*, 69.
80. "Dr. V. T. McGillycuddy's Recollections of the Death of Crazy Horse," in Brininstool, *Crazy Horse*, 47.
81. Clark to Crook, September 6, 1877, in Hardorff, *The Death of Crazy Horse*, 183.
82. Clark to Crook, September 9, 1877, Box 53, DP, Entry 3731, LR, June-July 1877, RG 393, Part 1.
83. Crook to Clark, telegram, September 10, 1877, Entry 3727, RG 393, Part 1.
84. Clark to Commissioner of Indian Affairs, September 10, 1877, in Hardorff, *The Death of Crazy Horse*, 186–88.

CHAPTER 8

1. Clark to AG, DP, September 14, 1877, NAMP, *SF, MDM*.
2. Ibid.
3. Thomas R. Buecker, "Lt. William Philo Clark's Sioux War Report and Little Big Horn Map," *Greasy Grass* 7 (May 1991): 14.
4. Clark to AG, DP, September 14, 1877.
5. "Heap Big Injun," *National Republican* (Washington, DC), September 26, 1877.
6. Bray, *Crazy Horse*, 394.
7. NAMP, *LR by the Office of the AG, 1871–1880*, File 6031 AGO 1877, Roll 369, 1877.
8. "Indians—The Sioux Delegation," *Chicago Daily Tribune*, September 22, 1877.
9. "The Indians," *Chicago Daily Tribune*, September 23, 1877.
10. "Big Injuns," *National Republican* (Washington, DC), September 25, 1877; "Heap Big Injun," *National Republican* (Washington, DC), September 26, 1877 (quotation).
11. "Heap Big Injun."
12. "The Sioux Delegation," *National Republican* (Washington, DC), September 27, 1877.
13. "The Sioux at the White House," *Evening Star* (Washington, DC), September 27, 1877.
14. Ibid.
15. "The Sioux Council," *New York Tribune*, September 29, 1877.
16. "Another Conclave," *National Republican* (Washington, DC), September 29, 1877.
17. "The Sioux Delegation"; "The Sioux Nation," *New York Herald*, October 1, 1877.
18. "A Final Talk with the Sioux," *New York Tribune*, October 2, 1877.
19. Ibid.; "The Indians at the White House," *National Republican* (Washington, DC), October 2, 1877.
20. "The Indian Chiefs Again," *New York Tribune*, October 3, 1877; "The Indian Delegations," *New York Times*, October 3, 1877.

21. "The Indian Chiefs Again"; "The Indian Delegations."
22. Clark to Mallery, November 5, 1879, W. P. Clark Letters, 1879–81, BAE, LR, 1879–88, NAA, Smithsonian Institution, Washington, DC.
23. "Departure of the Sioux," *National Republican* (Washington, DC), October 4, 1877; "Twenty-Three Red Warriors," *New York Times*, October 5, 1877; "Indian Chiefs in New York," *New York Tribune*, October 5, 1877.
24. "Farewell to the Braves," *New York Times*, October 6, 1877.
25. File 6119 AGO 1877, NAMP, *LR by the Office of the AG, 1871–1880*, Roll 369, 1877.
26. "Farewell to the Braves"; "Farewell to the Indians," *New York Tribune*, October 6, 1877.
27. "The Indian Chiefs," *Chicago Daily Tribune*, October 8, 1877.
28. Bray, "We Belong to the North," 34, 34n12, 39.
29. Ibid., 32, 34, 37.
30. Clark to Secretary of Interior Carl Schurz, November 7, 1877, NAMP, *LR by the Office of Indian Affairs, 1824–1881*, Publication No. M234, RG 75, Records of the BIA, 1793–1989, Roll 841, Spotted Tail Agency, 1875–80.
31. Lawson to AG, DP, December 4, 1877, Box 54, DP, Entry 3731, LR, 1877, RG 393, Part 1.
32. Clark to Schurz, November 7, 1877.
33. Bray, "We Belong to the North," 37–38.
34. Clark to Schurz, November 7, 1877.
35. Ibid.
36. Bray, "We Belong to the North," 37, 40.
37. Lawson to AG, DP, December 4, 1877.
38. Clark to Crook, telegram, November 2, 1877, File 4163 AGO 1876, NAMP, *LR by the Office of the AG, 1871–1880*, Roll 283, 1876.
39. Bray, "We Belong to the North," 38, 40.
40. Fanny McGillycuddy "The Diary of Fanny McGillycuddy, April 11, 1977–October 31, 1878," November 11, 1877, South Dakota State Historical Society, Pierre.
41. Mari Sandoz to Eleanor Hinman, Thanksgiving [November 27], December 10, 1947; Hinman to Sandoz, December 7, 1947: Mari Sandoz Collection (MS 080).
42. McGillycuddy, "The Diary," November 16, 1877.
43. Bray, "We Belong to the North," 40–41.
44. Lawson to AG, DP, December 4, 1877.
45. Bray, "We Belong to the North," 41.
46. Lawson to AG, DP, December 4, 1877.
47. Bray, "We Belong to the North," 41–42.
48. Clark to J. H. Hammond, telegram, November 24, 1877, NAMP, *LR by the Office of Indian Affairs, 1824–1881*, Roll 721, Red Cloud Agency, 1871–80, Year 1877; Lawson to AG, DP, December 4, 1877.
49. November 1877 PR, Red Cloud Agency, D.T., Roll 1535, NAMP, *Returns from U.S. Military Posts*.
50. Sheridan to Sherman, telegram, December 1, 1877, File 4163 AGO 1876, *LR by the Office of the AG, 1871–1880*, Roll 283.

51. Powers, *The Killing of Crazy Horse*, 431.
52. Brig. Gen. Alfred H. Terry to Col. Nelson A. Miles, telegram, January 10, 1878; Gen. William T. Sherman endorsement of telegram, File 4163 AGO 1876, *LR by the Office of the AG, 1871–1880*, Roll 284 (quotation).
53. November 1877 PR and January 1878 PR, Red Cloud Agency, D.T., Roll 1535, NAMP *Returns from U.S. Military Posts*.
54. McGillycuddy, "The Diary," December 31, 1877, January 1, 1878.
55. SO 6, January 17, 1878, SO, MDM, vol. 343.
56. Bray, "We Belong to the North," 43.
57. McGillycuddy, "The Diary," January 7, 1878.
58. "The New Indian Agencies," *New York Times*, January 15, 1878.
59. Jeffrey Ostler, *The Plains Sioux and U.S. Colonialism from Lewis and Clark to Wounded Knee* (Cambridge: Cambridge University Press, 2004), 122–26.

CHAPTER 9

1. SO 5, January 16, 1878, SO, MDM, vol. 343.
2. W. P. Clark to Dr. Valentine McGillycuddy, January 27, 1878, Miscellaneous Correspondence Received, Pine Ridge Agency, RG 75, Records of the BIA, NARA, Kansas City, MO.
3. Representative G. A. Bagley to AG E. D. Townsend, January 28, 1878; George Crook to President Rutherford B. Hayes, telegram, January 29, 1878, William P. Clark, File 330 ACP 1877.
4. Representative A. G. McCook to Hayes, February 10, 1878; Crook to AG, February 23, 1878, ibid.
5. Clark to AG, DD, April 1, 1878, Box 58, DD, LR, RG 393, Part 1.
6. SO 33, April 20, 1878, SO, MDM, vol. 343, 1878–79; SO 48, April 23, 1878, SO, DD, vol. 192, Entry 44; Robert W. Frazer, *Forts of the West* (Norman: University of Oklahoma Press, 1965), 67–68.
7. May 1878 PR, Fort Snelling, MN, Roll 1197, NAMP, *Returns from U.S. Military Posts*.
8. June 1878 RR, Second Cavalry, Roll 19, NAMP, *Returns from Regular Army Cavalry Regiments*; Frazer, *Forts of the West*, 82.
9. Nelson A. Miles, *Personal Recollections and Observations of General Nelson A. Miles*, vol. 1 (Lincoln: University of Nebraska Press, 1992), 283, 286.
10. June 1878 RR, Second Cavalry, *Returns from Regular Army Cavalry Regiments*; July 1878 PR, Fort Keogh, MT, Roll 572, *Returns from U.S. Military Posts*.
11. July 1878 RR, Second Cavalry, *Returns from Regular Army Cavalry Regiments*.
12. July 1878 RR, Second Cavalry, *Returns from Regular Army Cavalry Regiments*; Testimony of Sergeant Haver Dollmair, November 20, 1878, NAMP, *LR by the Office of the AG, 1871–1880*, File 147 AGO 1879, Roll 455.
13. File 147 AGO 1879. The following discussion of this issue is also from this source (including the quotation).
14. Miles, *Personal Recollections*, 294–95 (quotation); James S. Brust and Lee H. Whittlesey, "Roughing It up the Yellowstone to Wonderland: The Nelson Miles/

Colgate Hoyt Party in Yellowstone National Park, September 1878," *Montana The Magazine of Western History* 46, no. 1 (Spring 1996): 56–57.
15. Brust and Whittlesey, "Roughing It up the Yellowstone to Wonderland," 58–59*n*3; August 1878 PR, Fort Keogh, MT, *Returns from U.S. Military Posts*.
16. Brust and Whittlesey, "Roughing It up the Yellowstone to Wonderland," 56–57; Hunt, "A Purposeful Picnic," caption and group photo opposite 233; Carroll Van West, "Roughing It up the Yellowstone to Wonderland: An Account of a Trip through the Yellowstone Valley in 1878," *Montana The Magazine of Western History* 36, no. 2 (Spring 1986): 28.
17. Brust and Whittlesey, "Roughing It up the Yellowstone to Wonderland," 56–57; Van West, "Roughing It up the Yellowstone to Wonderland," 23–24, 28; "The Custer Battlefield," *Cleveland Leader*, September 11, 1878.
18. Van West, "Roughing It up the Yellowstone to Wonderland," 28.
19. "St. Paul Ladies," *Saint Paul Daily Globe*, September 12, 1878.
20. "John B. Sanborn," *Wikipedia*, last modified October 8, 2016, https://en.wikipedia.org/wiki/John_B._Sanborn.
21. Clark, *The Indian Sign Language*, 405.
22. "Telegraph to Tribune," *Bismarck* (ND) *Tribune*, November 12, 1880.
23. Hunt, "A Purposeful Picnic," 233; "Gen. Miles' Victory," *Daily Inter Ocean* (Chicago), September 13, 1878; First Lt. Frank D. Baldwin to Clark, August 13, 1878, and Baldwin to Commanding Officer, Fort Custer, August 13, 1878, Letter Book, DY, August 6, 1878 to August 1879, RG 393, Part 3, Entry 889.
24. "Gen. Miles' Victory."
25. Jerome A. Greene, *Yellowstone Command: Colonel Nelson A. Miles and the Great Sioux War, 1876–1877* (Lincoln: University of Nebraska Press, 1991), 208–10.
26. "Gen. Miles' Victory."
27. "The Custer Battlefield."
28. Hunt, "A Purposeful Picnic," 233, 245; "Gen. Miles' Victory."
29. Van West, "Roughing It up the Yellowstone to Wonderland," 29–31; "Upper Yellowstone," *Cleveland Leader*, September 19, 1878; Baldwin to Lt. Col. George P. Buell, August 20, 1878, Letter Book, DY.
30. "Upper Yellowstone."
31. George F. Brimlow, *The Bannock Indian War of 1878* (Caldwell, ID: The Caxton Printers, 1938), 8.
32. Ibid., 182; "Upper Yellowstone"; Miles, *Personal Recollections*, 295–96.
33. "Upper Yellowstone"; "On the Warpath," *Cleveland Leader*, October 2, 1878.
34. "On the Warpath." The following account of the encounter with the Bannocks is also from this source.
35. Baldwin to Clark, September 1, 1878, Letter Book, DY.
36. "On the Warpath."
37. Miles, *Personal Recollections*, 297–300; George W. Webb, *Chronological List of Engagements between the Regular Army of the United States and Various Tribes of Hostile Indians Which Occurred during the Years 1790 to 1898, Inclusive* (St. Joseph, MO: Wing Printing and Publishing Co., 1939), 84.

38. Miles, *Personal Recollections*, 300.
39. "The Yellowstone Park," *Cleveland Leader*, October 10, 1878; Van West, "Roughing It up the Yellowstone to Wonderland," 32; Brust and Whittlesey, "Roughing It up the Yellowstone to Wonderland," 58.
40. Brust and Whittlesey, "Roughing It up the Yellowstone to Wonderland," 59; "The Yellowstone Park."
41. "Yellowstone Expedition," *Daily Inter Ocean* (Chicago), October 10, 1878.
42. "The Yellowstone Park"; Brust and Whittlesey, "Roughing It up the Yellowstone to Wonderland," 61–63.
43. "The Yellowstone Park."; Brust and Whittlesey, "Roughing It up the Yellowstone to Wonderland," 63.
44. "The Yellowstone Park."
45. Miles, *Personal Recollections*, 305.
46. Brust and Whittlesey, "Roughing It up the Yellowstone to Wonderland," 63; "An Alarming Report," *Cleveland Leader*, September 12, 1878; "The Indians Bagged," *Cleveland Leader*, September 13, 1878.
47. Van West, "Roughing It up the Yellowstone to Wonderland," 33–34; "Miles Excursion Party," *Cleveland Leader*, October 29, 1878; "Wild Sport in Montana," *Cleveland Leader*, November 20, 1878; "Gen. Nelson A. Miles" and "Personal," *Independent Record* (Helena, MT), September 24, 1878.

CHAPTER 10

1. October and November 1878 RR, Second Cavalry, Roll 19, NAMP, *Returns from Regular Army Cavalry Regiments*; October 1878 PR, Fort Keogh, MT, Roll 572, NAMP, *Returns from U.S. Military Posts*; SO 119, October 9, 1878, DD, SO, vol. 192, Entry 44, RG 94; First Lt. Frank D. Baldwin to First Lt. W. E. Kingsbury, October 13, 1878, Baldwin to Maj. E. M. Baker, October 13, 1878, and Baldwin to Baker, November 2, 1878, Letter Book, DY, August 6, 1878 to August 1879, RG 393, Part 3, Records of the United States Army Continental Commands, 1821–1920, Entry 889, NARA, Washington, D.C.
2. November 1878 RR, Second Cavalry, *Returns from Regular Army Cavalry Regiments*.
3. Clark, *Indian Sign Language*, 381–82.
4. Clark to Acting AAG, Headquarters, DY, November 27, 1878, NAMP, File 37 AGO 1879, Roll 454.
5. Ibid.
6. Clark to Dr. Valentine McGillycuddy, December 1, 1878, Miscellaneous Correspondence Received, Pine Ridge Agency.
7. NAMP, File 4362 AGO 1879, *LR by the Office of the AG, 1871–1880*, Roll 518.
8. Thomas W. Dunlay, *Wolves for the Blue Soldiers: Indian Scouts and Auxiliaries with the United States Army, 1860–90* (Lincoln: University of Nebraska Press, 1982), 201.
9. Clark to Brig. Gen. Alfred H. Terry, January 25, 1879, Box 61, DD, LR, June–July 1877, RG 393, Part 1.
10. Ibid.

11. Richard Upton, comp. and ed., *The Indian as a Soldier at Fort Custer, Montana* (El Segundo, CA: Upton and Sons, 1983), 20, 121–23; Dunlay, *Wolves for the Blue Soldiers*, 195–96.
12. January and February 1879 PR, Fort Keogh, MT, Roll 572, NAMP, *Returns from U.S. Military Posts*; Robinson, *The Diaries of John Gregory Bourke*, 1:424.
13. Douglas C. McChristian, *Uniforms, Arms, and Equipment: The U.S. Army on the Western Frontier, 1880–1892* (Norman: University of Oklahoma Press, 2007), 13–15.
14. Clark to Recorder, Board of Equipments, February 20, 1879, NAMP, File 7721 AGO 1878, *LR by the Office of the AG, 1871–1880*, Roll 441.
15. McChristian, *Uniforms, Arms, and Equipment*, 15.
16. Clark to First Lt. William C. Rawolle, February 23, 1879, James T. Peale, File 2626 ACP 1876, Box 707, Folder 2, RG 94, Entry 297, LR 1863–94, ACP Branch Records, NARA, Washington, DC.
17. Lt. Col. J. N. G. Whistler to HQ, DD, telegram, March 22, 1879, NAMP, File 6470 AGO 1878, *LR by the Office of the AG, 1871–1880*, Roll 430; Nelson A. Miles, 1879 Yellowstone District Annual Report, September 1879, NAMP, *LR by the Office of the AG, 1871–1880*, Roll 545.
18. Heitman, *Historical Register and Dictionary*, 601, 962.
19. Clark to Post Adjutant, Fort Keogh, April 2, 1879, File 6470 AGO 1878, Roll 430.
20. John H. Monnett, *Tell Them We Are Going Home: The Odyssey of the Northern Cheyennes* (Norman: University of Oklahoma Press, 2001), 24–25, 27–38, 43–103.
21. Ibid., 106, 109–10.
22. Clark to Post Adjutant, Fort Keogh, April 2, 1879, File 6470 AGO 1878, Roll 430.
23. Monnett, *Tell Them We Are Going Home*, 113–14, 122–61.
24. Clark, *The Indian Sign Language*, 80.
25. Monnett, *Tell Them We Are Going Home*, 162–65.
26. Clark to Post Adjutant, Fort Keogh, April 2, 1879, File 6470 AGO 1878, Roll 430. The following account of Clark's pursuit of Little Wolf's band is also from this source (including quotations).
27. Lt. Gen. P. H. Sheridan to AG E. D. Townsend, telegram, April 2, 1879, File 6470 AGO 1878, Roll 430.
28. Clark to Post Adjutant, Fort Keogh, April 2, 1879, ibid.
29. Ibid.
30. "Indian Affairs," *Army and Navy Journal*, May 3, 1879.
31. "Indian Affairs," *Army and Navy Journal*, May 17, 1879.
32. Clark to AG, DD, April 6, 1879, File 6470 AGO 1878, Roll 430.
33. Ibid.; Monnett, *Tell Them We Are Going Home*, 170.
34. Clark to AG, DD, April 6, 1879, File 6470 AGO 1878, Roll 430. The following discussion of Clark's defense of Little Wolf's band is also from this source (including quotations).
35. Ibid.; Monnett, *Tell Them We Are Going Home*, 191.
36. Clark, *The Indian Sign Language*, 106.
37. Clark to AG, DD, May 26, 1879, Box 62, DD, LR, RG 393, Part 1.
38. Ibid.; Whistler to AAG, DD, May 30, 1879, and enclosed "Proceedings of a Board of Officers," Box 61, DD, LR, RG 393, Part 1.

39. Clark to AG, DD, May 26, 1879.
40. Ovenshine and Bailey Affidavit enclosed with Clark to AG, DD, May 26, 1879.
41. Whistler to AAG, DD, May 30, 1879, and enclosed endorsement by Whistler, May 8, 1879; Clark to AG, DD, May 26, 1879.
42. Clark to AG, DD, May 26, 1879.
43. Whistler to AAG, DD, May 30, 1879, and enclosed endorsement by Whistler, May 8, 1879.
44. Clark to AG, DD, May 26, 1879.

CHAPTER 11

1. Crook to Col. William D. Whipple, telegram, May 24, 1879, and endorsement of AG E. D. Townsend, File 330 ACP 1877, RG 94, Entry 297.
2. AG E. D. Townsend endorsement of Crook telegram to Whipple.
3. Clark to AG, DD, June 1, 1879, File 3897 AGO 1879, NAMP, *LR by the Office of the AG, 1871–1880*, Roll 496.
4. Endorsements to Clark to AG, DD, June 1, 1879.
5. Endorsements to Clark to AG, DD, September 14, 1879, NAMP, File 3897 AGO 1879.
6. Crossman correspondence, ibid.
7. "The Line," *Army and Navy Journal*, May 24, 1879.
8. Mark H. Brown and W. R. Felton, *The Frontier Years: L. A. Huffman, Photographer of the Plains* (New York: Bramhall House, 1955), 41.
9. Dunlay, *Wolves for the Blue Soldiers*, 97.
10. Brown and Felton, *The Frontier Years*, 38–41.
11. June 1879 RR, Second Cavalry, Roll 19, NAMP, *Returns from Regular Army Cavalry Regiments*; June 1879 PR, Fort Keogh, MT, Roll 572, NAMP, *Returns from U.S. Military Posts*.
12. John F. Finerty, *War-Path and Bivouac; or, The Conquest of the Sioux* (Chicago: Donohue Brothers, 1890), 297–98, 319, 330–31; Greene, *Yellowstone Command*, 227; Miles to AG Ruggles, July 18, 1879, NAMP, *LR by the AG, 1871–1880*, File 4163 AGO 1876, Roll 286.
13. July 1879 PR, Fort Keogh, *Returns from U.S. Military Posts*; June and July 1879 RR, Second Cavalry, *Returns from Regular Army Cavalry Regiments*; Finerty, *War-Path and Bivouac; or, The Conquest*, 321–22; Miles, *Personal Recollections*, 310.
14. Finerty, *War-Path and Bivouac; or, The Conquest*, 322. The following account of the party's experiences is also from this source (321, 323–28, 333).
15. Ibid., 333–36; Nelson A. Miles, 1879 Yellowstone District Annual Report, September 1879, NAMP, *LR by the Office of the AG, 1871–1880*, Roll 545.
16. Miles, 1879 Yellowstone District Annual Report, September 1879.
17. Robert M. Utley, *The Lance and the Shield: The Life and Times of Sitting Bull* (New York: Henry Holt and Co., 1993), 208.
18. Edward J. McClernand, *With the Indian and the Buffalo in Montana, 1870–1878* (Glendale, CA: Arthur H. Clark Co., 1969), 109.
19. Utley, *The Lance and the Shield*, 208.
20. Ibid.; Miles, 1879 Yellowstone District Annual Report, September 1879.

21. McClernand, *With the Indian and the Buffalo*, 109–10.
22. George W. Baird, "General Miles's Indian Campaigns," in *Eyewitnesses to the Indian Wars, 1865–1890: The Army and the Indian*, vol. 5, ed. Peter Cozzens (Mechanicsburg, PA: Stackpole Books, 2005), 196.
23. Utley, *The Lance and the Shield*, 208; "Gen. Miles's Column," *Army and Navy Journal*, July 26, 1879.
24. Utley, *The Lance and the Shield*, 208.
25. Finerty, *War-Path and Bivouac; or, The Conquest*, 338–41; Miles to AG Ruggles, July 20, 1879, File 4163 AGO 1876, NAMP, *LR by the AG, 1871–1880*.
26. Clark, *The Indian Sign Language*, 203–4; Finerty, *War-Path and Bivouac; or, The Conquest*, 381.
27. Finerty, *War-Path and Bivouac; or, The Conquest*, 341–43, 350.
28. Ibid., 348–49; Capt. Frank D. Baldwin to Maj. E. M. Baker, July 30, 1879, Letter Book, DY, August 6, 1878, to August 1879, RG 393, Part 3, Entry 889; Utley, *The Lance and the Shield*, 186, 209–10; Miles, *Personal Recollections*, 310.
29. July 1879 RR, Second Cavalry, *Returns from Regular Army Cavalry Regiments*; Finerty, *War-Path and Bivouac; or, The Conquest*, 388–89, 392–93.
30. Miles, *Personal Recollections*, 310.
31. August 1879 RR, Second Cavalry, *Returns from Regular Army Cavalry Regiments*.
32. Miles to AAG Ruggles, August 19, 1879, File 4163 AGO 1876, NAMP, *LR by the AG, 1871–1880*; Baldwin to Maj. E. M. Baker, August 15, 1879, Baldwin to Clark, August 16, 1879, Baldwin to Lt. Col. Joseph N. G. Whistler, August 16, 1879 Letter Book, DY, August 8, 1879, to October 1880, RG 393, Part 3, Entry 889; August 1879 RR, Second Cavalry, *Returns from Regular Army Cavalry Regiments*.
33. SO 118, October 27, 1879, SO, DD, vol. 193, Entry 44.
34. Monnett, *Tell Them We Are Going Home*, 173–79.
35. Ibid., 180–82; Todd D. Epp, "The State of Kansas v. Wild Hog, et al.," *Kansas History: A Journal of the Central Plains* 5, no. 2 (Summer 1982): 143, 145.
36. "Personal," *Saint Paul (MN) Daily Globe*, October 27, 1879.

CHAPTER 12

1. November 1879 PR, Fort Keogh, MT, Roll 572, NAMP, *Returns from U.S. Military Posts*.
2. Martin F. Schmitt, ed., *General George Crook: His Autobiography* (Norman: University of Oklahoma Press, 1960), 220–21.
3. Thrapp, *Encyclopedia of Frontier Biography*, 2:933.
4. Clark to Garrick Mallery, November 5, 1879; cover to Clark to Mallery, December 10, 1879, W. P. Clark Letters, 1879–81, Smithsonian Institution, Washington, D.C., NAA, BAE, LR, 1879–88.
5. Thrapp, *Encyclopedia of Frontier Biography*, 3:1169.
6. Clark to John Wesley Powell, December 10, 1879, BAE, LR, 1879–88.
7. Ibid. and cover to the letter.
8. Clark to Powell, January 23, 1880, two letters under same date, BAE, LR, 1879–88.
9. Brown and Felton, *The Frontier Years*, 41.

10. Clark, *The Indian Sign Language*, 15.
11. W. P. Clark, "The Sign-Language of the North American Indians," *United Service* 3, no. 1 (July 1880): 23–33.
12. 1880 PR, Fort Keogh, *Returns from U.S. Military Posts*; James T. Peale, Reports of House Committees, 51st Cong., 1st sess., 1889–90, vol. 10, HR Rep. 3076.
13. Clark to AAG, DD, February 19, 1880, Box 64, DD, LR, RG 393, Part 1.
14. March 1880 PR, Fort Keogh, *Returns from U.S. Military Posts*.
15. Capt. Frank D. Baldwin to Miles, March 13, 1880, File 3677 AGO 1880, NAMP, *LR by the Office of the AG, 1871–1880*, Roll 568.
16. March 1880 PR, Fort Keogh, *Returns from U.S. Military Posts*; March 1880 RR, Second Cavalry, Roll 20, NAMP, *Returns from Regular Army Cavalry Regiments*.
17. Huggins Report, contained in Capt. E. L. Huggins to AAAG, DY, April 6, 1880, Box 65, DD, LR; and First Lt. John H. Coale to Post Adjutant, Fort Custer, April 15, 1880, Box 65, DD, LR, RG 383, Part 1.
18. Col. John W. Davidson to AAG, DD, April 2, 1880, File 4163 AGO 1876, NAMP, *LR by the Office of the AG, 1871–1880*, Roll 287.
19. Clark to Post Adjutant, Fort Keogh, April 7, 1880, Box 65, DD, LR. Clark erroneously dates his departure as April 3.
20. Ibid.; Huggins Report, April 6, 1880; Capt. Samuel T. Hamilton to AAAG, DY, April 7, 1880, Box 65, DD, LR.
21. Clark to Post Adjutant, Fort Keogh, April 7, 1880.
22. Maj. Guido Ilges to First Lt. Edmund Rice, Post Adjutant, Fort Keogh, June 10, 1880, File 3418 AGO 1880, NAMP, *LR by the Office of the AG, 1871–1880*, Roll 567.
23. General Orders 49, June 10, 1880, Orders and Circulars, 1797–1910, RG 94, NARA, Washington, DC.
24. Huggins to AG, July 1, 1880, File 3847 ACP 1880, RG 94, ACP Branch Records, NARA, Washington, DC.
25. "Gen. Liggett, 78, War Hero, Indian Fighter, Is Dead," *Chicago Daily News*, December 31, 1935.
26. Clark to AG, DD, October 7, 1880, File 7596 AGO 1880, NAMP, *LR by the Office of the AG, 1871–1880*, Roll 585; July 1880 PR, Fort McKinney, WY, Roll 703, *Returns from U.S. Military Posts*.
27. Clark to AG, DD, October 7, 1880.
28. Clark, *The Indian Sign Language*, 84.
29. Frazer, *Forts of the West*, 182–83.
30. Clark to AG, DD, October 7, 1880; Lt. Liggett Itinerary attached to Clark to AG, DD, October 7, 1880.
31. Clark to AG, DD, October 7, 1880; July and August 1880 PR, Fort McKinney, *Returns from U.S. Military Posts*.
32. Clark to AG, DD, October 7, 1880. The following description of the journey is also from this source.
33. Hedren, *Great Sioux War Orders of Battle*, 101; *War-Path and Bivouac: The Big Horn*, 173–96.

34. Clark to AG, DD, October 7, 1880. The following description and quotations from Clark are also from this source.
35. Ibid.; September 1880 PR, Fort Keogh, NAMP, *Returns from U.S. Military Posts*; Lt. Liggett Itinerary attached to Clark to AG, DD, October 7, 1880.

CHAPTER 13

1. September and October 1880 PR, Fort Keogh, MT, Roll 572, NAMP, *Returns from U.S. Military Posts*; October 1880 RR, Second Cavalry, Roll 20, NAMP, *Returns from Regular Army Cavalry Regiments*; SO 116, September 28, 1880, SO, DD, vol. 193.
2. October 1880 PR, Fort Keogh NAMP, *Returns from U.S. Military Posts*; Utley, *The Lance and the Shield*, 216; Col. N. A. Miles to AAG, DD, telegrams, October 28 and November 9, 1880, File 4163 AGO 1876, NAMP, *LR by the Office of the AG, 1871–1880*, Roll 288.
3. Miles to AAG, DD, November 16, 1880, File 4163 AGO 1876, NAMP, *LR by the Office of the AG, 1871–1880*.
4. SO 157, November 23, 1880, SO, DD, vol. 193.
5. "Telegraph to Tribune," *Bismarck* (ND) *Tribune*, November 12, 1880.
6. Ibid.; "Montana and Dakota," *Bismarck* (ND) *Tribune*, November 12, 1880.
7. "City Globules," *Saint Paul* (MN) *Daily Globe*, November 13, 1880; "Died" and "Personal," *Saint Paul* (MN) *Daily Globe*, December 6, 1880; "The City," *Chicago Daily Tribune*, December 9, 1880.
8. SO 120, December 9, 1880, SO, MDM, vol. 344.
9. Office of Chief Engineer, "Yellowstone National Park, Big Horn Mountains, and Adjacent Territory" (map, 1881) Chicago, MDM, Norman B. Leventhal Map Center, Boston Public Library, maps.bpl.org/id/16055.
10. Heitman, *Historical Register and Dictionary*, 477.
11. Monnett, *Tell Them We Are Going Home*, 195–98.
12. Clark, *The Indian Sign Language*, 401.
13. SO 126, December 22, 1880, SO, MDM, vol. 344.
14. Clark, *The Indian Sign Language*, 89; "Some Personal Items," *Army and Navy Journal*, January 1, 1881.
15. "Some Personal Items," *Army and Navy Journal*, February 12, 1881; Clark to John W. Powell, January 27, 1881, BAE, LR, 1879–88.
16. William P. Clark, File 330 ACP 1877 and File 1176 ACP 1881, RG 94, Entry 297.
17. "Some Personal Items," *Army and Navy Journal*, February 12, 1881.
18. W. P. Clark, "Sign Language of the North American Indians and Some of Their Peculiar Customs," *Journal of the Military Service Institution of the United States* 2, nos. 5–8 (1881): 60–61.
19. Hugh Lenox Scott, *Some Memories of a Soldier* (New York: Century Co., 1928), 217.
20. Hugh Lenox Scott, "The Sign Language of the Plains Indians," in *The International Folk-Lore Congress of the World's Columbian Exposition*, vol. 1, edited by Helen Wheeler Bassett and Frederick Starr (Chicago: Charles H. Sergel Co., 1898), 210.
21. Clark, "Sign Language of the North American Indians and Some of Their Peculiar Customs," 63–66, 69–76.

22. Ibid., 67–68, 76.
23. Lt. Gen. Sheridan to Clark, telegram, February 19, 1881, File 330 ACP 1877, RG 94.
24. Robinson, *The Diaries of John Gregory Bourke*, 4:301, 313.
25. Clark to Powell, telegram, March 11, 1881, BAE, LR, 1879–88.
26. Clark to Powell, telegram, March 21, 1881, BAE, LR, 1879–88; James C. Pilling to Clark, March 22. 1881, BAE, LS, Photocopies and Transcripts, 1879–1902.
27. Robinson, *The Diaries of John Gregory Bourke*, 4:315–16. The following Bourke quotations are also from this source (316, 302, 317).
28. Clark to Powell, March 26, 1881, BAE, LR, 1879–88.
29. Lt. Gen. P. H. Sheridan to Gen. of the Army W. T. Sherman, March 28, 1881, Reel 12, General Correspondence, Philip Henry Sheridan Papers, Library of Congress, Washington, DC.
30. Clark, *The Indian Sign Language*, 7–8, 13, 15.
31. Joseph C. Porter, *Paper Medicine Man: John Gregory Bourke and His American West* (Norman: University of Oklahoma Press, 1986), 75–76.
32. Clark, *The Indian Sign Language*, 8, 19. The following quotations from Clark are also from this source (18–20, 148, 6).
33. SO 38, April 4, 1881, SO, MDM, vol. 344; J. W. Powell to S. J. Kirkwood, Secretary of the Interior, April 12, 1881, Box 5, and Clark to A. Bell, May 10, 1881, Box 7, Entry 653, LR, Indian Division, 1881–1907, RG 48, Records of the Office of the Secretary of the Interior, NARA, Washington, DC.
34. Clark, *The Indian Sign Language*, 329.
35. SO 54, May 25, 1881, SO, MDM, vol. 344.
36. Clark, *The Indian Sign Language*, 194.
37. *Army and Navy Journal*, July 16, 1881.
38. Clark, *The Indian Sign Language*, 68.
39. "Personals," *Daily Independent* (Helena, MT), July 12, 1881.
40. Hyde, *Spotted Tail's Folk*, 312–32; Clark, *The Indian Sign Language*, 379.
41. Clark, *The Indian Sign Language*, 365. The following Clark quotations are also from this source (366–68).
42. *Army and Navy Journal*, September 17, 1881.
43. SO 93, September 21, 1881, SO, MDM, vol. 344.
44. October 1881 PR, Fort Washakie, WY, Roll 1364, NAMP, *Returns from U.S. Military Posts*; Clark, *The Indian Sign Language*, 27.
45. Clark, *The Indian Sign Language*, 27–28. The following account of Clark's trip is also from this source (40–41, 60, 388, 390, 391 [quotation]).
46. "Personal Items," *Army and Navy Journal*, November 12, 1881.
47. *Army and Navy Journal*, November 26, 1881.
48. Ibid.; Clark, *The Indian Sign Language*, 365.
49. *Critic* (Washington, DC), January 21, 1882.
50. *Army and Navy Journal*, November 26, 1881.
51. Viola, "Red Horse and the Battle Drawings," 82–84.
52. *Army and Navy Journal*, November 26, 1881; Clark, *The Indian Sign Language*, 410.

CHAPTER 14

1. AAG R. Williams to Dr. Philip Gillett[e], January 16, 1882, MDM, 1866–1891, Entry 2538, Letters Sent, 1882–83, vol. 7, RG 393, Part 1.
2. Commanding General, DD to Headquarters, MDM, January 17, 1882, MDM, 1866–91, Entry 2545, Registers of LR, 1880–83, vol. 22, RG 393, Part 1.
3. AAG R. Williams to AG, February 1, 1882, Entry 2538, vol. 7, RG 393, Part 1; E. Ballou to President Chester Arthur, December 3, 1881; Charles Hatton to H. Price, Commissioner of Indian Affairs, December 30, 1881, Box 76, MDM, Entry 2546, LR, 1882, RG 393, Part 1.
4. Hatton to Price, December 30, 1881.
5. Williams to AG, February 1, 1882.
6. *Army and Navy Journal*, February 11, 1882; "Visiting Indian Children," *National Republican* (Washington, DC), February 4, 1882; "His Friends Visit Him," *Bismarck* (ND) *Tribune*, February 17, 1882.
7. Henry E. Stamm IV, *People of the Wind River: The Eastern Shoshones, 1825–1900* (Norman: University of Oklahoma Press, 1999), 234.
8. "Personal Items," *Army and Navy Journal*, February 25, 1882.
9. Dave Jones, Swinburne Cemetery sexton, telephone interview with author, March 11, 2014.
10. "Military Division of the Missouri," *Army and Navy Journal*, March 11, 1882.
11. File 2185 ACP 1882, Box 772, RG 94, Records of the AGO, 1780s-1917, Entry 297, LR, 1863–94, ACP Branch Records, NARA, Washington, DC.
12. Alfred Theodore Andreas, *History of Chicago*, vol. 3 (Chicago: A. T. Andreas Co., 1886), 576–77.
13. *Army and Navy Journal*, July 12, 1884; "Marital Engagements," *Daily Inter Ocean* (Chicago), June 29, 1884.
14. Robert E. Hartley, *Saving Yellowstone: The President Arthur Expedition of 1883* (Westminster, CO: Sniktau Publications, 2007), 28–29.
15. Ibid., 23–24.
16. *Report of an Exploration of Parts of Wyoming, Idaho, and Montana, in August and September, 1882, Made by Lieut. Gen. P. H. Sheridan, Commanding the Division of the Missouri, with the Itinerary of Col. Jas. F. Gregory and a Geological and Botanical Report by Surgeon W. H. Forwood* (Washington, DC: Government Printing Office, 1882), 5 (hereafter cited as *Sheridan Report*: Gregory's report is on 19–35 and Forwood's report is on 36–69, as cited below). The following descriptions of the trip are also from this source (6, 9, 11–12, 19, 21–27, 39).
17. Hartley, *Saving Yellowstone*, 29–30.
18. *Sheridan Report*, 11, 28. The following information on the expedition is also from this report (11–13, 28 (quotation)–30).
19. Ibid., 13, 31; Hartley, *Saving Yellowstone*, 31.
20. *Sheridan Report*, 13. The following description of the trip is also from this source (14–18, 31–35).

21. *Army and Navy Journal*, September 23, 1882.
22. SO 112, October 19, 1882, SO, MDM, vol. 345.
23. "The Reception at Gen. Sheridan's," *Chicago Daily Tribune*, December 24, 1882.
24. SO 29, March 21, 1883, SO, MDM, vol. 345; *Journal and Republican* (Lowville, NY), March 29, 1883.
25. "General Crook," *Daily Inter Ocean* (Chicago), May 30, 1883.
26. Hartley, *Saving Yellowstone*, 78–80; Frank H. Goodyear III, *A President in Yellowstone: The F. Jay Haynes Photographic Album of Chester Arthur's 1883 Expedition* (Norman: University of Oklahoma Press, 2013), 3, 14, 18.
27. Hartley, *Saving Yellowstone*, 81–82; Goodyear, *A President in Yellowstone*, 8, 18, 22–23.
28. Goodyear, *A President in Yellowstone*, 6.
29. Ibid., 18, 22–23, 43; Hartley, *Saving Yellowstone*, 78–79, 81–83.
30. SO 72, July 5, 1883, SO, MDM, vol. 345; AAG R. Williams to Commanding Officer, Fort McKinney, Wyoming Territory, July 5, 1883, Entry 2538, vol. 7, RG 393, Part 1.
31. AAG R. Williams to Brig. Gen. Alfred H. Terry, July 5, 1883, Entry 2538, vol. 7, RG 393, Part 1; July and August 1883 PR, Fort Washakie, WY, Roll 1364, NAMP, *Returns from U.S. Military Posts*; July 1883 PR, Fort McKinney, WY, Roll 703, *Returns from U.S. Military Posts*; Jack Ellis Haynes, "The Expedition of President Chester A. Arthur to Yellowstone National Park in 1883," *Annals of Wyoming*, 14, no. 1 (January 1942): 31–33.
32. Lt. Gen. Phillip Sheridan to Lt. Col. James F. Gregory, July 29, 1883, Entry 2538, vol. 7, RG 393, Part 1.
33. Goodyear, *A President in Yellowstone*, 23, 44–46; Hartley, *Saving Yellowstone*, 95.
34. Goodyear, *A President in Yellowstone*, 48–52. The following account of the expedition is also from this source (24, 76, 54–58).
35. Ibid., 60; Hartley, *Saving Yellowstone*, 82.
36. Goodyear, *A President in Yellowstone*, 4, 6; Hartley, *Saving Yellowstone*, 83–84; Haynes, "The Expedition of President Chester A. Arthur," 34; August 1883 PR, Fort Washakie, WY, Roll 1364, *Returns from U.S. Military Posts*.
37. Goodyear, *A President in Yellowstone*, 3, 104; Hartley, *Saving Yellowstone*, 96, 102.
38. Goodyear, *A President in Yellowstone*, 82, 88. The following information on the expedition is also from this source (90–116, 12, 118–22, 14, 20, 29).
39. Ibid., 30, 124; Hartley, *Saving Yellowstone*, 96.
40. Grace Logan, "Memoirs," typescript copy of selected pages provided by Dr. James S. Brust, Author's Collection; Dr. James S. Brust to the author, October 29, 1995.
41. Goodyear, *A President in Yellowstone*, 30–31; Hartley, *Saving Yellowstone*, 129–31; "The President in Chicago," *Army and Navy Journal*, September 22, 1883.

CHAPTER 15

1. SO 123, October 20, 1883, SO, MDM, vol. 345.
2. Hutton, *Phil Sheridan and His Army*, 346–49; "Division of the Missouri," *Army and Navy Journal*, November 10, 1883.

3. SO 126, November 1, 1883, SO, MDM, vol. 345; "Proceedings of a Board of Officers," November 2, 1883, Box 91, MDM, LR, RG 393, Part 1, Entry 2546.
4. SO 137, November 26, 1883, SO, MDM, vol. 345; *Army and Navy Journal*, December 8, 1883; Lt. Col. Michael V. Sheridan to AG, December 1, 1883, William P. Clark, File 330 ACP 1877, RG 94, Entry 297.
5. *Army and Navy Journal*, December 8, 1883.
6. *Army and Navy Journal*, January 5, 1884; "The Army and Navy German," *National Republican* (Washington, DC), January 12, 1884.
7. "The Longevity Pay Decision," *New York Sun*, April 10, 1882; "The New Army Act," *New York Sun*, July 25, 1882; *Army and Navy Journal*, January 5, 1884.
8. "The American Derby," *Daily Inter Ocean* (Chicago), June 29, 1884.
9. *Army and Navy Journal*, July 12, 1884; "Marital Engagements," *Daily Inter Ocean* (Chicago), June 29, 1884.
10. Clark to Lt. Gen. P. H. Sheridan, July 7, 1884; Sheridan to Secretary of War Robert T. Lincoln, July 8, 1884; Lincoln to Sheridan, July 12, 1884, General Records, 1821–1903, Correspondence, Entry 21, Registers of LR, vol. 27, RG 108, Records of the Headquarters of the Army, 1828–1903, NARA, Washington, DC.
11. *Army and Navy Journal*, July 12, 1884.
12. "The Late Capt. Clark," *Carthage* (NY) *Republican*, September 30, 1884.
13. Ibid.; "Death of Captain William Clark of Gen. Sheridan's Staff," *Journal and Republican* (Lowville, NY), September 25, 1884.
14. L. R. Hamersly and Co. circular filed with L. R. Hamersly and Co. to AG, October 17, 1884, NAMP, *LR by the Headquarters of the Army, 1827–1903*, Publication No. M1635, Roll 122, RG 108.
15. "Recent Deaths," *Army and Navy Journal*, September 27, 1884; "Death of Capt. Clark," *Carthage* (NY) *Republican*, September 23, 1884; Surgeon Basil Norris to AG, September 22, 1884, William P. Clark, File 330 ACP 1877; William Philo Clark, Certificate of Death, Division of the Department of Human Resources, District of Columbia, Vital Records Division (copy provided by the Lewis County Historical Society).
16. William Philo Clark, Certificate of Death; Wallace L. Chambers, MD, "Contributions to American History by Physicians," *American Journal of Surgery* 142, no. 6 (December 1981): 643.
17. "Recent Deaths," *Army and Navy Journal*, September 27, 1884; "Death of Capt. Clark."
18. "The Late Captain Clark," *Carthage* (NY) *Republican*, October 14, 1884; "Recent Deaths," *Army and Navy Journal*, September 27, 1884.
19. "The Late Capt. Clark," *Carthage* (NY) *Republican*, September 30, 1884 (quotation); "Death of Captain William Clark of Gen. Sheridan's Staff," *Journal and Republican* (Lowville, NY), September 25, 1884.
20. "Mrs. Cornelia Houghton, 68, Former Chicagoan, Is Dead," *Chicago Daily Tribune*, January 8, 1929; "Mrs. Cornelia McA. Houghton," *Winchester* (MA) *Star*, January 11, 1929; Ellen Knight, *Winchester Hospital: Our First Century* (Winchester, MA: Winchester Hospital, 2011), 5.

21. Fred A. Hunt, "A Purposeful Picnic," *Pacific Monthly* 19, no. 3 (March 1908): 238; John Gibbon, "Reviews: Clark's 'Indian Sign Language,'" *Journal of the Military Service Institution of the United States* 6, no. 21 (March 1885): 80.
22. Lt. Col. James F. Gregory to Lt. Gen. P. H. Sheridan, October 16, 1884; and AG R. C. Drum to Commanding Officer, Fort Keogh, MT, October 18, 1884, File 330 ACP 1877.
23. L. R. Hamersly and Co. to AG, October 17, 1884, and accompanying circular.
24. Clark, *The Indian Sign Language*, 20.
25. Gibbon, "Reviews: Clark's 'Indian Sign Language,'" 80.
26. Anonymous, "Clark's Sign Language," *Nation* 40, no. 1035 (April 30, 1885): 366–67.
27. Ernest Thompson Seton, *Sign Talk: A Universal Signal Code, without Apparatus, for Use in the Army, the Navy, Camping, Hunting, and Daily Life* (New York: Doubleday, Page, and Co., 1918), vii.
28. "The Late Captain Clark," *Carthage* (NY) *Republican*, October 14, 1884.
29. Alfred E. Bates, "William P. Clark," *Sixteenth Annual Reunion of the Association of the Graduates of the United States Military Academy at West Point, New York, June 12, 1885* (1885): 44, 46. The following quotations are also from this source (45–47).
30. "Miscellaneous: A Noble Soldier," *Journal and Republican* (Lowville, NY), October 9, 1884.
31. "Indian Fighter Leaves a Legacy and a Language," *Star-Ledger* (Newark, NJ), May 4, 1979.

BIBLIOGRAPHY

ARCHIVAL MATERIALS

Author's Collection
    Garnett, William. "Report of William Garnett, Interpreter to General H. L. Scott and Major James McLaughlin." 1920. Copy of original typescript.
    Logan, Grace. "Memoirs." Typescript copy of selected pages provided by Dr. James S. Brust.

Boston Public Library, Norman B. Leventhal Map Center
    Office of Chief Engineer. "Yellowstone National Park, Big Horn Mountains, and Adjacent Territory" (map, 1881). Chicago: Military Division of the Missouri. maps.bpl.org/id/16055.

Lewis County Historical Society, Lyons Falls, NY
    Cemetery Records, Deer River, Town of Denmark, NY.
    Clark, William Philo, Family File.

Library of Congress, Washington, DC
    Sheridan, Philip Henry, Papers.

Montana Historical Society, Helena
    Clark, William P. "Memo: Of a Voyage from Benson's Landing on the Yellowstone, 27 Miles from Fort Ellis, to the Mouth of Powder River." Typescript. [The Historical Society catalog identifies Clark as the author, while research revealed that the diarist was most likely First Lieutenant William I. Reed.]

National Archives and Records Administration (NARA), Kansas City, MO
    Record Group 75, Records of the Bureau of Indian Affairs, Pine Ridge Agency, Miscellaneous Correspondence Received; Rosebud Agency, General Correspondence.

National Archives and Records Administration (NARA), Washington, DC
- Record Group 48, Records of the Office of the Secretary of the Interior, Indian Division, Letters Received, 1849–80, Entry 649, and 1881–1907, Entry 653.
- Record Group 94
  - Records of the Adjutant General's Office: Appointment, Commission, and Personal Branch records, Entry 297, Letters Received, 1863–94, William P. Clark, Files 3407 ACP 1876; 4199 ACP 1876; 330 ACP 1877; 1176 ACP 1881; 2185 ACP 1882. James T. Peale, File 2626 ACP 1876. William I. Reed, File 3387 ACP 1880.
  - Records Relating to the United States Military Academy, Rolls, Registers, and Reports, Entry 232, Monthly Class Reports and Conduct Rolls, 1831–66.
  - Records Relating to the United States Military Academy, U.S. Military Academy Cadet Application Papers, 1864, No. 25.
  - Special Orders, Department of Dakota, vols. 192–93, 1878–80, Entry 44.
  - Special Orders, Department of the Platte, vols. 447–50, 1869–74, Entry 44.
  - Special Orders, Military Division of the Missouri, vol. 341, 1874, vols. 343–45, 1878–83, Entry 44.
- Record Group 107, Records of the Office of the Secretary of War, Register of Letters Received (Main Series), 1800–1889, vol. 211, Entry 17.
- Record Group 108, Records of the Headquarters of the Army, General Records, 1821–1903, Correspondence, Registers of Letters Received, vol. 27, Entry 21.
- Record Group 153, Records of the Office of the Judge Advocate General–Army: Court Martial Case Files, 1809–94, Box 2264, File 00-2531.
- Record Group 391, Records of the U.S. Regular Army Mobile Units, 2nd Cavalry, 1837–1907, Miscellaneous Records, Entry 644 and Special Orders Issued, 1847–81, Entry 639.
- Record Group 393, Part 1
  - Records of United States Army Continental Commands, 1821–1920, Department of Dakota, Letters Received, March 1878–November 1880, Entry 1175.
  - Department of the Platte, Letters Received, 1877, Entry 3731.
  - Department of the Platte, Telegrams Sent by General Crook's ADC, 1877–78, Entry 3727.
  - Division of the Missouri, Letters Received, 1866–91, Entry 2546.
  - Division of the Missouri, Letters Sent, 1866–91, vols. 6–7, Entry 2538.
  - Division of the Missouri, Registers of Letters Received, 1880–83, vols. 19–22, Entry 2545.
  - Record Group 393, Part 3, District of the Yellowstone, Letter Books—Letters and Telegrams Sent by Aide-de-Camp and AAG Baldwin, 1876–81, 4 vols., Entry 889.
- Record Group 393, Part 5
  - Forts and Posts, Records of Districts, 1841–1920, Special Orders, 1873–76, Headquarters, Fort Sanders, Wyoming Territory, vols. 4–5, Entry 7.
  - Special Orders, 1876–81, Fort Keogh, Montana Territory, vols. 1–3, Entry 16.

Smithsonian Institution, Washington, DC, National Anthropological Archives
- Bureau of American Ethnology (BAE), Letters Received, 1879–88; Letters Sent, Photocopies and Transcripts, 1879–1902.

South Dakota State Historical Society, Pierre
  McGillycuddy, Fanny. "The Diary of Fanny McGillycuddy, April 11, 1877–October 31, 1878."
University of Nebraska–Lincoln Libraries. Archives and Special Collections
  Sandoz, Mari, Collection (MS 080).
U.S. Army Military History Institute, Carlisle Barracks, PA
  Order of the Indian Wars Papers, File C-6.

GOVERNMENT PUBLICATIONS

Heitman, Francis B. *Historical Register and Dictionary of the United States Army, from Its Organization September 29, 1789 to March 2, 1903.* Vol. 1. Washington, DC: Government Printing Office, 1903.

Library of Congress, Washington, DC *Journey through the Yellowstone National Park and Northwestern Wyoming, 1883.* Washington, DC: Government Printing Office, 1883. Call Number 13414 (H). http://www.loc.gov/pictures/item/2002696055/.

National Archives Microfilm Publications (NAMP), Washington, DC *Letters Received by the Appointment, Commission, and Personal Branch of the Adjutant General's Office, 1871–1894.* Publication No. M1395, William Van Wyck Reily, File 4087 ACP 1875, Record Group 94, Records of the Adjutant General's Office, 1780s–1917.

———. *Letters Received by the Commission Branch of the Adjutant General's Office, 1863–1870.* Publication No. M1064, Record Group 94, Records of the Adjutant General's Office, 1780s–1917.

———. *Letters Received by the Headquarters of the Army, 1827–1903.* Publication No. M1635, Roll 122, Record Group 108, Records of the Headquarters of the Army, 1828–1903.

———. *Letters Received by the Office of Indian Affairs, 1824–1881.* Publication No. M234, Record Group 75, Records of the Bureau of Indian Affairs, 1793–1989, Roll 841, Spotted Tail Agency, 1875–80, 1876 (H345)–77 and Roll 721, Red Cloud Agency, 1871–80, Year 1877.

———. *Letters Received by the Office of the Adjutant General, Main Series, 1871–1880.* Publication No. M666, Record Group 94, Records of the Adjutant General's Office, 1780s–1917.

———. *Returns from Regular Army Cavalry Regiments, 1833–1916.* Publication No. M744, Rolls 18–20, Second Cavalry, Record Group 94, Records of the Adjutant General's Office, 1780s–1917.

———. *Returns from U.S. Military Posts, 1800–1916.* Publication No. M617, Rolls 347, 365, 572, 596, 597, 703, 879, 1028, 1050, 1094, 1364, 1535, Record Group 94, Records of the Adjutant General's Office, 1780s–1917.

———. *Special Files, Military Division of the Missouri.* Publication No. 1495, Roll 4, Record Group 393, Records of United States Army Continental Commands, 1821–1920.

New York Secretary of State. New York State Census, 1865. Albany, State Library.

Report of an Exploration of Parts of Wyoming, Idaho, and Montana, in August and September, 1882, Made by Lieut. Gen. P. H. Sheridan, Commanding the Military Division of the Missouri, with the Itinerary of Col. Jas. F. Gregory and a Geological and Botanical Report by Surgeon W. H. Forwood. Washington, DC: Government Printing Office, 1882.

Revised United States Army Regulations of 1861. Washington, DC: Government Printing Office, 1863.

U.S. Congress. House. Annual Report of the Chief of Engineers, United States Army, to the Secretary of War, 1881, part 3. 47th Cong., 1st sess., 1881. Ex. Doc. 1, pt. 2, vol. 2.

———. House. Clothing to Certain Enlisted Men of the Army. 43rd Cong., 1st sess., 1873–74. Vol. 8, Ex. Doc. 18.

———. House. Reports of House Committees. James T. Peale. 51st Cong., 1st sess., 1889–90. Vol. 10, HR Rep. 3076.

United States Military Academy (USMA). *Official Register of the Officers and Cadets of the U.S. Military Academy, West Point, New York.* Vols. 1865–67. New York: Baldwin and Jones, Printers, 1865–67.

———. *United States Military Academy, West Point: Register of the Officers and Cadets and Report of the Board of Visitors, 1868.* Washington, DC: Government Printing Office, 1868.

NEWSPAPERS

Army and Navy Journal (NY)
Bismarck (ND) *Tribune*
Carthage (NY) *Republican*
Carthage (NY) *Republican Tribune*
Chicago Daily Tribune
Cleveland Leader
Critic (Washington, DC)
Daily Independent (Helena, MT)
Daily Inter Ocean (Chicago)
Evening Star (Washington, DC)
Independent Record (Helena, MT)
Journal and Republican (Lowville, NY)
National Republican (Washington, DC)
New York Herald
New York Sun
New York Times
New York Tribune
Republican Daily Journal (Lawrence, KS)
Saint Paul (MN) *Daily Globe*
Star-Ledger (Newark, NJ)

BOOKS

Ambrose, Stephen E. *Duty, Honor, Country: A History of West Point.* Baltimore: Johns Hopkins University Press, 1966.

Andreas, Alfred Theodore. *History of Chicago.* Vol. 3. Chicago: A. T. Andreas Co., 1886.

Baird, George W. "General Miles's Indian Campaigns." In *Eyewitnesses to the Indian Wars, 1865–1890: The Army and the Indian,* vol. 5, edited by Peter Cozzens, 174–202. Mechanicsburg, PA: Stackpole Books, 2005.

Billings, John S. *Circular No. 4: Report on Barracks and Hospitals with Descriptions of Military Posts*. New York: Sol Lewis, 1974. Reprint, with an introduction by Herbert M. Hart. First published 1870 by War Department, Surgeon General's Office.

———. *Circular No. 8: A Report on the Hygiene of the United States Army with Descriptions of Military Posts*. United States: Palala Press, 2015. Facsimile. First published 1875 by War Department, Surgeon General's Office.

Bordeaux, W. J. *Conquering the Mighty Sioux*. Sioux Falls, SD: privately published, 1929.

———. *Custer's Conqueror*. Compiled and edited by Paul R. Morrison. Philadelphia: Xlibris Corp., 2010. Reprint. First published n.p.: Smith and Company, n.d.

Bourke, John G. *On the Border with Crook*. Lincoln: University of Nebraska Press, 1971.

Brady, Cyrus Townsend. *Indian Fights and Fighters*. Lincoln: University of Nebraska Press, 1971.

Bray, Kingsley M. *Crazy Horse: A Lakota Life*. Norman: University of Oklahoma Press, 2006.

Brimlow, George F. *The Bannock Indian War of 1878*. Caldwell, ID: Caxton Printers, 1938.

Brininstool, E. A., ed. *Crazy Horse: The Invincible Ogalalla Sioux Chief*. Los Angeles: Wetzel Publishing Co., 1949.

Brown, Mark H., and W. R. Felton. *The Frontier Years: L. A. Huffman, Photographer of the Plains*. New York: Bramhall House, 1955.

Buecker, Thomas R. *Fort Robinson and the American West, 1874–1899*. Lincoln: Nebraska State Historical Society, 1999.

Buecker, Thomas R., and R. Eli Paul, eds. *The Crazy Horse Surrender Ledger*. Lincoln: Nebraska State Historical Society, 1994.

Capron, Thaddeus Hurlbut. *Marching with General Crook*. Edited by Ray Meketa. Douglas, AK: Cheechako Press, 1983.

Child, Hamilton. *Gazetteer and Business Directory of Lewis County, N.Y. for 1872–3*. Syracuse, NY: Hamilton Child, 1872.

Clark, Robert A., ed. *The Killing of Chief Crazy Horse*. Lincoln: University of Nebraska Press, 1988.

Clark, W. P. *The Indian Sign Language*. Lincoln: University of Nebraska Press, 1982. Originally published Philadelphia: L. R. Hamersly and Co., 1885.

Cozzens, Peter, ed. *Eyewitnesses to the Indian Wars, 1865–1890: The Long War for the Northern Plains*. Vol. 4. Mechanicsburg, PA: Stackpole Books, 2004.

Cutter, William Richard. *Genealogical and Family History of Northern New York*. Vol. 3. New York: Lewis Historical Publishing Co., 1910.

Danker, Donald F., ed. *Man of the Plains: Recollections of Luther North, 1856–1882*. Lincoln: University of Nebraska Press, 1961.

De Barthe, Joe. *Life and Adventures of Frank Grouard*. Edited by Edgar I. Stewart. Norman: University of Oklahoma Press, 1958.

Dunlay, Thomas W. *Wolves for the Blue Soldiers: Indian Scouts and Auxiliaries with the United States Army, 1860–90*. Lincoln: University of Nebraska Press, 1982.

Finerty, John F. *War-Path and Bivouac; or, The Conquest of the Sioux*. Chicago: Donohue Brothers, 1890.

———. *War-Path and Bivouac: The Big Horn and Yellowstone Expedition* (1955). Edited by Milo Milton Quaife. Lincoln: University of Nebraska Press, 1966.

Frazer, Robert W. *Forts of the West*. Norman: University of Oklahoma Press, 1965.

Goodspeed, Jerome Washington. *Life of Col. James Fisk, Jr.* Chicago: J. W. Goodspeed, 1872.

Goodyear, Frank H., III. *A President in Yellowstone: The F. Jay Haynes Photographic Album of Chester Arthur's 1883 Expedition*. Norman: University of Oklahoma Press, 2013.

Gray, John S. *Centennial Campaign: The Sioux War of 1876*. Norman: University of Oklahoma Press, 1988.

Greene, Jerome A., comp. and ed. *Battles and Skirmishes of the Great Sioux War, 1876–1877: The Military View*. Norman: University of Oklahoma Press, 1993.

———. *Slim Buttes, 1876: An Episode of the Great Sioux War*. Norman: University of Oklahoma Press, 1982.

———. *Yellowstone Command: Colonel Nelson A. Miles and the Great Sioux War, 1876–1877*. Lincoln: University of Nebraska Press, 1991.

Grinnell, George Bird. *Two Great Scouts and Their Pawnee Battalion*. Cleveland: Arthur H. Clark Co., 1928.

Hardorff, Richard G., ed. *The Death of Crazy Horse: A Tragic Episode in Lakota History*. Lincoln: University of Nebraska Press, 2001.

Hartley, Robert E. *Saving Yellowstone: The President Arthur Expedition of 1883*. Westminster, CO: Sniktau Publications, 2007.

Hedren, Paul L. *Great Sioux War Orders of Battle: How the United States Army Waged War on the Northern Plains, 1876–1877*. Norman: University of Oklahoma Press, 2011.

Hutton, Paul Andrew. *Phil Sheridan and His Army*. Lincoln: University of Nebraska Press, 1985.

Hyde, George E. *Red Cloud's Folk: A History of the Oglala Sioux Indians*. Norman: University of Oklahoma Press, 1975.

———. *Spotted Tail's Folk: A History of the Brule Sioux*. Norman: University of Oklahoma Press, 1974.

Jensen, Richard E., ed. *Voices of the American West*. Vol. 1, *The Indian Interviews of Eli S. Ricker, 1903–1919*. Lincoln: University of Nebraska Press, 2005.

Kime, Wayne R., ed. *The Powder River Expedition Journals of Colonel Richard Irving Dodge*. Norman: University of Oklahoma Press, 1997.

King, Charles. *Campaigning with Crook*. Norman: University of Oklahoma Press, 1964.

———. *Trials of a Staff-Officer*. London: FB &c, 2015. Facsimile. First published 1891 by L. R. Hamersly and Co.

Knight, Ellen. *Winchester Hospital: Our First Century*. Winchester, MA: Winchester Hospital, 2011.

Liddic, Bruce R., and Paul Harbaugh, eds. *Custer & Company: Walter Camp's Notes on the Custer Fight*. Lincoln: University of Nebraska Press, 1998.

Marquis, Albert Nelson, ed. *Who's Who in New England*. Vol. 2. 2nd ed. Chicago: A. N. Marquis and Co., 1916.

Marquis, Thomas B. *Wooden Leg: A Warrior Who Fought Custer*. Lincoln: University of Nebraska Press, 1962.

McChristian, Douglas C. *Regular Army O!: Soldiering on the Frontier, 1865–1891.* Norman: University of Oklahoma Press, 2017.

———. *Uniforms, Arms, and Equipment: The U.S. Army on the Western Frontier, 1880–1892.* Norman: University of Oklahoma Press, 2007.

McClernand, Edward J. *With the Indian and the Buffalo in Montana, 1870–1878.* Glendale, CA: Arthur H. Clark Co., 1969.

Miles, Nelson A. *Personal Recollections and Observations of General Nelson A. Miles.* Vol. 1. Lincoln: University of Nebraska Press, 1992.

Monnett, John H. *Tell Them We Are Going Home: The Odyssey of the Northern Cheyennes.* Norman: University of Oklahoma Press, 2001.

Ostler, Jeffrey. *The Plains Sioux and U.S. Colonialism from Lewis and Clark to Wounded Knee.* Cambridge: Cambridge University Press, 2004.

Porter, Joseph C. *Paper Medicine Man: John Gregory Bourke and His American West.* Norman: University of Oklahoma Press, 1986.

Powers, Thomas. *The Killing of Crazy Horse.* New York: Vintage Books, 2011.

Price, Sir Rose Lambart. *The Two Americas: An Account of Sport and Travel.* Philadelphia: J. B. Lippincott and Co., 1877.

Regan, James. *Manual of Guard Duty and Kindred Subjects for the Regular Army, Volunteers and Militia of the United States: Being a Thorough Compilation of Rules, Regulations, and Principles, Collected from the Most Authentic Sources.* New York: Harper and Brothers, 1883.

Robinson, Charles M., III, ed. *The Diaries of John Gregory Bourke.* 4 vols. Denton: University of North Texas Press, 2003–2010.

———. *General Crook and the Western Frontier.* Norman: University of Oklahoma Press, 2001.

———. *A Good Year to Die: The Story of the Great Sioux War.* New York: Random House, 1995.

Sandoz, Mari. *Crazy Horse: The Strange Man of the Oglalas.* Lincoln: University of Nebraska Press, 1961.

Schmitt, Martin F., ed. *General George Crook: His Autobiography.* Norman: University of Oklahoma Press, 1960.

Schneider, George A., ed. *The Freeman Journal: The Infantry in the Sioux Campaign of 1876.* San Rafael, CA: Presidio Press, 1977.

Scott, Douglas D., Peter Bleed, and Stephen Damm. *Custer, Cody, and Grand Duke Alexis: Historical Archaeology of the Royal Buffalo Hunt.* Norman: University of Oklahoma Press, 2013.

Scott, Hugh Lenox. "The Sign Language of the Plains Indians." In *The International Folk-Lore Congress of the World's Columbian Exposition*, vol. 1, edited by Helen Wheeler Bassett and Frederick Starr, 206–20. Chicago: Charles H. Sergel Co., 1898.

———. *Some Memories of a Soldier.* New York: Century Co., 1928.

Seton, Ernest Thompson. *Sign Talk: A Universal Signal Code, without Apparatus, for Use in the Army, the Navy, Camping, Hunting, and Daily Life.* New York: Doubleday, Page and Co., 1918.

Stamm, Henry E., IV. *People of the Wind River: The Eastern Shoshones, 1825–1900.* Norman: University of Oklahoma Press, 1999.
Thrapp, Dan L. *Encyclopedia of Frontier Biography.* 4 vols. Glendale, CA: Arthur H. Clark Co., 1988, 1994.
Tucker, William Warren. *His Imperial Highness the Grand Duke Alexis in the United States of America during the Winter of 1871–1872.* Cambridge, MA: Riverside Press, 1872.
Upton, Richard, comp. and ed. *The Indian as a Soldier at Fort Custer, Montana.* El Segundo, CA: Upton and Sons, 1983.
Utley, Robert M. *The Lance and the Shield: The Life and Times of Sitting Bull.* New York: Henry Holt and Co., 1993.
Viola, Herman J. *Little Bighorn Remembered: The Untold Indian Story of Custer's Last Stand.* New York: Times Books, 1999.
Webb, George W. *Chronological List of Engagements between the Regular Army of the United States and Various Tribes of Hostile Indians Which Occurred during the Years 1790 to 1898, Inclusive.* St. Joseph, MO: Wing Printing and Publishing Co., 1939.
Wheeler, Homer W. *Buffalo Days.* Indianapolis: Bobbs-Merrill Co., 1925.
Wilhelm, Thomas. *A Military Dictionary and Gazetteer.* Rev. ed. War College Series. Charleston, SC: BiblioLife, 2015. Facsimile. First published 1881 by L. R. Hamersly and Co.
Willert, James, ed. *The Cuthbert Mills Letters to New York Times during the Indian War of 1876.* La Mirada, CA: privately published, 1984.

ARTICLES

Anonymous. "Clark's Sign Language." *Nation* 40, no. 1035 (April 30, 1885): 366–67.
Bates, Alfred E. "William P. Clark." *Sixteenth Annual Reunion of the Association of the Graduates of the United States Military Academy at West Point, New York, June 12, 1885* (1885): 43–48.
Bray, Kingsley M. "We Belong to the North: The Flights of the Northern Indians from the White River Agencies, 1877–1878." *Montana The Magazine of Western History* 55, no. 2 (Summer 2005): 28–47.
Brininstool, E. A., ed. "Chief Crazy Horse, His Career and Death." *Nebraska History* 12, no. 1 (January–March 1929): 1–78.
Brust, James S., and Lee H. Whittlesey. "Roughing It up the Yellowstone to Wonderland: The Nelson Miles/Colgate Hoyt Party in Yellowstone National Park, September 1878." *Montana The Magazine of Western History* 46, no. 1 (Spring 1996): 56–65.
Buecker, Thomas R. "Lt. William Philo Clark's Sioux War Report and Little Big Horn Map." *Greasy Grass* 7 (May 1991): 11–21.
Chambers, Wallace L., MD. "Contributions to American History by Physicians." *American Journal of Surgery* 142, no. 6 (December 1981): 640–45.
Clark, W. P. "The Sign-Language of the North American Indians." *United Service* 3, no. 1 (July 1880): 23–33.
———. "Sign Language of the North American Indians and Some of Their Peculiar Customs." *Journal of the Military Service Institution of the United States* 2, nos. 5–8 (1881): 60–77.

Epp, Todd D. "The State of Kansas v. Wild Hog, et al." *Kansas History: A Journal of the Central Plains* 5, no. 2 (Summer 1982): 139–46.

Freedom, Gary S. "Moving Men and Supplies: Military Transportation on the Northern Great Plains, 1866–1891." *South Dakota History* 14, no. 2 (Summer 1984): 114–33.

Gibbon, John. "Reviews: Clark's 'Indian Sign Language.'" *Journal of the Military Service Institution of the United States* 6, no. 21 (March 1885): 80–81.

Haynes, Jack Ellis. "The Expedition of President Chester A. Arthur to Yellowstone National Park in 1883." *Annals of Wyoming* 14, no. 1 (January 1942): 31–38.

Hedren, Paul L. "The Crazy Horse Medal: An Enigma from the Great Sioux War." *Nebraska History* 75, no. 2 (Summer 1994): 195–99.

Hunt, Fred A. "A Purposeful Picnic, Part 1: The Inception, the Progress, and the Survey of the Custer Battlefield." *Pacific Monthly* 19, no. 3 (March 1908): 233–45.

Lee, Jesse M. "The Capture and Death of an Indian Chieftain." *Journal of the Military Service Institution of the United States* 54 (January, March, and May 1914): 323–40.

Pfaller, Reverend Louis. "The Fort Keogh to Bismarck Stage Route." *North Dakota History* 21, no. 3 (July 1954): 91–125.

Riley, Paul D., ed. "Oglala Sources on the Life of Crazy Horse: Interviews Given to Eleanor H. Hinman." *Nebraska History* 57, no. 1 (Spring 1976): 1–51.

Van West, Carroll. "Roughing It up the Yellowstone to Wonderland: An Account of a Trip through the Yellowstone Valley in 1878." *Montana The Magazine of Western History* 36, no. 2 (Spring 1986): 22–35.

INDEX

References to illustrations appear in italics.

adjutant duties: Fort D. A. Russell, 16–17; Fort Sanders, 21–27; Omaha Barracks, 17–18, 20–21
aide-de-camp assignments, 31–32, 198
Alexis, Grand Duke, 18–20, *98*
Alum Creek, 187
American Horse, 36, 86–87
Andrus, Edwin P., 192
Armstrong, John H., 187
Army and Navy German . . . Club, 198
Army and Navy Journal, 54
Arthur, Chester A., *103*, 191, 192–96
Assiniboine scouts, Sitting Bull engagement, 149, 151
Autochthonic Theory, 174

Badger Creek, 177
Bagley, G. A., 118
Bailey, Hobart K., 122, 125, 128, 129
Baird, George W., 151
Baker, Eugene M., 121, 131, 148, 152, 153
Baker's battlefield, 124

Baldwin, Alice, 122
Baldwin, Frank D., 122, 124, 128, 158
Baldwin, Millie, 122
Baldwin, Nita, 122
Bancroft, Hubert Howe, 190
Bannocks: post-reservation conflicts, 124–28, 130; scouts during Sioux War, 42, 43–44; in sign language project, 179–80; Sitting Bull engagement, 149
Baronett, Jack, 187–88
Baronett's Bridge, 127–28, 187, 195
Battle of Slim Buttes, 33–36
Bear Tooth Mountains, 188, 189
Beaver Creek, 113, 150–51
Beebe's Ranch, 25–26
beef issue incident, 64
Belknap, William W., 22, 129
Belle Fourche River (and camp), 37, 45–47
Bemis and McAvoy Brewing Company, 184
Benjamin, S. N., 8, 10
Bennett, Andrew S., 29, 122, 128

Benson's Landing, 28
Big Horn and Yellowstone Expedition, Sioux War, 32–39
Big Horn Canyon, 166
Big Horn Mountains, exploration expeditions, 65–66, 162–63; mapping, 168–69
Big Horn River, 124, 164, 165
Billings community, 189, 196
Bishop, Heber R., 185, 187–88, 189
Black, Henry M., 6, 10
Black Canyon, 166
Black Coal, 106, 108, 110, 183, 185, 193
Black Coyote, 61, 143
Black Crane, 143
Black Crow, 89
Blackfeet Agency, 177
Black Fox, 86–87
Black Hills area: evasion by Northern Cheyennes, 137; in relocation dispute, 114; Sioux War period, 32–33, 37, 45
Black Shawl, 87
Blacksmith, 153
Blood Indians, in sign language project, 177
Bodmer, Karl, 156
Bordeaux, Louis, 69, 80, 88–90, 93, 94
Bordeaux, William J., 69
Borden, George P., 150
Bourke, John G. (before Sioux War), 23, 25, 26
Bourke, John G. (during Sioux War): comment on sign language, 46; at Powder River camp, 31–32; Slim Buttes–area fighting, 36; in surrender/peace negotiations, 49; travel to Fort Laramie, 37–38
Bourke, John G. (post–Sioux War): arrival of surrendering bands, 53; on Clark at Red Cloud Agency, 48; competition for Sheridan staff position, 176–77; in Crazy Horse conflicts, 82, 93; ethnographic assignment, 172–74; report from Clark about scouts, 52–53; and ring acquisition story, 54
Box Elder Creek (northern Montana), 150
Box Elder Creek (South Dakota and Montana), 139–40
Bracket, Albert G., 23, 24
Bradley, Luther P.: background, 63; discussions about buffalo hunt, 70, 73; incarceration plans for Crazy Horse, 88–89, 90–91, 92; in military move against Crazy Horse, 83, 84, 85, 87; and Nez Perce dispute consequences, 79–81; remembrance of Clark, 204
Bragg, Edward S., 190
Bragg, Margaret, 190
Brave Wolf, 141
Brett, Lloyd M., 159, 160
Brisbin, James S., 121, 128
Brotherton, David H., 133
Bruguier, John "Big Leggins," 148
Brule Lakotas, 19–20, 49–50, 65, 181. *See also* Spotted Tail
Buell, George P., 128
buffalo hunts, 18–20, 54, 70–71, 73, 75, 98, 162–63
Bull Head, 86
Bureau of American Ethnology, 155–56
Burke, D. W., 73, 78, 80, 88, 89
Burnham, Horace B., 55

Calhoun, Frederic, 91
Camp Alexis, 18–20
Campbell, James A., 192
Camp Brown, 65, 79, 84, 179
Camp Douglas assignment, 23
Camp Robinson: arrivals of surrendering Indians, 50, 55; Clark assigned to, 47; commander replacement, 63; council about buffalo hunt, 70; council about horse thievery, 69–70; Crook meeting with Agency Indians, 62; death of Crazy Horse, 91–96; incarceration plans for Crazy Horse, 88–91; military responsibilities, 48; moves against

Crazy Horse departure, 79–80, 83–84; Nez Perce conflict, 76–77; in remembrances of Clark, 204; during Sioux War, 38, 39, 46; surrender negotiation parties, 48–51; tobacco pipe anecdote, 44. *See also* Red Cloud Agency, Clark's activity
Camp Sheridan, 48, 53–54, 55
Cannonball River, 33
Cantonment Reno, 41–42, 45
Carling, Elias B., 23
Carlisle Indian School, 183
Carr, Eugene A., 31
Chadron Creek, 137
Cherry Creek, 167
Cheyenne, Wyo., 16, 40
Chicago, headquarters, Division of the Missouri, Clark's activity at: commissary examination, 190; equipment loss problem, 197; escort of Northern Arapahos, 182–83; friends' weddings, 179, 183, 190; horse purchase, 197; Indian delegation visits, 106–7, 112, 183–84; sign language manuscript work, 182, 183, 190; transfer to Washington, D.C., 197–98; Yellowstone map project, 168–69; Yellowstone National Park expeditions, *102–3*, 184–90, 191–96
Chicago Times, 37, 57, 59, 149
Church, Albert E., 7
Cinnabar community, 195
Civil War period, 4–6
Clark, Ambrose W., 5
Clark, Daniel (uncle), 3
Clark, Frances M. (sister), 3, 183
Clark, Harriet A. (sister), 3, 4
Clark, J. C., 8
Clark, John W. (brother), 3, 4–5, 200–201
Clark, Prudency Taylor (mother), 3, 203
Clark, Sarah P. (sister), 3, 4
Clark, William Durant (father of Clark), 3, 5

Clark, William Philo (biographical highlights): childhood/youth, 3–4; courtships/engagements, 122–23, 168, 184, 199; illness and death, 200–202; military commission, 13, 15; military training, 5–13; photos of, *97–98, 100–104*; remembrances of, 204–5. *See also* Fort Keogh posting, Clark's activity; Red Cloud Agency, Clark's activity; sign language project
Clark, William R. (grandfather of Clark), 3
Clark's Fork, 125–26, 128, 188, 189
Clay Mountain, 188
Clear Fork, 163, 164
Cleveland Leader, 122
Clitz, Henry B., 6
Cloud Peak, 165
Coale, John H., 187
Cody, William F. "Buffalo Bill," 18–19, 35
Commissary Department, Clark's appointment pursuit, 118–19
commissary duties, 26
company units. *See* Second Cavalry *entries*
Conquering Bear, 19
Cooke City, 188
Cosgrove, Tom, 43–44
Countryman, Horace, 124, 125, 130
court-martial duty, Clark's: at Fort D. A. Russell, 16–17, 26; at Fort Fred Steele, 23; at Fort Hartsuff, 25, 26; at Fort Keogh, 148, 158; at Fort Sanders, 22
court-martial proceedings, Clark's at West Point, 8–12
Cowles, Edwin, 122, 124, 125, 130
Cozzen's Hotel, in West Point court-martial proceedings, 9
crayfish, 86
Crazy Horse (and Red Cloud Agency): alienation from other Indians, 75–76; beef issue incident, 64; buffalo hunt promise, 64, 65, 70–71, 73, 75; burial during relocation journey, 113–14; Clark's appeasement efforts, 60,

Crazy Horse (and Red Cloud Agency) (*continued*)
75; council about horse thievery, 69–70; death of, 82, 91–96; departure confusion and dispute, 76–81, 85; escorted return, 89–91; Irwin conflicts, 72; marriage to Nellie Larrabee, 68–69, 72; meeting with Crook, 62; military move against, 79, 80–81, 83–87; Nez Perce debate, 76–79; prisoner status, 89, 91; pursuit of, 87–88; Red Cloud conflict, 70–71, 82; relocation dispute, 57, 71, 72, 76; return negotiations, 88–89; rides/journeys with Clark, 65; rumor of planned Crook murder, 82–83; sun dance ceremony, 66–67; Washington, D.C., delegation conflict, 68, 71–72, 73–75

Crazy Horse: during Sioux War, 27, 36, 42, 63, 105; surrender/peace period, 49–50, 52, 55–58

Crazy Woman's Fork camp, 42, 45

Crook, George (during Sioux War): at Belle Fourche camp, 37, 45–47; march ordeal, 32–33, 37; at Powder River camp, 31–32; Powder River Expedition, 40–47; Rosebud Creek battle, 27; Slim Buttes–area fighting, 33–36; surrender/peace period, 48–49, 51, 52, 53–54, 57; travel to Fort Laramie, 37–39

Crook, George (post–Sioux War): buffalo hunt promise, 62, 70, 71, 74; confidence in Clark, 59, 60; councils with Crazy Horse, 62, 81; and Crazy Horse conflicts, 80–81, 82–84, 87, 89, 93, 95–96; and Crazy Horse's departure dispute, 80–81, 82–84, 87; dispatch from Clark about departing Indians, 63; newspaper article about, 191; and Nez Perce dispute, 79; Pine Ridge grievances, 155; report request, 105; support for Clark's promotion, 119; on value of Indian scouts, 60–61; Washington, D.C., delegation, 74, 75, 107, 108; West Point recommendation, 147; on Yellowstone–Big Horn valley exploration expedition, 65–66

Crook, George: and Fort Sanders personnel, 23; photos of, *98*, *101*; remembrance of Clark, 204

Crook City, 38

Crosby, John Schuyler, 190, 191, 195

Crossman, George H., 148

Crow Agency, 125, 130, 165

Crow Creek Agency, 181

Crow Dog, 177

Crow Indians: Bannocks engagement, 125, 126–27, 128; horse thefts from, 159; along Little Big Horn River, 165; Rosebud Creek engagement, 159–60; Sanger dispute during Sioux War, 29; settler conflicts, 132; Sitting Bull engagement, 149, 151; and Yellowstone Park expedition, 189

Cullum, George Washington, 6

Cushing, Frank H., 183–84

Custer, George A., 18–20, 27, *98*, 148. *See also* Little Big Horn battle

Custer Creek, 131

Custer's Conqueror (Bordeaux), 69

Daily Inter Ocean, 191

Dakota Column, Sioux War, 27–28

Darlington Agency, 136–37

Davidson, John W., 159–60

Deadwood community, 38

deaf sign language, 170, 182, 203

Deer River community, 3–4, 201

De Lany, Hayden, 40, 43, 179

demerits at West Point, Clark's, 7–8, 12–13

deserters, Fort Sanders, 26

Devils Lake Reservation, 180

Dewees, Thomas B., 16, 149–50

Dodge, R. I., 170

dog feasts, 53, 60, 62
Dost, George W., 23
Douglas, Samuel R., 122
Dry Fork camp, 45
Dull Knife, 43, 45, 55, 137
Dull Knife Fight, 43–45, 56, 63, 163

education, Clark's, 5–13
Egan, James, 19, 121
Egan, John, 9–11
Evans, A. W., 53
Ewers, Ezra P., 121
Ewers, Sylvia, 122
Ewers, Willie, 122

Farrar, Henry W., 162
Far West steamer, 29–30
Fast Bull, 64, 81
Few Tails, 48–49
Field, Georgiana, 179
Fifth Cavalry, 43–45, 193
Fifth New York Heavy Artillery Regiment, 4–5
Finerty, John F., 37–38, 149–50, 190, 205
Firehole River, 187
fires, 21, 133–34
Fleury, George, 138, 139, 140
forage change requests, 147–48
Ford, John W., 59
Forsyth, George A., 19, 176
Forsyth, James, 19
Fort, Greenbury L., 187–88
Fort Assiniboine, sign language project, 176
Fort Berthold, sign language project, 176
Fort Buford, mixed-bloods escort journey, 153
Fort C. F. Smith, Big Horn Mountains exploration, 165–66
Fort Custer: and Big Horn Mountains exploration, 165, 166; horse delivery, 119; and Little Big Horn battlefield inspections, 119–20, 123, 124; pursuit of escaped Northern Cheyennes, 131; pursuit of horse thieves, 159; Sitting Bull engagement, 150; and Yellowstone Park expeditions, 128, 189, 192, 193
Fort D. A. Russell, 15–17, 26
Fort Ellis, 28, 125, 127, 128, 130, 193
Fort Fetterman, 26, 41, 45, 47
Fort Fred Steele, court martial assignment, 23
Fort Hall, and sign language project, 179–80
Fort Hartsuff, court martial assignment, 25–26
Fort Keogh: location, 119; storage of Clark's belongings, 202; Yellowstone presidential party, 196
Fort Keogh posting, Clark's activity: Bannock Indians engagement, 125–28; Beaver Station conflict investigation, 160–61; Big Horn Mountains exploration party, 162–66; clothing/equipment recommendations, 135–36; Crow camp investigation, 132; defense of Northern Cheyenne Indians, 142–44, 153–54; forage change requests, 147–48; horse delivery escort, 119; kitchen fire, 133–34; leave of absence, 169–71; Little Big Horn battlefield inspection, 120–21; mapping project, 168–69; Newman's horses conflict, 144–46; O'Fallon Creek conflict, 159–60; Peale fitness report, 136; Pine Ridge grievances, 155; property shortage problem, 132–33; pursuit of Northern Cheyennes, 131–32, 136–42; Red River mixed-bloods capture/escort, 152–53; scout reorganization, 134–35, 148; sign language project, 155–57, 177–78; Sitting Bull campaign, 148–52; temporary company commands, 157–58, 167; Yellowstone Park expedition, 121–25, 128–30

252 INDEX

Fort Laramie, during Sioux War, 38–40, 47
Fort Leavenworth, Northern Cheyenne prisoners, 153–54
Fort McKinney, 162–63, 164, 192
Fort Missoula, and sign language project, 176, 177
Fort Peck, Sitting Bull engagement, 149, 152, 153
Fort Robinson, Northern Cheyenne surrender, 137, 143. *See also* Camp Robinson
Fort Sanders posting, Clark's activity, 17, 21–26
Fort Snelling posting, Clark's activity, 119
Fort Thornburgh, in sign language project, 180
Fort Washakie, 179, 185, 192–93
Forwood, W. H., 185, 189, 192
Four Crows, 64
Fourth Cavalry, 42–43, 56
Fowler, Joshua L., 19, 23, 24, 184
Frenchman's Creek, 152
Friday (Arapaho), 106

Garfield, James A., 171–72
G.A.R. gathering, 190–91
Garnett, William "Billy": on Clark–Red Cloud meeting, 51–52; on Clark's Indian interests, 60, 66; in Crazy Horse conflicts, 82–83, 84, 85, 92; criticism of Crazy Horse enlistment, 61; on Nellie Larrabee, 68; in Nez Perce debate, 77; at surrender of Crazy Horse, 56–58; Washington, D.C., delegation, 106
Geer (rancher), 188
Gibbon, John, 27, 190, 202, 203
Gibson, Francis, M., 187
Gillette, Philip, 182, 203
Girard, Alfred C., 133
gold search, Big Horn Mountains, 163–64
Goose Creek, 27, 32, 164

Government Printing Office, and sign language manuscript, 199
Grand Army of the Republic gathering, 190–91
Grand Island, 25
Grand River, 33
Grant, Ulysses S., 11, 25
Green River, 180, 185, 192
Gregory, James F.: American Derby event, 199; Chicago staff appointment, 176–77; at Clark's death, 200, 201, 202–3; in *Sign Language* acknowledgments, 203; Yellowstone map project, 168–69; on Yellowstone Park expeditions, *103*, 184, 187, 189, 193, 197
Gros Ventre Indians, in sign language project, 176
Gros Ventre River, 186, 194
Grouard, Frank: in Crazy Horse departure conflict, 83; illness, 40; mistranslation of Nez Perce debate, 76–78, 80, 95; during Sioux War, 33–34, 35–36; at surrender of Crazy Horse, 57–58; on Yellowstone–Big Horn valley exploration expedition, 65–66

Hamersly and Company, 200, 202
Hamilton, Samuel T., 128, 158, 160
Hatch, Rufus, 195
Hat Creek camp, 50
Hatton, Charles, 183
Hayden, Ferdinand V., 129
Hayes, Edward M., 193
Hayes, Rutherford B., 108–9, 110
Haynes, Frank Jay, 192
Hayt, Ezra, 134
health issues, Clark's, 5, 8, 200
Heart River, 32
He Dog: and Crazy Horse conflicts, 81, 84, 86–87; at death of Crazy Horse, 92; Little Wound's feast, 60; surrender

of Crazy Horse, 56; Washington, D.C., delegation, 106
Hell Roaring Creek, 188
Higgins, Caroline, 183
High Bear, 78, 80, 89
Hole in the Rock Creek, 140
Holt, Joseph, 11, 12
Hoppin, Curtis B., 150, 151
horse racing, 84, 198–99
Houghton, Henry L., 201
Hoyt, Colgate, 122, 123, 130
Hoyt, Wayland, 122, 129
Huffman, L. A., 148, 157
Huggins, Eli L., 149, 159, 160
Hughes, Robert P., 187
Hunkpapa Indians, in sign language project, 180–81. *See also* Sitting Bull
Hunts the Enemy, 48–49, 50

Ilges, Guido, 160–61
Index Peak area, 126–27, 188
Indian artifacts, Clark's, 169–70, 205
Indian Sign Language, The. *See* sign language project
interpretation problems, 46, 50, 76–78
Irwin, James S.: in Crazy Horse conflicts, 68, 71, 72, 74, 84; relocation of Agency Indians, 113, 116; Washington, D.C., delegation, 74, 106, 110

Janis, Antoine, 106
Jetmore, Mr., 154
Johnson, Andrew, 12
Johnson, Charles A., 64
Johnson, Ellen Roche Reily, 55
Johnson, Joseph, 159
Jordan, Charles P., 58
Journal of the Military Service Institution, 170, 203

Kansas, Northern Cheyenne trial, 153–54
Kennington, James, 90–91, 92
Key, Francis Scott, 54

King, Charles, 17–18, 35, 36
Kingsbury, Frederick W., 136

Lake Station, 161
Lakota Indians, during Sioux War: battles against, 27–28, 33–36; scout allies, 40, 41, 42, 43–44, 46–47; surrender/peace negotiation period, 48–50, 52, 55–58, 63. *See also* Red Cloud Agency, Clark's activity; *names of specific bands*; *names of specific leaders*
Lame Deer, fight with Miles, 63–64, 123
Laramie Peak area, 24–25, 48
Larrabee, Helen "Nellie," 68–69, 72, 99, 115
Last Bull, 61
Lawson, Joseph, 113, 115, 116
Lawton, Henry W., 63, 136–37
leaves of absence: from Army Headquarters, 199–200; from Division of the Missouri Headquarters, 169–70, 190–91; from Fort Sanders, 23; from Red Cloud Agency, 118; after West Point commission, 18
Lee, Jesse M.: on Clark's personality, 59–60, 85; and Crazy Horse conflict, 79, 80, 85, 87–91; and death of Crazy Horse, 95; relocation of Agency Indians, 113; and Washington, D.C., delegation, 72
Lee, Lucy, 95
Lewis County Democrat, 4
Lewis Lake, 186, 194
Liggett, Hunter, 162
Lincoln, Abraham, 5
Lincoln, Robert Todd, 184, 191, 194, 196, 199
Lincoln Pass, 186, 194
Little Big Horn battle: belongings of soldiers, 54, 61; investigations/reports about, 105–6, 120, 124, 166; map/narrative from Sitting Bull,

Little Big Horn battle (*continued*) 183; outcome, 27, 56; reenactment of battle, 66
Little Big Horn River, 164, 165
Little Big Man: at buffalo hunt discussions, 70; in Crazy Horse conflicts, 76, 86, 89, 91–92, 96; and death of Crazy Horse, 91–92, 94; at Pine Ridge Reservation, 155; Washington, D.C., delegation, 106
Little Hawk, *100*
Little Missouri River, 32, 49, 138, 139
Little Missouri Station, 161
Little Porcupine Creek, 158
Little Powder River, 49, 64
Little Rocky Creek, 188
Little Wolf, Lincoln, 183
Little Wolf (Lakota), in Crazy Horse conflict, 82, 83
Little Wolf (Northern Arapaho), son at boarding school, 183
Little Wolf (Northern Cheyenne): Big Horn Mountains exploration party, 162; flight from/evading agency, 137–41; killing of Starving Elk, 169; in sign language project, 157; Sioux War fighting, 43, 44, 45; surrender of, 50, 141–42
Little Wound, 19, 52, 60
Logan, Grace, 196
Logan, John A., 192
Logan, Thomas H., 196
Lone Bear, 82
Long, Oscar F., 122
Long Dog, 152
longevity pay, court case, 198
Looking Horse, 86
Lord, James H., 192
Lower Brule Agency, 181
Lyon, William H., 111

Mackall, James B., 9, 10–11
Mackenzie, Ranald S., 42–43, 45, 47, 58

mackinaw travel, Yellowstone River, 28–30
Magpie, 151
Mahan, Dennis Hart, 6–7, 30
Mallery, Garrick, 155–56, 157, 170, 203
Mammoth Hot Springs, 127–28, 129–30, 195
maps/mapping projects: Big Horn Mountains explorations, 162; Indian-provided, 180–81, 182; Laramie Peak-area exploration, 24; Little Big Horn battle, 106; for sign language fieldwork, 156; Yellowstone explorations, 126, 168–69
Mason, Julius W., 47, 49, 50, 80–81, 86
Masterson, Bat, 153
McAvoy, Charles, 201
McAvoy, Cornelia, 184, 199, 200–201
McAvoy, John H., 184
McChesney, Charles E., 181
McClernand, Edward J., 151
McCook, A. G., 119, 134
McCrary, George W., 111
McCree, Henry, 183
McCullough, John, 185, 186, 188
McGillycuddy, Fanny, 115, 116, 117
McGillycuddy, Valentine T., 92–93, 94, 95, 117, 118, 132–33
McKinney, John A., 38, 44, 163
Medicine Stand, 151
Merrivale, Jose, 106
Miles, Cecilia, 122
Miles, John D., 154
Miles, Mary, 122
Miles, Nelson A.: on clothing/equipment board, 135; conflict with Bannock Indians, 124–25, 127–28; Crow camp investigation, 132; forage change debate, 148; Lame Deer fight, 63–64, 123; Little Big Horn examination, 119–20, 124; Powder River camp, 29–30; remembrance of Clark, 204–5; Sitting Bull campaign, 149, 150–52,

150–53; Yellowstone Park expedition, *102*, 121–22, 128–30
Military Service Institution, 170
Milk River, 150–52
Mills, Anson, 33–34
Miniconjou Indians: in sign language project, 181; surrender process, 49, 53–54, 63–64, 65, 81; Yellowstone Park expedition, 123
Missouri River, 46, 108, 149, 152–53. *See also* relocation plan
Mix, John, 170
Mohler, J. G., 153–54
Montana Column, 27, 28
Moore, Thomas, 185, 192
Morris Museum, 205
Mounts, Matthew "Cy," 28
Mount Washburn, 128–29, 187, 194
Muddy Creek, 123
Mud Volcano, 129
Murphy Ranch, 132

Nation, The, 203
National Hotel, Yellowstone National Park, 195
National Republican, 55
Newman, E. S., 144–46
New Red Cloud Agency, 116–17
New Spotted Tail Agency, 117
New York City, Indian delegation visit, 110–12
New York Herald, 20, 29
Nez Perce Indians, 76–78, 79
Nickerson, Azor H., 147
No Flesh, 87
Noisy Walking, 153
No Neck, 89
Norris, Basil, 200
North, Frank, 41, 43
North, Luther, 41, 43
Northern Arapahos, and Powder River Expedition, 40, 42, 43–44, 45, 46–47

Northern Arapahos (post–Sioux War): Big Horn Mountains exploration party, 162, 163–64; in Nez Perce conflict, 76; in sign language project, 179; Washington, D.C., trips, 106, 107, 108, 110, 182–83; Yellowstone Park expeditions, 185, 193
Northern Cheyennes (during Sioux War): battles against, 27–28, 33–34, 42–45, 165; scout allies, 40, 42, 43–44, 46–47; surrender of, 48–49, 50, 55–56, 61, 64–65, 136–37
Northern Cheyennes (post–Sioux War): Big Horn Mountains exploration party, 162, 163; Clark's defense of, 142–45, 153–54; departure for reservation, 63, 136–37; O'Fallon Creek conflict with Lakota band, 159; pursuit of, 131–32, 137–42; Red River mixed-bloods escort, 153; Sitting Bull engagement, 149, 150, 151; sweat lodge experience, 177–79. *See also* Little Wolf (Northern Cheyenne)
Northern Pacific Railroad, 168, 189, 195–96
No Water, 83, 87, 96
Nowood Creek, 163–64

O'Fallon's Creek, 32, 136, 138, 159–60
O'Fallon's Station, 161
Oglala Indians. *See* Crazy Horse *entries*; Red Cloud; Red Cloud Agency, Clark's activity
O'Kelly, James J., 29, 30
Old Crow, 153
Old Faithful, 129, 187, 194
Omaha Barracks, 17–18, 20–21
One Bull, 180–81
Ord, E. O. C., 19
ordnance officer, rifle ruling, 121
Otter Creek camp, 49
Ouray Reservation, 180

256 INDEX

Ovenshine, Samuel, 145
Owl Creek camp, 37

Paint Pots, 129, 187
Palladay, Leon, 106
Palmer, Innis N., 17–20, 22, 23, 27, 28
Pass Creek Canyon, 165
Pawnee Indians, 41, 42, 43–44, 176
Pawnee Killer, 19
Peale, James T., 26, 136, 157–58
Pearce, Henry S., 16
Peters, Samuel M., 154
Piegan Indians, in sign language project, 177
Pine Ridge Agency, 137, 155
Piney Creek, 164
Pitcher, Thomas Gamble, 6
Pittsburgh Dispatch, 122
Plenty Wolves, 89, 92
Ponca Agency, 112
Poor Elk, 132
Poor Wolf, 176
Pope, James W., 122, 124, 130
Poplar Creek, 167
Poplar River, 149
Porcupine (member of Dull Knife band), 153
Pourier, Baptiste "Big Bat": in Crazy Horse conflicts, 82–83, 89; criticism of Crazy Horse enlistment, 61; and death of Crazy Horse, 93, 94; during Sioux War, 35–36; on Yellowstone–Big Horn valley exploration expedition, 65–66
Powder River Expedition, 40–47, 179
Powder River: gold search, 164; Indian engagements, 137–39, 160; military depot, 30–32; rifle loss, 120–21
Powell, John Wesley, 155–56, 170, 172, 173
Powell, William H., 24
Prairie Dog Creek, 164
Price, Rose Lambart, 24–26

quartermaster duties, 26

railroads: boundary celebration, 168; Crook travel, 23; Grant travel, 25; military protections, 16, 21; Yellowstone Park expeditions, 189, 192, 195–96
Rain-in-the-Face, 167
ranches, expansion of, 164
Randall, Edward L., 160
Rawolle, William C., 22
recruit delivery assignment, 28–31
Red Bear, 115, 116
Red Cloud, Jack, 51
Red Cloud Agency, Clark's activity: beef issue incident, 64; on condition of surrendering bands, 56; confusion/dispute about Crazy Horse's departure, 77–82; council about buffalo hunt, 70; council with Crook, 62; death of Crazy Horse, 92–93, 94–96; escort to new agency locations, 113–17; and expectations of fleeing Northern Cheyennes, 137; feast attendance, 60, 62, 70–71, 81; incarceration plan for Crazy Horse, 89, 90–91; meetings with surrendering parties, 56–58, 61–62, 64–65, 87; in military move against Crazy Horse, 83–88; monitoring network, 59–60, 69, 75, 81–82; recruiting of Crazy Horse, 60–61; and resident relocation debate, 61, 62, 71, 76; response to rumor about Crook murder plot, 82–83; scout command, 48, 52–53, 63; sun dance observation, 66–67; in surrender/peace negotiations, 48–49, 50; Washington, D.C., delegation, 72–75; "working" of Crazy Horse, 62, 64, 68–69, 75; "working" of Red Cloud, 50–52, 53. *See also* Camp Robinson; Crazy Horse (and Red Cloud Agency)
Red Cloud: Clark relationship, 50–52; at council about buffalo hunt, 70;

in Crazy Horse departure conflict,
83; and death of Crazy Horse, 94;
leadership position, 53; power
struggle with Crazy Horse, 68, 70–71;
and surrender of Crazy Horse, 56, 57;
Washington, D.C., delegation, 74, *101*,
106, 109, 112
Redd, Rosten G., 122
Red Feather, 86
Red Fork, 43, 56, 163
Red Horse, 181
Red River mixed-bloods, 152–53
Red Willow Creek, 18–20
Reed, William I., 28, 30
regimental adjutant assignments. *See*
adjutant duties
Reily, William Van Wyck, 54–55
relocation plan: follow up discussions,
118; implementation process, 112–17;
opposition of Agency Indians, 61,
62, 70, 71; Washington delegation
discussions, 108–10
Rhodes, Charles D., 185, 186, 187–88
Rice, Edmund, 122, 133
Rice, Rachel, 122, 129
Ricker, Eli S., 61
Riley, Thomas, 20–21
ring acquisition story, 54–55
Robinson, Levi, 48
Rock Creek, 151, 152
Rocky Fork, 189
Rollins, Daniel G., 191
Roman Nose, 49
Rosebud Creek (southeastern Montana):
battle at, 27, 32, 51; camps, 28–29,
30, 42; Indian reserve near, 144;
post–Sioux War conflicts, 158–59; in
Yellowstone Park expedition, 123, 124
Rosebud Creek (southwestern Montana),
125
Rosebud Reservation, 177
Rosenquest, J. Wesley, 56
Rouse, Henry Clark, 122, 130

Rowland, William, 50, 55
Rowley, George B., 201
Running Hawk, 50

Sabin, W. E., 141
Sacket, Delos B., 184, 199, 201
Sanborn, Hattie, *102*, 122, 129, 154, 168
Sanborn, John B., 122
Sand Hills area, evasion by Northern
Cheyenne, 137
Sandoz, Mari, 68, 115
San Francisco assignment, 18
Sanger, Louis H., 29
Sans Arc Indians, 49, 53–54, 167
Saunders, Alvin, 18
sawmill scandal, Fort Sanders, 22
Schofield, John M., 197
Schoolcraft, Henry R., 190
Schriver, Edmund, 12
Schurz, Carl, 108, 109–10, 113–14
Schuyler, Walter S., 36, 37–38, 43–44,
64–65
Scott, Hugh Lenox, 170, 204
scouts, Indian (during Sioux War):
in battles, 40–47; in surrender
negotiation period, 48–49, 52–53,
57–58
scouts, Indian (post–Crazy Horse
surrender): in agency monitoring
network, 59–60, 75, 81–82; Big Horn
Mountains exploration party, 162;
Clark's command/organization
of, 63, 134–35, 148; in Crazy Horse
confrontation, 85–87, 90–91, 93, 96;
Crook's opinion of, 60–61; horse thief
apprehensions, 70; after Little Wolf's
surrender, 144, 148; meeting with
Crook, 62; at New Red Cloud Agency,
117; in Nez Perce conflict, 76–77, 79;
property shortage problem, 132–33;
pursuit of Northern Cheyennes,
132, 138–41; Red River mixed-bloods
escort, 153; in relocation journey, 113,

scouts, Indian (post–Crazy Horse surrender) (*continued*) 115, 116; reorganization plan, 134–35, 148; Rosebud Creek engagement, 159–60; search for Miniconjou camp, 64; Sitting Bull engagement, 149, 150, 151; with Yellowstone–Big Horn valley exploration expedition, 65–66

Second Cavalry, Clark's service (before Sioux War): buffalo hunt with Grand Duke Alexis, 18–20; commission, 13, 15; escort assignments, 18, 20–21; frontier posts, 14; Laramie Peak area exploration, 24–25; scouting assignment, 24. *See also* adjutant duties

Second Cavalry, Clark's service (during Sioux War): assignment to Camp Robinson, 47; at Belle Fourche camp, 37, 45–47; march ordeal, 32–33, 37, 98; at Powder River camp, 29–32; Powder River Expedition, 40–47; recruit delivery to Rosebud Creek camp, 28–29; Slim Buttes–area fighting, 33–36; travel to Fort Laramie, 37–39; at Whitewood Creek camp, 37. *See also* Camp Robinson; Fort Keogh posting, Clark's activity

Second Cavalry, field activity (post–Sioux War): Beaver Station investigation, 160–61; escort of surrendering Sans Arcs, 167–68; pursuit of Lakota bands, 159–60; Sitting Bull engagement, 148–52; Yellowstone Park expeditions, 185–90, 193

Seminole, Jules, 139
Seton, Ernest Thompson, 204
Seventeenth Infantry, Sioux War, 30
Seventh Cavalry, 28, 29, 34, 44, 54, 187. *See also* Little Big Horn battle
Shadow Come Out, 151
Sharp, Colonel, 54
Sharp, Jeter, 145
Sharp Nose, 43, 106, 108, 110, 179, 183, 185
Shave Elk, 57
Shell Creek, 165
Sheridan, Michael V., 19, 184, 192, 193, 195, 198
Sheridan, Philip H.: buffalo hunt with Grand Duke Alexis, 18–20; at Division of the Missouri Headquarters, 117–18, 171–72, 176–77; ethnographic projects, 172–74; incarceration plan for Crazy Horse, 89; Nez Perce conflict, 76, 79; promotion to General of the Army, 197; remembrance of Clark, 204; rifle loss ruling, 121; and sign language manuscript, 199; during Sioux War, 39; Washington Park Club racetrack, 198–99; on Yellowstone–Big Horn valley exploration expedition, 65–66; Yellowstone National Park expeditions, 102–3, 184–90, 191–96
Sheridan Pass, 186
Sherman, Francis H., 190
Sherman, William T., 116–17, 121, 129, 136, 173–74, 197
Shoshone Dick, 185, 187, 193
Shoshone Lake, 187, 194
Shoshone reservation, 108, 110, 179
Shoshones: Sioux War scouts, 42, 43–44, 45; Yellowstone Park expeditions, 185, 187, 193
Sibley, Frederick W., 38, 135, 165
signal officer assignment, 22–23
sign language project: deaf language component, 170, 182, 203; earliest interests, 41, 43, 46; evolutionary perspectives, 174–75; field assignment, 172–74, 176–81; during Fort Keogh posting, 155–57; during leave of absence, 169–71; methodology, 174–75; publication of manuscript, 199, 200, 201, 202–3; responses to published book, 203–4

Sign Talk (Seton), 204
Sinclair, William, 9, 10
Sioux War: summary report, 105–6; summer campaign, 27–39, 123, 165; surrender/peace negotiations, 48–58; winter campaign, 40–47. *See also names of specific battles and expeditions*
Sitting Bear, 42
Sitting Bull: Baker's battlefield, 124; in Crazy Horse's claim about scouts, 79; final engagement, 148–52; and fleeing Northern Cheyenne, 140; as Lakota headman, 27; map/narrative about Little Big Horn, 182; in report about Little Big Horn battle, 105; reports/rumors about, 50, 63–64, 76, 117; in sign language project, 180; sweat lodge description, 177
Slim Buttes, area, 33–36, 138
Slough Creek, 188
Smith, J. Q., 72
Snake River, 186
Soap Creek, 166
Soda Creek Butte, 188
Spirit Lake Reservation, 180
Spotted Bear, 148
Spotted Eagle, 167
Spotted Tail Agency, Indian residents: arrival of surrendering bands, 53–54, 81; exodus to Missouri River location, 112–17; number of, 58; relocation opposition, 53, 61, 62, 68; role in surrender/peace negotiations, 49–50; scout recruitment, 52, 68; Washington, D.C., delegation concerns, 72–73. *See also* Red Cloud Agency, Clark's activity
Spotted Tail: buffalo hunt with Grand Duke Alexis, 19–20; in Crazy Horse conflict, 85, 88–89; death of, 177; leadership position, 53; in Red Cloud–Crook conflict, 51; relocation process, 113; role in surrender negotiations, 49–50; Washington, D.C., delegation, 74, 106, 107, 108, 109, 111
Spring Creek, 21
Stager, Anson, 185, 192
Standing Elk, 44
Standing Rock Agency, 180
Stanton, Edwin M., 5
Stanton, Thaddeus H., 31
Starving Elk, 169
Stephens, N. T., 154
Strahorn, Robert E., 60
Strong, William E., 185, 186, 187–88
Strong Left Hand, 153
Sturgis, James G., 123, 124
Sturgis, Jerusha, 123, 124
Sturgis, Samuel, 123
sun dance ceremony, 66–67
Sunday Creek, 135, 158
Sutton, Mike, 154
sweat lodge experience, 177–79
Sweetwater River, 192
Swift Bear, 88, 89

Tabby, 180
Tall Man, 50
Tangle Hair, 153
Taylor, Prudency (later Clark), 3, 203
Terry, Alfred H.: Dakota Column command, 27, 28; Little Wolf's people, 142, 144; Newman horses episode, 146; Powder River camp, 30–31, 32; remembrance of Clark, 204; scout reorganization plan, 134
Third Cavalry, 49, 80–81, 86, 113
Thornburgh, Thomas T., 180
Three Bears, 41
Tibbetts, Ben, 64
Tidball, John C., 6
Tillson, John C. F., 136
Tongue River area, 29–30, 57, 114, 144, 164–65
Tosar, 186

Touch the Clouds: in Crazy Horse conflict, 88–89, 91, 96; at death of Crazy Horse, 93; invitation of Crazy Horse, 73; and Nez Perce conflict misunderstanding, 76–77, 80; in relocation journey, 116; surrender negotiations, 49; Washington, D.C., delegation, 106
Tower, Zealous Bates, 6
Townsend, E. D., 11, 12, 118, 147, 161
Treasury Department, 18, 198
Tullock's Fork, 124
Turtle Mountain, 153
Two Belly, 132
Two Lance, 19
Two Moon, 141
Two Moon Creek, 169
Tyhee, 180
Tyler, United States v., 198

Union Pacific Railroad, 16, 21, 130, 162, 172
United Service journal, 157
United States Military Academy, 5–13, 97, 147
Ute Indians, 162, 163, 172, 173, 180

Valentine, Ezra G., 203
Van Voast, James, 16
Vest, George G., 191–92, 195
Vest, George G., Jr., 191–92

Walsh, James M., 152
Wardman, George, 122, 124
Washakie, 179, 185, 193
Washington, D.C., visit (Agency Indians delegation), *101*; preparation and planning, 62, 68, 70, 71–73; relocation discussions, 108–10; reservation conditions discussions, 182–83; sightseeing activity, 107, 110–12; travel periods, 106–7, 112
Washington, D.C., visit, Zuni headmen group, 183–84

Washington, D.C., Army Headquarters assignment, 197–99
Washington Park Club, racetrack, 198–99
Wasson, Joseph, 37–38
Weir, Robert W., 7
Wells, Elijah R., 119
Welsh, William, 107
West Point, 5–13, 97, 147
Wheelan, James N., 185, 189
Whistler, J. N. G., 144, 145, 146
Whistler (Lakota), 19
White, Charles, 35
White Clay Creek, Crook's council, 81–83
White Hat, name origins, 16, 40
White River, 86, 180
Whitewood Creek camp, 37–38, *98*
Wied-Neuwied, Maximilian von, 156
Wild Hog, 153–54
Williams, Robert, 203
Williamson, John P., 182
Willow Creek, 37, 164
Wind River, 185–86, 194
Wolf Moccasin, 179
Woman Dress, 82–83, 85, 86
Woodbridge, Francis, 28, 30
Wooden Leg, 61–62
Wounded Knee Creek, 115
Wyoming Column, 27

Yellow Bear, 112
Yellow Medicine Creek, 113, 116
Yellowstone Lake, 129, 194
Yellowstone National Park: expeditions to, *102–3*, 121–25, 128–30, 184–90, 191–96; mapping project, 168–69
Yellowstone River: Fort Keogh location, 119; Indian hunting rights, 132; interpreter confusion, 46; mackinaw travel, 28–30; for sweat lodge experience, 178–79
Young Man Afraid of His Horses, 70, 115, 133, 155

Zuni Indians, 183–84